Who Cares Who Wins?
Combat Para, SAS Rebel's story

by Nigel Mumford

Told by a soldier in his own words, in a soldiers language, uncensored & unchanged. Some things are shocking and will offend people, but the truth hurts ......

First published in 2007 by
Nigel Mumford, Spain

Copyright © Nigel Mumford
[Sunday Times article © News International Newspapers]

All rights reserved. No part of this publication may be reproduced, stored in a retrieval system, or transmitted, in any form, or by any means, electronic, mechanical, photocopying, recording or otherwise, without the prior permission of the publisher and copyright holder, except for a reviewer who may quote brief passages in connection with a review for insertion in a newspaper, magazine, website, or broadcast.

Nigel Mumford hereby asserts his moral right to be identified as the author of this work.

British Library Cataloguing in Publication Data
A catalogue for this book is available from the British Library.

ISBN 978-84-611-5049-6

Typeset in Book Antiqua 11pt on 14pt lead

Contents

Chapter One
The murder of Private Francis Bell and the
blood-stained hands of Gerry Adams — page 5

Chapter Two
Aftermath — page 24

Chapter Three
Tell the truth, Gerry Adams — page 38

Chapter Four
Geordie Boy — page 49

Chapter Five
We're in the Army now — page 62

Chapter Six
23rd Parachute Field Ambulance — page 70

Chapter Seven
The Day of Internment 9th August 1971 — page 82

Chapter Eight
Ballymurphy — page 105

Chapter Nine
New Lodge and another Tour — page 125

Chapter Ten
Life as a Para — page 151

Chapter Eleven
South Armagh - Bandit Country — page 170

Chapter Twelve
The 22nd SAS Regiment — page 185

Chapter Thirteen
South Oman - first combat mission — page 198

Chapter Fourteen
Beach Landings, 'Drowning Practice' and Dying for a Shit — page 209

Chapter Fifteen
Four months in combat — page 229

Chapter Sixteen
Attack on the Sherishitti Caves — page 249

Chapter Seventeen
My discharge from the Army — page 271

Preface

Driving down the road, approaching my home after a hard day's work, I saw a man lying in the road and a group of people looking at him from the pavement. No one had gone to his aid, so I stopped my car and ran to him. Unconscious, not breathing, blue in the face, the man's life was in the balance! His crash helmet was still in place and the chin-strap was impeding me clearing his airway, so I started to undo the strap. A woman shouted from the crowd. "Do not do that he may have a fractured skull". Her ignorance and only a little knowledge could lead this man into dying and worse than death, permanent brain damage from lack of oxygen, thus the saying a little knowledge is often more dangerous than no knowledge at all. I replied, "Yes, you may be right, but the fractured skull is not killing him at the moment, the lack of air is! I am an SAS trained combat medic. If you know better than me, take command of the situation". The strap removed, I opened his mouth to find his false teeth and tongue blocking his airway. The teeth removed and his tongue pulled forward, the man started to breathe and soon recovered consciousness. An ambulance arrived on the scene and I handed over to them, telling them that he had been unconscious for a few minutes. Yes, it felt good, I had helped save this stranger's life because those first few minutes after an accident are so vital, get the person breathing first, then stop bleeding, and only then worry about broken bones. My training and experience in combat had saved the day for one man and his family!

Over-enthusiasm as a young man gave me a lot to regret and apologise for, but young men all tend to think they know better. Later, with age and maturity, you realise you were wrong. This enthusiasm in young men is what the system manipulates and has led many a young man into doing things he later regrets, but we cannot turn the clock back. Talking about what has happened helps a lot of people to live with their conscience. Talk about the good times and bad times, tell it how it was and do not be afraid to put your finger up at the system.

A hero, a coward, a bully, a Samaritan, a killer, a saviour, immature, mature, stupid, clever, a teacher. I have been all these things in my life. I served in the Royal Army Medical Corps, the 23rd Parachute Field Ambulance, the 2nd Battalion Parachute Regiment and finally in the 22nd Special Air Service. A witness to State terrorism, murder, police corruption that caused an innocent man to be sentenced to death by hanging. First-hand witness to the conflict in North Ireland at the sharp end with all the blood and guts that came with that experience.

In the 1970s I was unfortunate enough to be present at some historic and tragic events, such as the Ibrox football disaster in Glasgow, involved in the riots after Bloody Sunday, the Day of Internment, witness to the comradeship and professionalism of Parachute Regiment after the IRA had blown up the officers' mess in Aldershot, killing our Catholic priest and civilian women cleaners. Operation Motorman to clear out the no go areas of the IRA, a tour of duty in "bandit country" (South Armagh) and with the SAS in the secret war in the Oman.

I have been nearly killed on a number of occasions and after some people have read this book, I will be keeping my head down again. The truth hurts people with a guilty conscious. I have killed two men, and I have tried to kill more but also saved the lives of a few while doing my job and duty. The book tells the truth about people who have murdered, shot, robbed, gang-banged, tortured, sodomised and committed political terrorism.

In the memoirs of Gerry Adams he writes about the murder of a British Officer in Ballymurphy and I finish his story by putting the true facts and names to his story!

I hope you find it an anti-war book and a call for change of attitude towards British soldiers, because without professional soldiers, it may be your son at the sharp end without the right equipment and in the hands of incompetent officers.

I will bore you slightly with what motivated me into joining the British Army, my up-bringing and views as an innocent 15-year old boy, what I witnessed that made me mature the hard way, scarring me for life. I signed a contract to serve 22 years in the British Army, taking the Queen's Shilling and still only an innocent boy!

Chapter 1

The murder of Private Francis Bell and the blood-stained hands of Gerry Adams

A four-month tour was worse than a prison sentence for soldiers serving in Northern Ireland. Could you just imagine putting more than one hundred prisoners in one room, on bunk beds with only leg room between each bed, forced to work seven days a week doing shift work, no contact with family and friends other than by telephone-which we had to pay for? Then having to walk the gauntlet, with verbal abuse, stones, petrol-bombs and sniper attacks from the local people; prisoners in the local jails had much better conditions than us soldiers!

An old woman was one of the few that liked our presence, "I am glad when you Paratroopers come to our area as all the trouble makers leave " referring to the IRA terrorists, but their supporters and collaborators stayed to organise attacks against us.

With our constant round-the-clock presence patrolling the area, the terrorists' activity was abated and we were sure that the indiscriminate car bomb attacks blowing the heart out of Northern Ireland did not originate from our area. Weeks without any contact led to complacency from a few soldiers, lowering their guard. Was that what the terrorists were waiting for? We were here for four months, but this was their home patch and they could sit, watch and wait for the right moment to attack. Find a weakness, a routine that the soldiers always took, and then plan an attack; they had the time, the skill and the brains that made them the most formidable terrorist group in the world.

A soldier found an Army torch on waste ground and his Corporal patrol leader did not stop the young soldier picking it up and bringing it back to base. I was standing with my mate Cpl Mike Harding waiting to get orders to take two patrols out on duty. The soldier came into the operations room and gave the torch to a Staff Sergeant who was also the company Quartermaster in charge of the stores. He was an experienced man with only a couple of years to finish his 22 years service and had won an MM (Military Medal) for fighting and killing Indonesian soldiers during the Malaya campaign in 1965. A veteran who should have known better to fall for such an obvious trap. He immediately tried to turn the torch light on by pushing the switch forward, but it was stuck with rust. He picked it up and hit the switch on the side of a table to move the switch forward, but it still was stuck fast. He hit it again, but it never moved even with the force used against it. He gave up and opened the clips to expose the battery. Yes it had a battery, a detonator and enough plastic explosive to kill everyone in the room. He was standing in dumb belief looking at it, his life passing before his eyes, Mike and I dived out of the door in perfect harmony, only laughing with relief when we were far enough from the room and the bomb. Was that another one of my lives gone or another miracle or does someone want me to write this book?

If a bullet has your name on it you cannot do a lot about it. If it is your unlucky day and the sniper picks you as his target, Ladbrooks would not give you good odds. A soldier on the practice range fires at a target which is pasted on a board and is officially called a number 11 target, which stands there and does not fire back. In Northern Ireland, British soldiers were the IRA's number 11 target, they got the chance to fire first. Even if you saw them with a gun, you had to shout that you were going to fire at them. We carried a green card which stated that you had to carry out certain procedures before you could engage and open fire at the enemy. This was introduced after "Bloody Sunday" so that the IRA had a better chance and so that officers could pass the blame onto the individual soldier who decided to pull the trigger. Every round fired had to be aimed and accounted for, or you could be faced with a court martial or worse, put on a murder charge. An example of this was the murder conviction and life sentence given to Private Lee Clegg of my battalion. A political prisoner to show that the government did not have a shoot-to-kill policy in Northern Ireland, (as an ex SAS soldier I know the truth on that score)! With the Paras, the card was always on our mind, but common sense prevailed, no witnesses, no card. In the case of Clegg, shooting at a car that had not stopped at a check point was fair game to any Para! Why have a road block if car thieves and terrorists have the right to ignore it? The terrorist needs to steal a car before making a car bomb. Why run if you have nothing to hide! Clegg was a hero. Had the stolen car been later used as a car bomb, how many lives would have been lost? Soldiers had killed and fired not using the card, but this time external pressure by America forced the government to sacrifice a soldier doing his job. If the Americans are so just, why not sign up to the international war crimes tribunal? Would they sacrifice a soldier to appease another nation?

As a soldier we lose the right to object about our orders, we have to do what our politicians order as they are democratically elected and it is part of our obligations as a professional soldier to carry out their demands, if we agree or not (democracy). If you do not vote you lose the right to cry, as you are the people who also put our lives at risk for not electing responsible, educated people that should be the voice of the majority. The best morale in the world for a soldier is when the country is behind you and you have a reason for fighting. In Northern Ireland we did not get the feeling that the British people were all for the use of troops but the Government had us there in the middle, in a no-win situation.

A patrol (a section of a platoon) normally consisted of a Corporal in command, a Lance Corporal second in command, a radio operator and the rest classed as riflemen, of whom we normally had five or six. Officers did not take to the field or the firing line on a regular basis unless the full platoon, consisting of three sections (patrols) were deployed, or the CO group, was doing an inspection, checking up on the lads on the ground. The officers and sergeants normally took duty in the command centre of a Company group within the secure base from which we operated and in this case was Saint Peter's Catholic School. On the radio you called them "Zero" and had to report in to them on regular basis and report your position. Now this can be noted to be stupid orders, as the IRA could easily pick up our radio frequency on an ordinary television and our officers were aware that they had stolen radios from other British units.

An IRA sniper normally had a number of men and women to give him the nod that we were coming and then cleared the killing ground of their own people before they took cover in numerous safe houses that left their doors open to them. The sniper could have his pick, he could choose the killing ground, his firing position, his weapon, the escape route and the British soldier carried his card. With a little intelligence gathering and back-up, he knew how many patrols were on the ground in his area and where. He would be briefed and given orders by Gerry Adams on whom to kill, especially in Ballymurphy where he was the terrorist commander (does anyone believe he got to the top by being a good Catholic or being a supporter of human rights)? With a little insight into military training, he would know the man in charge was normally followed by the radio operator, followed by two riflemen. The second in command normally took the other side of the road followed by three riflemen; military tactics seldom change in the British Army when the system and training drills it into you. This sniper was part of the Ballymurphy battalion of the IRA, so 90% of locals were on his side and helping him as his finger took the first squeeze on the trigger. He had been given all the information by his bosses, university students, their professors, ex-British soldiers, engineers, politicians and future politicians. Not stupid thick Paddies, but by men and women often better educated than most of our own officers who totally underestimated the enemy. They might not have pulled the trigger, but everyone that helped in any way shape or form, had blood on their hands and were as guilty as the man who finally pulled the trigger. How many people had blood on their hands before the 11th September? When terrorism happens to you and you are not immune from it, think back to what you inflicted on others in the name of a cause or religion. BUT, but nothing, if you helped in any way, you are as guilty as the man who pulled the trigger or detonated a bomb. Then 11th September opened your eyes to what you have been inflicting on others, that greenback should be a redback and every dollar donated gave the terrorist his ammunition. Nearly every bar in New York had collection boxes for the IRA. The movie industry and writers portray these men as freedom fighters, heroes, Poets and songs make fame for these men. The facts are different when you see what they have done and picked up the meat that once was a human being, men, women and yes children, blown to pieces all in the name of a cause.

They lived in a Catholic "ghetto" as they called it, Ballymurphy. The hardcore IRA and their best killers lived in this area. I mentioned ex-British soldiers, as a former paratrooper deserter Peter (The Para) McMullan was often deployed by Gerry Adams to carry out executions. That paratrooper now lives in America with a new identity, after telling the truth about Gerry Adams. He confirmed that no bomb or execution was carried out without Gerry's orders. The Para is still under sentence of death by the IRA, as are all informers. At this point I will mention what is a double agent. This was a man passing information to the police with the full knowledge of Gerry Adams; he passed on little bits of truth, but in the main, false information to waste police and army time. This agent could also frame innocent Catholic people that were a threat to the IRA, and to cap it all they were paid by the police for their false information.

The peace treaty did not include true IRA informers; ask

Martin McGartland who was gunned down in South Shields, England, on the 12/5/99, after the peace treaty was agreed. He was also guilty of naming Gerry Adams as the head terrorist who ordered his execution. He sat tied to a chair with a blindfold around his face, but he could see the bright light coming through a window. He heard Gerry Adams come into the house, he personally knew him so there was no mistaking his voice. He heard Adams order the two IRA men holding him captive to go upstairs and execute him for being a British spy. With nothing to lose, he lifted the chair and made for the window, going head-first through it. Desperate and knowing his death sentence, this was his last and only chance, out through the window and falling, landing in the front garden. This must be what you call the luck of the Irish, as a British Army foot patrol was moving down the street just at that moment and saved his life. Gerry still ordered his execution wherever he was hiding in the world with the protection of the British government. They found him living in South Shields, and being a lucky informer survived the six bullets that hit him.

Then, more recently, they executed Danny Morrison in April 2006 for being a spy for the British . No peace treaty for anyone that was a true informer who told the truth about Adams!

A central Catholic church, with three large Catholic schools, halls, a few corner shops, not a bad place to live if it was not for the IRA The estate was much better than most areas I had ever lived in and they had gardens the size of allotments, a Geordie paradise! If this is what they called a ghetto us Geordies had it a lot tougher in life in comparison. Most Geordies passed their spare time in allotments where they grew their home vegetables, they would enter competitions to show who could grow the best leeks and flowers. Then many would be into racing pigeons with a coop on the land or dog kennels where they would keep whippet dogs for racing. It was a pity we could not educate the Irish into more peaceful activities.

The Irish had their hatred for each other, which stems back generations with their open bigotry, they blame everyone but themselves, how sad! For this reason the streets were dirty, walls painted with graffiti supporting the different terrorist groups, the open areas were neglected, the shops boarded up and closed, the schools occupied by company-strength Army units. While searching a house I knocked on the door and a man in council work clothes answered it, I told him of my orders to search the house and to my amazement, he shouts "Outside lads, the soldiers want to search the house". Out wander over twenty men who turned out to be council workers. The foreman says the IRA would not let them work so they sat there every day playing cards and dominoes till knocking off time at 5pm, this house was located in Springfield Avenue.

It was a nice sunny day, 17th September 1972; the patrol of Paras was slowly working its way up Springhill Avenue, towards Springhill Road and the patrol was commanded by Corporal Yorky Hill. He was followed by his radio operator and two riflemen; they had taken the right side of the avenue, the same side that the sniper had chosen to hide. This did not give the sniper the right angle to fire on the patrol commander, the intended target. Now the sniper had to make a secondary choice and on this occasion he chose the last man working his way up Springhill on the left side of the Avenue, towards the pre-planned kill zone. It would have been observed that halfway up the Avenue there was a wide gap that soldiers had to cross, open ground, which gave a good firing position from Divismore Park. Any well-trained soldier would stop and observe towards Divismore before committing himself to cross an obvious danger point. You do not rush into a danger area. Stop and observe, only commit enough of your body so that you can observe for any movement, anything out of the ordinary. Step back, let the next patrol member get close to you so if you come under fire he can quickly come to your assistance with cover fire. Then you make the dash over to the other side, the adrenaline is getting pumped through your heart, now working faster, the hairs on the back of your neck stand up, you weave back and forwards, change your pace, up and down till you reach the safer area and cover. You then turn back, cover and observe for the next man to cross, you aim your rifle towards Divismore Park. This same action had been carried out by many soldiers, myself included, in the past months of patrolling the streets of Ballymurphy. We had all done the same at this point and it had also been noted by the enemy! Private Francis Bell reached this hazard, the youngest soldier who had just joined from basic training; Corporal Hill and his men covered the danger area from garden walls that gave protection to the men on the right side of the avenue, keeping an eye on the men that had little or no cover. Hill was also looking towards the obvious danger as Bell was preparing to make his move, the loud crack of a rifle firing echoed in the Avenue before Bell had moved.

Gerry Adams has written in his own words, where he describes in great detail the ambush and killing of a Paratrooper Officer by an IRA sniper. Adams knows and I know, we are both describing the same murder; no paratrooper officer was ever killed in Ballymurphy! He, as a politician, has only promoted Private Bell in his description of the incident, to that of an officer to make it sound better than killing one of the youngest soldiers in Northern Ireland. A seventeen-year old boy, to the Government he was now an adult. He still did not have the right to vote or drink alcohol in a bar but our politicians saw no wrong in allowing boys to die for their country. He was a good kid that settled in well with our Company and soon made many friends. He was too young and immature to know about religion or politics, this was his first job after leaving school and as with the rest of us, being a soldier was just a job.

The rifle sight was zeroed into the exact range, the

soldier, a perfect figure 11 from the shooting position carefully chosen; a head shot was easy at 100 metres. The sniper took the second squeeze on the trigger; he was no amateur, the bullet hit the target before he even lowered his sights. The Red Beret flew into the air as the bullet impacted into Bell's head. The bullet hit the baseline of the beret just above the left ear, but then ricocheted off. The damage was done, a large 50 mm hole in the skull, the force of the bullet sucking out brain tissue. A portion of brain tissue was sucked out of the gaping hole like a segment of cauliflower which was hanging onto his ear. Blood, brain fluid came out as Bell was spun round landing on his back. The blood loss was always heavy from a head wound; it ran into the road gutter. Unfortunately instant death did not occur with the angle that the bullet hit, nor deep unconsciousness either. Every muscle in his body contracted with the pain he suffered, his body arched like a banana as he lay on his back, only his feet and shoulders touching the ground. Bell's teeth and jaw were like a vice, literally crushing bits of his teeth.

I was tired. I felt as if I had grown eyes in the back of my head, my feet ached and I was looking forward to a bit of nosh and then getting my head down. I was just about to enter our camp after patrolling the streets of "the Murph" for the last four hours. Camp was another local school which had been converted into an Army post, accommodating over a hundred men of "B" Company 2nd Battalion Parachute Regiment. A four-month tour of duty and for the Paras always at the sharp end, with endless patrolling to maintain some sort of law where the police dare not enter. Four hours patrol and eight hours in camp, seven days a week for four months. Prison was luxury compared to our living conditions; most of the lower ranks were all accommodated in the school hall, the bunk beds had been squeezed in with just enough space to slide in and out. The constant movement of soldiers, changing for guard duty, patrol and for food, made it difficult to get a good sleep, so most people after the first month were in the zombie mode, as an undisturbed sleep was impossible, farting and snoring in close proximity did not help either.

I could already smell the kitchen, no complaints about the food or the cooks, they did their best, pots of tea and plenty of grub. Nobody would think of accepting tea from any of the locals in the "Murph" after one of the lads tried a cup from a nice old lady to find broken glass in the last slurp. Nice people, they just did not know what went into a good cup of English tea. The school was transformed with sandbags, corrugated sheeting, barbed wire, sentry posts. We lived with the enemy like being circled by the Indians in a wagon train. A mutual hatred built up, the Catholics were doing the shooting and for soldiers it becomes natural to hate the enemy whatever religion, especially when they are trying to kill you. They never asked our opinion and only saw us as a political tool.

A shot echoed through the deserted streets. Different rifles have distinct sounds and this sounded like it was an American-made Armalite. My radio operator was receiving the contact report from the patrol that had just replaced our patrol. "Man down", no orders were needed, the men had all cocked their weapons putting a 7.62 round in the breach of their rifles, and were heading back into Ballymurphy. A fast, watchful pace ready for action, to help our mates, a Para down was the incentive to throw caution to the wind.

The crack and thump of a bullet, gave you some idea of the distance from where you had been shot at by counting the seconds in between. In open fields you could work out the range of a sniper but in a built-up area the crack echoed and it was difficult to locate the sniper's position. The thump was the bullet impacting near or passing close by, or in many cases hitting you or one of your comrades.

The crack was not far away, the radio op was shouting, "Springhill Avenue". The Catholic church on our left, boarded -up shops to the approach of Springhill Avenue, nobody in sight, the locals had been warned. No movement, nobody running away. I led my patrol into Spinghill Avenue, now at a cautious walk, rifle ready to fire. First glance and the soldier could be seen lying on the pavement in the open, then the rest of the patrol trying to take the best cover in doorways. I could hear the patrol commander calling on the radio so I approached him. Private Francis Bell, the wounded soldier, was directly opposite the patrol commander, Yorky Hill and his radio operator. No one had gone to the assistance of the seventeen-year old Paratrooper, and the blood loss was obviously heavy. You could see the blood in three distinct layers where it was congealing, then fresh blood running and making another layer, mixed with cerebral fluid, it glistened in the strong sunlight. My training as a medic was not forgotten. I knew I had to go to his aid. I looked back and my men had taken cover, I said to Yorky Hill "No fucker got a shell dressing in your patrol?"

The sniper position had not been located, but the IRA had seldom been known to stand and fight. Shoot you in the back and run was the tactic, thus their nickname 'I Run Awaymen', which was more correct than the 'Irish Republican Army'. Now with two patrols on the ground and able to give cover fire I went for it, and went to help the boy. When you are anticipating a shot coming your way, your senses are working to their maximum and yes your hair stands up. I made it to Bell, no shot, so I was sure the terrorist had made his escape.

The gaping hole above his left ear exposed his brain, a lump of brain and bone resting on the side of his ear. He was still alive, as his back was arched and every muscle in his body was in contraction. His face was a mask of pure unadulterated pain and agony. A shiver went through my body; I could feel his pain as I knelt down beside him. "God give me a hand," I whispered and that from the mouth of an Atheist! I fumbled in my belt pouch as I had kept an airway in my first aid kit. His jaw and teeth were clamped so tight with his muscle contraction that I could not prize them open to insert the airway. I pulled out a bandage, known in Army terms as a shell dressing, a large absorbent yellow lint pad with brown bandage attached, well wrapped in a waterproof cover, a bitch to get off in a hurry. After a few curses, I got the dressing from the packing. I put the piece of brain back into the hole and tied on the bandage. "It's me, Geordie Mumford the medic, try and relax, open your mouth, you're going to be alright, relax." I pulled him into my arms to comfort him and then I felt his body relax. His stomach pulled in and he spewed out congealed dark blood and the contents of his stomach, it went over the both of us. His blood and spinal fluid had soaked into my trousers, with the amount of blood on me you would think we were both shot. I put my fingers in his mouth and cleaned out the bits of sick, mixed with congealed blood. His tongue was forward, so I put in the airway so the tongue could not fall back and stop him breathing. I still held Bell in my arms and I spoke to him "You're going to be OK. We are just waiting for the ambulance." I felt Bell going heavy on me, going into a deep coma. I still held him, would it not comfort you if someone was comforting you when you were dying? He was now at peace and no longer in pain and now I wanted him to pass away, as I loved him as a fellow human being and out of humanity, I only wanted him to be at peace. As a twenty-year old veteran, this horrific incident would be an experience and nightmare for the rest of my life, only talking and writing about it has helped me to live with it but I could never forget that boy's death.

    I was now thinking about where the sniper had fired from, who was watching and at the same time thinking about the consequences of Bell's injury. An old woman came to the door were Yorky Hill was in cover and offered a blanket. It was a brave thing to do as the IRA had executed people for helping wounded soldiers, even Catholics that put Christianity before this evil. At the Southern General Hospital in Glasgow where I had done a month's casualty training, I remembered a staff nurse showing me round the neuro surgical department which was one of the best in the world. She had said that they actually reduced the body temperature with people with head wounds before surgery, so that is why I declined the use of the blanket. Then I was thinking, with the loss of blood, spinal fluid and obvious brain damage this lad was going to be in a vegetative state the rest of his life if he survived. As a fit young person I thought I would rather be dead than live like that.

I imagined his position before he had been shot and came to the conclusion from the position he was now in that the bullet had come up Springhill Ave. The church was a good position but a long shot, the shops or the two alleyways near them were the angle I concluded the shot had come from. We had found a large cache of weapons and bomb-making material in the church. The priest had denied any knowledge of it, but he must have tripped over it on a daily basis. Thou shall not kill, love thy enemy, two-faced fucking hypocrite, I would love to ask the Pope if he was aware what these people were doing in God's name!

The big army Saladin ambulance broke the silence as it powered up the street. This was meant for conventional war, heavy armour, and massive tyres so it could take the impact from bullets and shrapnel, but slow in an urban environment. It took a good driver to manage it in narrow streets. The IRA did not honour the Red Cross, as I had experienced in previous tours of duty. They had fired on ambulances evacuating wounded soldiers and had even ambushed them to execute the wounded. So now we had to use the Saladin which was slow and every second counts when you are trying to save lives. This ambulance came from Musgrave Park Hospital which also had been attacked by a terrorist bomb killing patients, doctors and nurses and again on the orders of that Saint, Gerry Adams. The doors swung open, two medics and the battalion doctor jumped out. The crew looked at the boy soldier, we looked at each other and that look said everything. I had worked with this Scots doctor, Captain McCray and this was yet another statistic of the dead and dying that made us veterans of this terrorist war. I gave him a quick briefing of the injury as we got him on the stretcher. No pissing about, in the ambulance and away, I was pushing the doors shut as it moved off.

At this moment the company commander Major Patton in his Land Rover, driver, radio op, and sergeant major turned up, "How is Private Bell, Mumford?" To which I replied, "Better off dead," He gave me a funny look, seeing I was covered in blood. The major jumped back in his Land Rover and sped off after the ambulance. His job should have been to coordinate a search for the sniper, the rifle and even the shell case. If I had been the commanding officer I would have sealed the area with the hundred men in the Company and then searched every house, taking into custody any likely suspects for carbon tests on their hands. He did not even give the task to a junior officer to carry out a coordinated search. Only he can answer for his actions to not take direct command in the kill zone and leave the company without a CO.

Corporal Hill had moved his men into and around the shops, as he had assumed this to be the sniper position. I decided on the flats and alleyway to the left of the shops. Taking the ground-floor flat with a window that you could have a good line of vision was my first objective. We badly all wanted to find the IRA sniper who had shot Bell. With no orders from our commander or any other officer we used our own initiative. Kicking the door, it quickly opened, I saw two men behind the one that opened the door, my rifle lined up and I pushed it into his stomach. My men pushed past and covered the other two, who were quickly made to spread against the wall. I had the lads search the one bedroom, bathroom, dining room cum kitchen flat, in fact tear it apart. The reply to my first question "You heard the shot?" I asked. "What shot? We never heard anything," came from the tall thin lad with a spotty, plucky face. He was smiling, "What's the problem?" he said, smirking to a soldier covered in his comrade's blood. He was the self-appointed mouthpiece for the other two, the gang leader. The other two said nothing but their names and addresses. They did not live in this flat, they did not know the name of the owner, they had no house keys either, so they were obviously involved!

Never in my life had I wanted to kill anybody till this moment. Spotty face was trying to wind me up answering a question with a question. Practicing for his later political career, I remembered him. This guy had not just kissed the Blarney Stone but must have had oral sex with it. He came over as a student, well educated and full of himself, arrogant, without the least form of regret for the death of a fellow human being. A gang leader, with no mercy for the enemy, a tyrant in the same form as Hitler, and more recently Dr. Caraditch, well educated and with the same talent to inspire followers to throw away their morals and commit crimes against humanity. They are still looking for Caraditch to stand trial at The Hague for war crimes and mass killings, but this confuses me. How and why they distinguish between Adams and Caraditch, is it the amount of blood on your hands, is it a numbers game with how many you have ordered to be executed or is it because Adams is a British member of parliament?

From the flat window he had witnessed the whole incident and it could have been the sniper position. Any other soldier, in any Army would have wanted revenge and been justified in shooting these three bastards? Gerry was now using the democratic state and its laws to defend his rights, the same state he was fighting and hated and would put me in prison for any violation of his rights. Yet, in the name of a cause, he mocked every human right unless it affected him.

The democratic state tied my hands; they had no answer to this type of man, no punishment to fit his crime. This man needed killing. I was married and my life was good, could I jeopardise it for this bastard? I believed in a United Ireland then and now, but this man was only using this argument to run his gang. A Mafia, with money from extortion, drugs, collection boxes and the patriotic Irish Americans, they were rolling in money. That was the gang leader then and now, Gerry Adams!

On this occasion I did feel like a coward. I had to back off, the state protected him from instant justice. My natural instinct said this evil bastard needed to be dead. I had no doubt. These three had been taken part in the killing of my comrade. They were not worth ruining my own life; I had to overcome my anger.

I used my radio operator to send a situation report, that I had three suspects, check names and addresses. I was waiting for confirmation to take them into custody. Waiting for the police to come and do forensic tests, all this science that could convict these men, angle of fire, powder on hands, fingerprints, and check records for past involvement in terrorist activity, etc. etc. Then the order came, "Let them go," Adams was smiling, knowing I had to obey my orders. I could not look him straight in the eyes as I would have cracked and pulled the trigger. We left the rest of the lads searching the area for the rifle and returned to camp. Two days and twenty-eight pints of blood, all donated by his mates, seventeen-year old Private Francis Bell was one of the youngest soldiers to die at the hands of Gerry Adams and the IRA and everyone that had donated money to the them. I did not know the importance of Adams at the time of the shooting and it was only years later when giving an interview on television that I recognised him as the man with the mouth. Yes I remember you Gerry, you also described in your book the death of Private Bell, and did you promote him to an officer to help your conscience?

Why the fuck bother? We were only the middle men, keeping Catholic and Protestant Irish apart, dying because no politician had the balls to do their job and take the English out of Ireland. Oh, they will kill each other was the political argument to stay and occupy this part of Ireland, let them get on with it as it is an Irish problem not an English one, let the Americans be the middlemen. We English, Scottish and Welsh have a different mentality to this crowd who have the cheek to call themselves Protestants and Catholics but not a clue what is a CHRISTIAN. The thought of Ian Paisley, standing behind the Queen at the Armistice parade in London makes my blood boil. He being one of the main reasons the British were dying on the streets of Ireland. A friend told me he went on a world tour of friendly nations and was back in one day!

The Officers thought it might comfort Bell's family if they could speak with the soldiers that were with him when he had been shot. The mother, father and girlfriend sat in the middle and we circled them, sitting in chairs. For stupid ideas, I think that just about beat the lot, we could only sit and look at them, both groups in emotional pain. To a man we had a horrible lump in our throats and the odd tear. What could we say to comfort them? It could have been anyone of us that took the sniper's bullet, but it had "Dinga" Bell's name on it.

An intelligence report shortly afterwards stated that the fatal shot had indeed been fired from the shops from a well-concealed sniper who had remained hidden while the search had taken place. How did they come with that information when the shops had been well searched? If they knew so much why not give us his name and address? Justice is all we wanted!

The street photo shows an angle looking down Springhill Avenue from the side Corporal Hill was on. You can see the church and I have marked the shops where Hill searched, to the left of these was the apartment where I found Adams and two other men. The street walls have been painted to remove the IRA slogans and even after all these years no one lives in the houses on the right which were newly constructed at the time of Bell's murder.

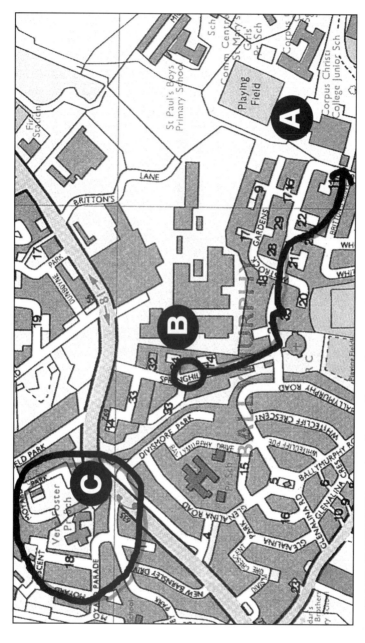

BALLYMURPHY: **A** - Army Barracks **B** - Springwell Avenue where Bell was shot **C** - Vera Foster School, Army post

THE KILL ZONE: Springhill Avenue: I treated the wounded Private Bell where he fell (Right of the picture) Cpl. Hill was left of picture when Bell was shot by the sniper located in the Shops on left.

Chapter 2

Aftermath

Bell's death was to be revenged; the junior ranks and privates were in total agreement to make life hell for the people of Ballymurphy. There were two weeks till the end of our tour of duty and we intended to make it a nightmare for the community. Communal punishment, as we believed they all had blood on their hands. Why did we feel so strong against these "Catholics" when we had many a Catholic within our Regiment and many an Irishman from North and South? They openly smiled and rejoiced that one of our comrades was murdered. Being a bit more aggressive than a normal Army unit we would not stand for it. Did we have any Human Rights or only them? A member of the Anglian Regiment was killed in a later incident, literally blown to pieces. A laughing member of this community handed over his eye, saying "your friend might need this." Not with our Unit, the wrong guys to fuck with!

Suggestions about how to get back at the locals flew thick and fast. Burn down their social centre was an instant hit with the lads. It was actually called the Ex-Serviceman's Club, but had bugger all to do with the British Legion. This club and another situated near the timber yard were the only safe, cheap, illegal drinking dens.

How about a curfew? Another suggestion carried by all. We can tell the Micks if we catch anyone on the streets after ten at night they will get seven barrels of shit kicked out of them. There were more suggestions, the talk went on and spirits lifted, in fact a good laugh.

We did not have the kit to make a bomb, the IRA were more professional and better equipped than us at laying their hands on that type of material. Bill Hastings had enough of talking, he filled a bottle with petrol and a little cloth to make the most basic bomb. We watched him walk out of the gates and two minutes later saw the flames shoot into the air followed by the bang. An officer coming out to go to the toilets saw us smiling. Looking at the orange glow in the night sky, he forgot the piss and ran back to the ops room to phone the fire brigade. Bill returned with a roar of approval from the lads. It just so happened, that it was Dinga Bell's patrol who were out on duty and they were ordered to the scene of the fire. The locals had gathered round and were watching the place burn. "It was them Protestant bastards," was the cry to the soldiers as they turned up. Corporal Hill moved his men away from the fire. He did not want his men to be the target of another sniper as they were silhouetted against the night sky. He had a smile of mischief on his face. He and his men waited out of sight in the next street. They did not have to wait long as the fire engine roared to the scene, lights flashing and sirens sounding. Hill stepped calmly into the middle of the street, raised his left hand, his right pointing his rifle towards the driver. The fire engine screeched to a halt! He walked over to confront the engine crew. "Where the fuck are you going in such a big hurry, making all that fucking noise?" The driver sat there lost for words, dumbfounded, but before he could respond he was dragged from the engine with the rest of the crew. "Spread them". They were all spread-eagled against the side of the fire engine. The officer in charge of the fire crew said "But we are going to the fire!" "What fucking fire?" screamed Hill, as the night sky exploded in an orange ball of flame. Smoke billowed and bits of burning wood and cinders began to rain down all around them, striking the fire engine and bouncing off into the street.

Hill reached to the fireman's belt. "What the fuck!" he shouted in the mans ear. "Carrying a fucking offensive weapon...cunt!!!! Face the front...CUNT!" Staring like a mad dog into the fireman's eyes. Hill embedded the sharp axe into the roll of fire hose. The officer seemed to take the hint. "We will be on our way and not make so much noise in the future" as he tried to appease the mad soldier. "Turn this wagon round, fuck off and I will not report the offensive weapon". The patrol were standing in the background, pissing themselves laughing as the fire engine did like a ten point turn, crashed its gears and raced back into the night. That night the Fire Brigade thought the Army was going mad.

The drinking den collapsed with a loud roar, sending a column of sparks up into the night air. The creosoted wooden building had not lasted long, but the lads had a good uplift and more to come for the Irish bastards. These events were talked about back at the school and obviously exaggerated, but the base of truth was there.

Every patrol that went out gave the local yobs hell and warned them about curfew-breaking. The gentle knee in the balls emphasised the point. What individual patrols got up to was the talk of the Company, morale and comradeship improved and no patrol wanted to be outdone in feats of mischief and revenge.

Being an ex-medic, I easily got some needles and syringes from our first aid post. The blocked smelly urinal had given me an idea. The full syringes I carefully put into my weapons pouch, out on early patrol, following the local milkman, a little bit of piss injected under the full cream top was all you wanted on your cornflakes in the morning. It was a pity AIDS had not been around at the time!

One patrol raided the local timber yard carrying, with great difficulty, heavy railway sleepers, quietly placing them against the doors of known IRA members. When someone displays a replica AK47 rifle made by inmates of Long Kesh internment camp above his fireplace for all passers-by to see, you know he is not a supporter of British democracy. Yes, you've got it, knock on the door and run away - good clean childish fun. It made your stomach sore crying with laughter, especially when they screamed! The lads were fighting for the privilege to ring the door bell.

There had always been a problem with the local dogs giving our positions away. Talking years later to a Catholic woman who had lived in the area, she put it down to the dogs smelling our fear. Well, every fucker must be frightened passing my house because my dogs bark, that's what you have them for. This problem was solved by injecting mouth watering steaks with poison. We felt sorry for the dogs. The poison was supplied by a policeman, who used to come round and sell stolen goods to the soldiers.

By this time the locals were sick of us. I have inserted some press cutting from the time. The Commanding Officer was snowed under with complaints from the local populace. We had kept him in the dark and he did not have a clue what was going on. At first he thought the complaints weren't justified and could not believe what he was being told. Then one day he saw the light. He was touring the area in a Land Rover checking on the lads. "What has that man got on his belt?" he enquired to the driver. "Looks like dogs' tails, Sir". Then the shit hit the fan.

They were frightened to break the curfew, they knew we were angry and some lads had to be restrained by other soldiers when a curfew breaker was caught.

On the third night of our retaliation, Paddy Devlin and another Member of Parliament for the area tried to break the curfew. Bawling through a hand held PA he shouted "there is no curfew." Corporal Fox accidentally broke the PA, which was not made very well. Then he found that MP's balls are the same size as the rest of us mortals, if not smaller. We made the papers again the next day as they were organising protests to get the Paras out! The CO was not going to get a medal out of this tour of duty and started getting the Sergeant Major to fuck the troops about, in an attempt to restore discipline.

The IRA was ordered into action again by our friend of

peace, Gerry Adams. Are those wings the Pope has given you? This time my friend Scouse was the Patrol Commander and I was the number two, leading the left side of the road going up Whiterock Gardens, another sunny day, you don't get many in Ireland. The sniper was on my side of the road, his target turned out to be a big popular Irish Paratrooper "Paddy McClay". He had to shoot at the last man, as he was the nearest, with his back as the target. I had stopped at a house as I could hear our radio operator from inside as the owner was monitoring our frequency; I turned and was just about to call on Scouse. The crack and thump were instant, again the Armalite rifle was used, the sniper was a nervous wanker, as at such close range, less than 50 metres, he missed and the bullet hit the concrete door support of the front gate, inches from the target. With the quick reaction from the lads diving for cover No chance of a second shot. I got up and started running for the sniper. He could not see me unless he exposed his position, he was on my side of the street and I was running head-on to a back-shooter. A guy with an English accent shouted from a doorway, "It's those lads at the corner that set you up". Brave man risking his life giving me that sort of information. Who the hell was he? I still don't know. Unfortunately I found myself on my own, as I had refused Scouse's order to take cover. I was against his orders as I thought he was being over-cautious, you have to take a risk when fighting these bastards and I was sure the sniper was on my side of the road and running.

"Down or I will shoot you fuckers," I shouted as I pointed my rifle at the youth section of the IRA. I had put fear into these kids as they all went to the ground. They were situated on the corner of a road that linked Whiterock Gardens and Whiterock Drive. I have put in this detail so, if they buy my book, they will remember the incident. Then I noticed them looking towards a woman with a pram. She shouted a warning to someone inside and the door was slammed closed. I am sure the sniper's weapon was to have been hidden in the pram with the baby, but my quickness on the scene stopped that plan. I shouted to Scouse but the patrol had not moved and without someone I realised I was out-numbered by the young IRA. Storming the house on my own was a bit silly, so I returned to Scouse and reported. We found the spent case from the rifle and it was a 5.56 mm case from an Armalite. The rifle had to be within a small area, but for some reason the CO did not send out more soldiers so that we could cordon off and search the small area between the shooting and the escape route. Again, as Commanding Officer, Major Patton, with over one hundred men at his disposal, did not react when he was less than two hundred metres from the shooting incident.

We did manage to round up the twelve young IRA volunteers, who were trying to move out of the area, all under sixteen years of age, future fodder for Gerry, get them in young and again, the democratic state protected young offenders, even for attempted murder. Child soldiers, was there no level too low for this man! These kids were killers being praised by their so-called betters so you could say it was not their fault but how would you feel if they tried to kill you or a member of your family! It is so sad that 18 of these children would die in the conflict fighting the British Army but the blood is on the hands of their parents and Gerry Adams for putting them in the front line. I do not doubt their courage and sacrifice for a united Ireland. They were just being used by a coward that would not put his own life on the line, but thought nothing of sacrificing these children. The battalion HQ sent an armoured car to take them into custody for questioning by the police. We gave them a good kicking onto the wagon, I suppose out of frustration on our part, as the system would not punish them. Then on arrival at Battalion HQ, situated at Black Mountain School a good friend of mine Ginge Shatford, gave them a good kicking off at the other end. Talk about bad luck, civil rights people, MPs and a group of crap-hat officers were looking into complaints from the locals. Then they witnessed "Ginge" kicking shit out of those kids. He got three months in Crumlin Road jail and was kicked out of the Army as we were working within the system.

The lads were taking revenge on the locals and some people you should not annoy. Geordie N, he may have once been good-looking but in a fight in Newcastle someone had bitten his nose off. The guy that had sewn it back on needed glasses, as it sure did not fit right. So fight him, he now had a thing about noses. Friend or nose, he went for it and tried to bite it off. If he liked you, he would give you the nose back to get stitched, back on but to an enemy, he would chew it and swallow it. I did mention to him that I would kill him if he did it to me, he knew I meant it, so we were good mates and fellow Geordies. It did not go down well in Aldershot when in a bar; he bit the balls off the owner's Labrador dog. Now he was let loose on the local Paddies.

The lads went over the top one night with one curfew-breaker, a rifle that got shoved down his throat got stuck coming back out. I heard it was the attachment where you fix your bayonet which caused the problem, it got stuck on some fleshy, sensitive spot at the back of his throat. Ammunition was found in his pocket. Was it planted on him? Well with the mood of the blokes anything could happen. If one side has no rules why should we obey rules and laws? In the beginning of the troubles the Paras were used against the Protestants who were trying to burn out the Catholics, now sympathy for the Catholics was at such a low I doubt if we would have helped without being ordered and then with little enthusiasm.

Then one night patrol, a woman came running up to me and begged me to come into her house and help her husband. You had to be wary. Is this a set-up? You could not trust anybody any more, so I undid my safety catch on my rifle. The woman was genuine; her old man was in a bad way, a stomach problem which looked like a burst ulcer, he was spewing up bile and blood. Why should I help? He lived near Springhill Avenue, they all knew a soldier was to be shot and did nothing, but I was not going to fall to the same level as Gerry, so I gave first aid and got an ambulance urgently sending him to hospital. I even phoned the hospital to prepare them for his arrival, I saved his life but would he have done the same for me? Another patrol had a similar experience trying to help a local woman and I reproduce the press cutting as proof we were not as bad as the IRA propaganda painted us.

Major Patton was a pure Rupert and a budding General, hard to think what book or famous person he was trying to copy. He gave me orders to take my patrol to set up an observation post in one of the empty houses in Springhill Avenue. It was a clear night and a full moon out, we moved into the allocated house. With men covering the front and back doors, I climbed into the loft with my radio operator and two riflemen. The loft had a skylight which we removed and we positioned the starlight scope. This nightscope was a brilliant piece of good kit; it literally made night into day. Everything had a green tinge about it but, you had good visibility and an edge over the enemy. It did strain your eyes with prolonged use, so we constantly changed rota observing through it.

There he was, a guy with a fag sitting in the back garden of 24 Divismoor Park and a rifle resting against the house wall. This was also the boundary between our company and a company from 1st Battalion Parachute Regiment, famous because of "Bloody Sunday". I sent a situation report and asked our HQ 'ZERO' as known on the radio, to locate any friendly forces in the area. The gunman had not moved and was still enjoying his fag. Then the HQ informed us that there were no friendly forces in the area. I carefully studied the situation, I would have to leave my observation post, move my patrol in open line to get closer and engage the now designated enemy position. I only had one night scope which was not zeroed in. That is to say it had not been tested at the ranges and was not in line with the rifle sights. So if I opened fire at night I would have to use the combined fire of the patrol to engage the target which was against the rule book I was carrying. I had a doubt in the back of my mind; if this was IRA he was one cool, relaxed son of a gun. The officer had to make the decision so I put the ball back in his court. "You have double checked that this is not friendly forces and you are giving me the order to engage". The voice was raised; "He is not, I repeat, not friendly". Well I had covered myself, I moved out from my Observation post and moved closer to engage the enemy, informing all units that I am going to open fire. Then, as we were moving out to do the job on this guy, the panic, a total breakdown in radio procedure. "Don't shoot don't shoot it is a Para patrol," My radio operator said it for me on the open air "You fucking idiot, you nearly caused the death of one of ours."

Another incident worth mentioning was when on the second last day of tour I stopped a group of people walking up Springhill Ave. Two IRA men were giving a guided tour to a group of Americans from NORAID. I couldn't resist stopping them and having a chat.

"Get your fucking hands on the wall and spread them", I shouted at the top of my voice. It was like the movies, and then this big fat American cow demands that her small weak husband Herbert takes a photo of this! "Take your hands off the wall Herbert and I'll blow your fucking head off." First round to me, as he quickly replaced his hands on the wall, which must have been the first time he had not obeyed his wife. I had the lads give them a search and I searched the two Paddies giving the tour. One had his dole card and the other his family allowance book which they carried to avoid us taking them in for an ID check up. I concentrated on the mouth, Herbert's wife. "Well who are you and what are you doing?" She was proud to tell me she was on a fact finding tour so she could report back to her NORAID Organisation in America, land of the brave and free. "Well I will help you with your mission from a soldier's point of view. Lads which of you are Catholics?" I did not honestly know till three of them put their hands up, two Scousers and a Paddy. One lad is from Southern Ireland serving with the British Army and even speaks Gaelic which the two IRA escorts did not, then they have the cheek to call themselves real Irishmen. "This is a dole card and this a family allowance book, the one with the family allowance is on over a hundred and thirty pound a week, twice my wages. So this means they do not work and are therefore paid by the British Government to feed them, they don't pay rent or rates either. So any money you raise for them is not for food as they are not that proud as to refuse a hand out from the British". I stated. "Yes but look at the state of the place," with this remark I remembered the council workers playing cards. "Well before you take your hands down I would like you to look up at the sky." They all like sheep look up; "Do you see any B52s dropping napalm on the natives?" "This is not Vietnam" she retorts. "Look over the wall do you see any Mai Ly massacre?", again she was not happy with my comments against American behaviour towards their communist enemy. "We have captured a few AK47s so you do not mind them buying guns with your money." Then I led them to where the council workers were so they could have a chat. "I hope you now tell your friends in America that they are giving money to terrorists and they all have blood on their hands".

In the school we were stationed, out of boredom, I picked up a kids' book and started to read it. The teacher had given them the task to write an essay "Why we hate the British Army." There is no end to this conflict when you realise what is meant by in-bred hatred.

As we moved out of Ballymurphy I was in an open Land Rover, I saw ahead of us a woman carrying a young baby, wrapped in a beautiful white christening shawl; she turned and spoke to the child, as we approached. With a proud smile she beamed as the child raised two fingers. She had taught her child to hate the British before it could talk, or walk, now I knew these ignorant people.

Protest by Falls M.P. at delay in sending ambulance

FALLS M.P., Mr. Paddy Devlin, last night protested to Lord Channon, Minister of State, about the two-hour delay in sending an ambulance to a Ballymurphy woman who died from loss of blood early on Sunday morning.

The woman was Mrs. Mary Catherine Cosgrave (39), mother of 12 children, of Ballymurphy Parade. She was expecting another child in a few weeeks' time.

Her husband, Mr. Charles Cosgrave (41), claimed yesterday that during two hours in which his wife was badly haemorrhaging efforts were made by him and soldiers of the 2nd Parachute Regiment to get an ambulance. But the ambulance was reluctant to come out.

Mr. Devlin told Lord Channon that he was greatly concerned at the way Mrs. Cosgrave lost her life.

"That a modern ambulance service, so highly efficient that it attracts great praise on the same day this happened, takes two hours to arrive properly equipped to deal with a simple haemorrhage case, completely and utterly baffles me."

Welcomed investigation

Mr. Devlin said he welcomed the suggestion from the Hospitals Authority that an investigation into the case would be held.

He pointed out to Lord Channon that an inquiry should be extended to cover the policy purporting to provide an ambulance service for the entire community.

If there was any doubt about a full and free service being withheld from the Lower and Upper Falls areas, service that is extended to that part of the community which that service's personnel favour."

Nurse contacted by Military

A nurse, Mrs. Lynn Turner, who was contacted by the military during the attempts to get the ambulance to Mrs. Cosgrave yesterday told of being wakened at about 2-45 a.m.

The soldiers told her that Mrs. Cosgrave could not get an ambulance because the ambulance said they could not come out without a line from the doctor.

"I went up to the house and found Mrs. Cosgrave lying on the floor with blood everywhere. I said: 'This woman is dying, ring 999.'

"The ambulance came out then but they could do nothing and they radioed for special equipment and the ambulance driver went off to get it.

"It was 40 minutes before they returned, despite the fact that I can drive to the Royal Victoria Hospital in seven minutes by private car."

Mrs. Turner added: "I am convinced that if this woman had had an ambulance at the beginning she would be alive to-day".

Devlin accuses Paras

SOCIAL Democratic and Labour Party M.P. for Falls, Mr. Paddy Devlin, last night complained to the "Irish News" that troops of the Parachute Regiment harassed people at the centre set up to hear complaints against the regiment.

Mr. Devlin said that, shortly after the centre opened at 7 p.m., two members of a foot patrol came in and began to ask the voluntary helpers their names, addresses and what they were doing.

'Get out'

"When they questioned me, I told them I was Member of Parliament for the area, but refused to give them my name or address," Mr. Devlin added. "I then told them to get out of the premises as they were interfering with my constituency duty."

The two soldiers then left the centre, but remained outside questioning people visiting it. Mr. Devlin claimed that they threatened one man, beaten by them earlier, that if he reported the incident "they would come back and get him."

Mr. Devlin also claimed that a woman worker at the centre, returning from investigating a complaint, was forced to open her handbag while the contents were examined.

"This general harassment continued until I contacted Mr. Frank Steele, the U.K. representative, and the C.O. of the 2nd Paras, Lt.-Colonel Geoffrey Howlett, and asked them to remove the soldiers from the vicinity of the centre. The soldiers were subsequently moved about 30 yards down the road," the M.P. added.

Mr. Devlin said he also told Colonel Howlett the names of the person who had loaned him the premises at 23 Britton's Parade, and the man threatened by the soldiers. "I did this to make certain that neither men suffers as a result of his actions," said Mr. Devlin.

disperse after a demonstration.

10/9/72

'Very serious'

A soldier was shot in the head while on foot patrol in Springhill Avenue, Ballymurphy, Belfast, yesterday. His condition was last night described at the Royal Victoria Hospital as "very serious."

The wounded soldier was serving with the Parachute Regiment and last night the families in the Upper Falls area reported that the "Paras are running riot" in the area. A Pressman from the Twenty-Six Counties who had been threatened by Paras last night was getting into his car when he heard a loud behind him and turned to find that a civilian had been viciously clubbed on the head with a rifle butt.

The injured man was taken to the Royal Victoria Hospital with severe head injuries. He is understood to be a barman from Whiterock Crescent.

People in the area reported that they had been subjected to threats from members of the Parachute Regiment throughout the day and had been told that anyone on the street after 11 p.m. "would be dealt with".

"They have been working themselves into a frenzy all night" a local housewife said. "They have the district in a grip of terror."

Another soldier shot outside St. Genevieve's school Army post last night was later said to be "not seriously" injured. He was entering the post after going off patrol when a sniper opened fire.

Mill fire

Fire, believed to have been started maliciously, badly damaged a big Lisburn mill late last night. The blaze was at the Island Mill, Canal Street. Fire Authority headquarters later reported that a section of the mill had been gutted.

And in Lurgan, fire destroyed an outhouse at the Ormeau Bakery farm. It was not immediately known how the fire started. The building will be examined to-day by forensic experts.

A privately-owned Customs clearance caravan at Mopaghan Road, Armagh, was destroyed by fire late last night. The caravan had replaced a hut gutted in a petrol bomb attack two weeks ago.

Strabane had two hours of rioting when stones and bottles were hurled at troops at Bridge Street and Mellmount Road yesterday.

The Army fired rubber bullets to disperse about 200 youths and one arrest was made.

An electricity van was hijacked but it was recovered by the Army undamaged. The rioting occurred as the result of the arrest of James Logue, Patrician Villas, Strabane, on Friday night who was later charged at a special court with the attempted murder of a British soldier by throwing a blast bomb. Townspeople claimed that he was not involved.

A meeting was held yesterday in the Fountain Street area of the town and it was decided not to send children to school to-day as a protest against the arrest. It was also decided to hold a public meeting to-night, which, it was hoped, would be addressed by Miss Bernadette Devlin, M.P.

Automatic gunfire was heard in the New Lodge Road-North Queen Street area of Belfast late last night but there were no reports of casualties.

Imperial Hotel incident

Two men are helping police with their enquiries after an early morning shooting incident outside Belfast's bomb-wrecked Imperial Hotel yesterday.

An Army spokesman said men had been firing at two unarmed civilians. When a military patrol appeared, the car by which two gunmen had been standing drove off.

The two unarmed men then attacked the other two men with their fists, said the spokesman.

The two men being questioned are both Protestants. The men fired on are Catholics, who were keeping watch on valuable property inside the hotel pending its removal.

In the rubble of the Imperial—as a result of Thursday's explosion two people died and 50 more were injured—soldiers found a pistol thrown there after the shooting.

Welsh Guardsmen have discovered an arms dump in the Markets area of Belfast.

In the rafters of a garage they found an American sten gun with two full magazines, an Armalite rifle with one magazine; two loaded Webley revolvers; a Luger pistol with 52 rounds, and more than 50 rounds of other assorted ammunition.

gun battle

OUTBREAK AFTER ARREST OF LOCAL PROVO LEADER

By BELFAST TELEGRAPH REPORTER

ONE MAN was shot dead and another man and a soldier were wounded during gun battles in the Ardoyne area of Belfast last night after the capture of a Provisional IRA leader.

Police said that ammunition for an Armalite rifle was found in the pocket of the dead man when his body was brought to the Royal Victoria Hospital.

They said his body was recovered after troops opened fire on a gunman on waste ground at Flax Street.

The gunman opened fire on troops in the area after he was handed a rifle by a woman who was with him.

But, according to the RUC, soldiers fired at him and he fell. The woman then ran off with the rifle.

Twenty minutes later, a gunman fired a number of high-velocity shots at troops in the Brompton Park area. The soldiers returned fire and claimed a hit.

But police said the body of the gunman was dragged away by friends.

Earlier, troops claimed a hit on a gunman when they engaged him in Butler Street.

A man was then admitted to the Mater Hospital with serious gunshot wounds in his head.

He was named by the RUC as Gerard Kane, of Jamaica Street in the Ardoyne area.

During the trouble, soldiers of the 1st Bn. The Light Infantry were attacked with stones, bottles and blast bombs. One soldier was slightly wounded when he was struck in the head by a bullet which ricocheted.

Troops fired rubber bullets to try and disperse stone-throwers.

The Army claimed three positive and one possible hit on gunmen during the night.

The commander of the Ardoyne battalion of the Provisionals was arrested when soldiers went into a house in Jamaica Street, yesterday afternoon.

Another soldier died in hospital in Belfast last night almost eight weeks after he was shot.

He was Pte. Thomas Stoker (18), single, of the 1st Bn. The Light Infantry. Pte. Stoker, who came from Wakefield, Yorks., was shot on July 29.

Earlier, 18-year-old Pte. Frank Bell, single, of the 2nd Bn. The Parachute Regt., died in hospital from wounds he sustained when he was shot by a gunman in Belfast on Sunday.

Pte. Bell was from New Ferry, Cheshire.

Police and troops last night dispersed a crowd after stone-throwing incidents in the Lepper Street/Duncairn area of the city.

Five men — three of them armed with pistols — held up staff of The Office Cleaning Company at Holywood Road in Belfast last night and escaped with a small sum of money.

Bangor — Residents of a house at Braeside Close put out a fire in the living room after a nail bomb with an incendiary device was thrown through a window. It exploded and set fire to a settee, but no-one was hurt.

Newry — Two bursts of automatic fire were directed at a mobile patrol of the Argyll and Sutherland Highlanders at the Derrybeg housing estate.

Magherafelt — An electricity pylon in Ballylaguily was damaged by an explosion caused by a device attached to one of the supporting legs.

Londonderry — There were only two shooting incidents involving troops in the city last night.

Three shots were fired at troops at Rosemount and one shot was directed at an Army post at Drumahoe.

In Bogside and the Creggan, rubber bullets and a water cannon were used to disperse small groups of young people stoning Army patrols.

No. 32,150   BELFAST, THURSDAY, SEPTEMBER 21, 1972

DOCUMENT

plan
;lo-
itrol

e policy document
l the Republic of
:ept joint interim re-
:hern Ireland through

an Assembly and an
themselves all powers
ind financial subven-

a declaration that it would
ities in both islands if Ire-
all the people of Ireland,
sitively encourage such a

PROVOS DENY R.V.H. THREAT

A spokesman for the Royal Victoria Hospital in Belfast reported yesterday that a message had been received from the 2nd Battalion Provisional I.R.A. saying that the second alleged threat against the hospital, announced this week in the Press, was totally without foundation.

Mr. Robert Spence, the R.V.H. group secretary, said it had been confirmed that there would be no attacks on the wards, clinical or residential units which were now functioning as an open site. There could be no similar guarantees given in respect of premises on the perimeter of the hospital at present occupied by troops.

Anti-internment

Curfew in Whiterock area
—Paddy Devlin

A MILITARY curfew is being operated in the Whiterock area of Belfast with people being ordered indoors after 11 p.m. under threat of being shot or arrested, said an angry Mr. Paddy Devlin, the SDLP M.P., for Falls, last night.

He advised residents to disregard the orders given by troops to get off the streets. "Under no circumstances must they observe any curfew or ban on their movements."

Mr. Devlin said that when he protested to the Whitelaw office the claim was denied. But the facts of the case were otherwise.

Said Mr. Devlin: "I would advise the people of the Whiterock district to come out of their homes to-morrow evening and, in a dignified way, thus make certain that no soldier groups attempt to place them under curfew.

The M.P. said that he and the SDLP secretary, Mr. Julian Jacottet were subjected to troop harassment and acts of humiliation when they were trying to interview constituents.

Both were made to stand with their hands against a wall with feet wide apart. A L-Corporal of the 2nd Paras stationed in the area was particularly objectionable. He insisted on seeing Mr. Devlin's identification papers while refusing to let him take his hands from the wall. In fact Mr. Devlin was well-known to the L-Corporal.

Eventually he told the individual that he was taking his hands from the wall to establish his identity . . ." and he could do what he damned well liked about it."

He continued to ask what Mr. Devlin was doing in the area. Eventually it got through to him that part of an M.P.'s job was to be with his constituents.

Mr. Jacottet described the treatment of the M.P. as intolerable and added that it would be put up with nowhere else.

To lead the Irish Government team

The Irish Attorney-General Mr. Colm Condon, and chief states solicitor, Mr. Liam Lysaght, will lead the Irish Government's team at the

Pictured at the meeting yesterday to launch t tion in Ireland (l. to r.): Mr. Denis Barrett, Governor of Northern Ireland; Dr. G. B. Newe; Co-Chairmen of PACE. See

Says he was forced to sig clearing Captain of char

EX-INTERNEI

X-RAYS WILL TRAP THE GUN RUNNER

The British Army's latest anti-terrorist device — nickname Flicker — yesterday made its first public appearance.

Using it, troops claim they will be able to stop and search a car within a matter of seconds—by means of X-Rays.

Flicker is a massive X-Ray machine attached to the back of a standard four-ton Army lorry.

It was developed for use in Northern Ireland by an English research and development company and, housed to its makers, it has already conclusively proved that it can detect hidden weapons and ammunition.

When a motorist is stopped, his vehicle is attached to a trolley. It is then winched into the back of the lorry, where it passes through the X-ray machine.

Fifty yards away, in a specially armoured landrover, the X-rays are monitored on four screens by trained troops. If anything suspicious

BRIT O

AN 18-year-old British Arm statement clearin beaten and insul

The officer is Ca Bibby, of the 2nd B the Royal Regimen iers — victors u colonel, John Chur Duke of Marlborou Boyne, Cork and 1690.

Mr. McNally's was made at a Pr ence in Belfast du full details were charges.

They began w young men, incl McNally, were a September 5 last day they made sta the Northern Ire Rights Association arrests and these were distributed to and published.

Article

On September 1

sure their premises were secure. The area had been cleared for about three-quarters-or-an-hour after a warning about the bomb was given. Shops in High Street, Edward Street and Market Street had windows shattered —many for the third time in the past six months.

In Belfast a furniture store in Upper North Street was wrecked yesterday by a "sofa bomb."

Three teenagers hijacked a vanload of furniture bound for the store. They ripped into a sofa and stuffed it with 200lbs. of explosives. They then delivered the load.

Building wrecked

The store owner, Mr. Fred Hewitt, said: "We suspected something was wrong when we sniffed the couch — we could smell the explosives. Then we tried to move it. It weighed four times what it should have done and we knew something was wrong."

Staff alerted troops nearby as police got a phone warning about the bomb. The store and street were cleared in five minutes and the bomb went off 45 minutes later.

No one was hurt but the three-storey building containing the store was wrecked. Hundreds of windows in nearby shops were shattered by the blast.

'Painters' breach the barrier

Two men posing as painters got through the strict security cordon around Derry City centre yesterday to plant a bomb in the former Northern Counties hotel building in Waterloo Place. The men carried gallon paint tins and went into an office of the building now occupied by the Community Relations Commission, wired the tins together and left.

The offices were being renovated and the painters on the job had gone to lunch. An Army spokesman said the bogus painters even had the colour of the paint right.

The 30 lb. bomb did not go

After four hours the Army experts took the explosives out of the building to what an Army spokesman said was 'a

1,000 AT 'PARAS OUT' MEETING IN BALLYMURPHY

29/9/72

NEARLY 1,000 people attended a "Paras Out" protest meeting in Ballymurphy last night.

Among the speakers at the open air meeting which was organised by local Republican clubs, were ex-internee Mr. Des O'Hagan of the County Antrim Executive of Republican Clubs and Mr. Raymond O'Hagan, a member of the NICRA Executive. The chairman was ex-internee Mr. Harry Flynn.

Another speaker, Ethel McAllister, the proposed Official Sinn Fein candidate for the area, urged the women of the district to unite in their efforts to safeguard their homes and the well-being of their men-folk by taking part in vigilante operations.

Afterwards, the Roger Casement Republican Club protested in a statement about the "continuous raiding of houses in the New Barnaley and Moyard area by the Parachute Regiment."

The statement said that one house in Moyard had been raided 15 times in the past two months. On several days the house had been raided four times.

'End it' call

"Each time they come they give no reason for the raids other than they are 'routine searches.' It has reached the stage where the woman of the house is attending her doctor for treatment for her nerves and her husband is seeking accommodation for the family in another area away from the Paras. We call for an

The blast happened 10 minutes later but the area was cleared. There were no casualties.

end to the harassment of this family immediately, and we fully support the activities of the Ballymurphy - Whiterock Republican Clubs in seeking the withdrawal of the Paras from all civilised areas."

In a joint statement after the meeting, the James Larkin the Betsy Gray, the Thomas Clarke and William Orr Republican Clubs said: "It is the purpose of our protest to clear the Paras out of the area for good, and while any regiment of Paratroops remain the protests will continue. The clubs will continue the fight for social and economic change that is so badly needed in the area and resolve not to lose sight of our final goal.

"To-night's meeting proved that the people will back all peaceful protest and we warn the Paras to beware of the risen people of Ballymurphy and Whiterock. The people's wishes will never be met unless they show unity of purpose. We asked on Tuesday for the help of any organisation or individual interested in peace and justice in this campaign. It is with regret that we say such offers have been few and far between."

The clubs will mount a picket next week at St. Peter's School which is still occupied by British troops. They asked for support for a meeting to be held by the Civil Rights Association on Sunday in the area.

TO PRAY FOR PEACE AND VISIT GRAVES

THE decision to hold an Act of Intercession for peace, in Belfast City Cemetery on Sunday, has met with widespread approval by both Catholics and Protestants.

Rev. Kenneth Ruddock, of the Church of Ireland parish of Lower Falls, said yesterday that the City Cemetery had been chosen for a number of reasons. There had been a lot of vandalism in it, but this had been spotlighted because it was a Protestant Cemetery in a Catholic district. People were reluctant to visit graves of relatives

the other clergy thought it would be a good idea to hold the service there and give the people an opportunity to visit the graves.

Among those who hope to attend is Most Rev. Dr. William Philbin, Bishop of Down and Connor.

Many Catholics living in the Whiterock area will also

was appalled at the amount of vandalism that was occurring in the cemetery and could not understand the mentality of those who resorted to such vile behaviour as damaging graves and smashing headstones. It was the act of uncivilised people, and the residents of Whiterock had to hang their heads in shame at some of the acts of vandalism committed.

He expressed the hope that Sunday's ceremony would bring home to these people that their acts were deplored by all sections of the community. It was, he added, a terrible state of affairs when

Chapter 3

Tell the truth, Gerry Adams.

Two lives were ruined the day Gerry organised the murder of Private Francis Bell. When I approached reporter Liam Clarke from the Sunday Times, he checked out my story to validate what I was saying. He brought to my attention that a man called Liam Holden had been arrested for the murder of Francis Bell, which took me by surprise as I had never heard about it. He also pointed out that Holden claimed he was innocent and arranged for me to speak with this convicted terrorist killer of my friend and comrade.

He had been a chef working long hours and did not have time to be involved with the IRA, and he also had an alibi for the time of the shooting of Francis Bell. A police double agent had fingered him as the killer and had said where a 303 Lee Enfield rifle could be found with two rounds fired from the magazine. Wrong rifle, and everyone in Ballymurphy, Army and civilians only heard one round fired. I say double agent as this informer still lives in Ballymurphy and had he been a true informer he would have been a long time dead or in hiding.

The police did not arrest Holden but passed on the information to the Army. A group of Paras from the 1st Battalion was despatched to arrest Holden. Now this is a murder involving a dead Para and they send Paras' to arrest him, just does not sound right from the start. He claims he was beaten up by the Paras, now nobody would believe nice Paras would do such a cruel thing to someone who had been fingered for killing a comrade! Obviously there had been witnesses or he might not have made it out of his house or is that what the police wanted?

Holden was taken to a Protestant area Spring Martin estate, where the locals were told this was an IRA killer and they were going to let him go. Now with the option of being lynched or signing a confession what would you have done? He signed the confession and that was the only evidence that convicted him. The confession he signed stated he had acted alone and had dumped the rifle, a 303 Lee Enfield, as he ran from the scene, on open ground, near Curry's timber yard. Also he had fired two shots and the recovered rifle had a magazine with two bullets missing, what a coincidence! The rifle had been found two weeks before his arrest in the house of an old couple who say the IRA forced them to hide it for them. It was never proved to be the rifle used in the killing or to have any link with Holden.

The statement from Corporal Hill was a pack of lies and this man was later given a commission in the SAS Regiment, I always wondered why! His actions in Ireland showed he had no love for them which I can understand but he owes an innocent man 18 years of his life. Hill in his statement said he had given first aid treatment to Bell and had carried him to safety. The ambulance arrived and he carried on with his patrol, short and sweet, but not the truth. Could you imagine him carrying on with the patrol as if nothing had happened! Why did you lie to the court, Sir?

Holden was sentenced to death by hanging, (fucking hell was my verbal expression on hearing that) the judge being very formal even wearing a black cloth on his head as he sentenced him to death. The first man since James Henratty, to be sentenced to death! On death row waiting for sentence to be carried out I could just imagine how he felt, especially when innocent OK, he could have done the crime or anyone else but the evidence against him was a joke. Fortunately a Protestant was also given the death sentence for murder and sentenced to hang. William Whitelaw reduced the death sentence for both men to life in prison or Holden would have hung. Another little fact that proves Holden was innocent puts doubt about his conviction was that the IRA never recognised the court but Holden had recognised the British court of law.

Then we make the claim that British justice is the best in the world. Is it not more the case of who you are with the British system and how much money you have with the American system? I think at the time the government was eager to execute a rebel to show an example, as I remember reading in the press that we still had the death sentence for treason and a short time later we have someone to hang. The IRA that started the first uprising in 1918 did not have the sympathy of the Irish as they were jeered and mocked by the public crowd that lined the route as they were taken to prison. Then the British government started to execute the ringleaders and made martyrs of the rebels which was over the top and united the Irish, with a backlash against the British that forced them to withdraw from Southern Ireland. Obviously our government did not know how to handle the situation then or learn from past history and were about to fall into the same over-reaction that would unite the Irish. If Holden had been hung and the IRA then admitted the crime what would have been the outcome, the whole world against the British for hanging an innocent Catholic. Was this another IRA plot the killings on "Bloody Sunday" which caused thousands to join the terrorist ranks and again millions of dollars in financial backing from America outraged by the so-called over reaction by the British Army.

Holden spent the next 18 years in prison and is now out on parole but cannot leave the country. To think I was always in favour of the death penalty, especially to terrorists but to frame a innocent man makes you lose credibility in the system. I would have no problem kicking the stool away from Gerry Adams as I was sure then and now he was part of this murder and to prove it he even writes about it in his memoirs. Then Gerry is best mates with Tony Blair and the Pope. Are they blind, does Blair not read the intelligence reports about Adams or does he only believe the ones about weapons of mass destruction? If you can let the IRA out of jail for the crimes they have committed then no person should be left in a British jail, as the majority of British criminals have never done crimes that even compare to those committed by the IRA!

Friends and family which includes high-ranking police officers and Catholics, even my own Catholic wife, say to me: Why say anything to help Holden? The fact that he was arrested and I was a principal witness that was never called to his trial, with evidence that implicated Gerry Adams and two other men. Why frame Holden, was it a punishment to his family as his sister had married a soldier? In Holden's statement admitting guilt he said he acted alone, why was that put into the statement, was someone getting protected so many years ago?

I firmly believe the law should be equal for all men and I do not give a shit what religion they are!

Another question put to me, was if the shoe was on the other foot would Holden help me? I can live with my conscience and it is up to Holden to live with his. Yes it would be easier for me not to help but I know right from wrong, be one of the sheep is what I feel people are saying to me; go with the system and let conviction stand, after all, he was a Catholic!

Then I believe that the men that went over the top in the First World War were like sheep, most did not know what they were fighting or dying for and they went over because all the sheep were doing the same, lambs to the slaughter. To me the brave man was the one that refused because his conscience said this was wrong as the class system was telling them to make the ultimate sacrifice without sufficient reason.

There is no doubt Holden did not have a fair trial as his lawyers had not been given all the facts in the case. He was in the hands of the paratroopers three hours before being handed over to the police and handed over with a signed confession. Does anyone believe in those three hours he was given a guided tour around the City of Belfast?

Then another twist in the story was that a sergeant with

the paratroopers claiming to be a member of the Special Air Service Regiment. SAS are trained to withstand torture for three days and thus they also know how to torture, very similar to what happens to Iraqi and other Arab prisoners. At this time in Northern Ireland there was no official acknowledgment of the use of Special Forces operating in Ireland. I have copied numerous newspaper cuttings from the time of Holden's arrest, trial, conviction and sentence of death by hanging. In one you will read that the court was indeed emptied so that someone of some importance in British counter-terrorism could give evidence against Holden. Only the judge at the trial would be able to say who this man really was and what evidence did he have that convinced him of Holden's guilt. Were the SAS operating in Ireland before the official proclamation sending in a Sabre Squadron in 1976? In a later chapter you will read a story that was told to me and you might have the same question as I have, did we have a General Pinochet with such power that he could have a free hand to torture and even execute people?

One reason why Holden may have been convicted is that solicitors in Northern Ireland seem to either defend Protestants or Catholics so you have the same partisan attitude within the law. Even with my information to the Criminal Cases Review Commission, it may not be used to help Holden, as some lawyers would not want to use my evidence as they do not want to cause damage to the Republican movement or Gerry Adams and would rather see an innocent man swing, even if he is a Catholic. It was pointed out to me by the members of the CCRC that while in jail he never complained about his sentence or claimed his innocence. If you had been locked up with the hardened killers of the IRA would you shout your mouth off that you were framed by the IRA and Gerry Adams?

When Liam Clarke of the Sunday Times told me about Holden's conviction, the statements and circumstances, I initially could not believe it. Then he put me in direct contact with Holden via the telephone and after that conversation I believed he was innocent. I immediately went to the police and made a statement that I believed a man had been wrongly convicted of murder. They never contacted me again after that but I was told by the CCRC that they considered I was a liar but did not give the reason for that statement.

Now that the CCRC have recommended that the conviction be overturned we have another problem. The British Government will not want the public to know that we sentenced someone to death without a fair trial and the only evidence against Holden was his statement which was made under torture. Then Adams, who is the friend of Tony Blair, will also not want the facts or a public inquiry into the case. He does not want the Americans to know the fact that he is a terrorist and not a freedom fighter.

I personally envisage that Liam Holden will be paid off with a million pound compensation plan; as long as he goes into hiding and keeps quiet. His other alternative is to be murdered, either on the orders of Adams or dare I say the British. If I am around to find out I would love to know how they intend to wriggle and lie out of this!

The next chapters recall my reasons for joining the British Army at 15 years of age and how and why I have the right to talk about the Irish problem and life within the British Army. If any story needs a public enquiry I believe it is this one!

Reprieve is likely for Para's killer

By DESMOND McCARTAN

SECRETARY OF STATE Mr. Whitelaw, who voted last night in the House of Commons to abolish the death penalty for murder in Northern Ireland, is expected to announce a reprieve for a young Belfast chef under sentence of death for the killing of a Paratrooper.

While MPs voted by a decisive majority for the new Government clause to the Emergency Provisions Bill, the sentence of death on 19-year-old William Gerard Holden, of Ballymurphy, could still be carried out under the law as it stands at present.

But it is understood that Holden, who was convicted of the shooting of Private Frank Bell of the Parachute Regiment, will not hang. Hanging was considered unlikely after Mr. Whitelaw granted a reprieve to Albert Edward Browne, a UDA man convicted of the murder of an RUC constable, and last night's vote in the Commons reinforced this view.

CHEF OF M

22 DEC 1972

A 19-year-old chef appeared at a special depositions court at Belfast Magistrate's Court yesterday accused of murdering a soldier.

Before the court was William Holden, a ch

Murder charge: another remand

4 DEC 1972

A 24-YEAR-OLD Belfast docker was again remanded in custody until December 20 when he appeared at Belfast Magistrate's Court yesterday on a murder charge.

He is Leo Patrick Morgan, of Spamount Street, and he is accused of murdering Inspector Alfred Devlin on October 29 last year.

He is also accused of attempting to murder a soldier in Belfast on March 3.

At the same court a 19-year-old Ballymurphy man was again remanded in custody until December 21 when he appeared on a charge of murdering a soldier on September 17.

He is William Gerald Holden, of Westrock Drive, and he is accused of the murder of Private Frank Bell in Belfast.

Five Belfast men were refused bail at the same court when they appeared on charges of armed robbery at the Northern Bank, Cregagh, on November 13.

They are William Russell (29), of Seaview Drive; Stewart Hamilton (24), of North Queen Street; Alfred Morrow (29), of Syringa Street; Robert Lambe (19), of Fortwilliam Parade, and James Claxper (36), of Clarendon Avenue.

The five are accused of the armed robbery of £13,890 from the Northern Bank at Cregagh. They were again remanded in custody until December 20.

Reprieve plea to Whitelaw

20 APR 1973

BELL MURDER CASE

THE Civil Rights Association to-day asked Mr. Whitelaw to immediately grant a reprieve to William Gerard Holden, who is under sentence of death.

Holden, a 19-year-old chef from Ballymurphy, was convicted at Belfast City Commission yesterday of the capital murder of a soldier last September.

See Page 11.

Fear made me admit to murder, says accused

A MAN accused of the capital murder of a soldier told Belfast City Commission yesterday he admitted the killing because he was afraid of being assassinated, and he claimed that at the time of the shooting of the member of the 2nd Parachute Regiment he was involved in an open-air card game with his brother and some friends.

William Gerard Holden (19) a chef from Westrock Parade, Belfast, denies the capital murder of Private Frank Bell of the 2nd Parachute Regiment last September.

He also denies a charge of possessing a .303 rifle and eight rounds of ammunition with intent to endanger life.

Holden claimed he had been beaten by the Army and taken by them in a car with a hood over his head: "I told them I shot the soldier because I was afraid of being taken to the Glencairn Estate and assassinated," he told the court.

Holden who went into the witness box yesterday afternoon said he and his brother Patrick had been arrested when they were in bed. They were brought to the Black Mountain Army post and there he was approached by a SAS man. He alleged this person held a lighter to his arm and that he was struck by an Army sergeant.

He told of being pushed into a cubicle and alleged that six men came into the room, held him down, put a towel over his head and slowly poured water from a bucket through the towel and on to his face.

"It nearly put me unconscious. It nearly drowned me and stopped me from breathing," Holden told the court, "This went on for a minute."

He said the SAS man twisted his nose, and a short time afterwards the "towel and water treatment was repeated". He was shown a bullet and told "this is for your head."

"I am an SAS man and I am one of yours," Holden was told. He assumed the man was Irish.

Later someone put a white hood over his head and he was trailed to a car. Some soldiers got in and the car moved off. Later on the hood was taken off and he noticed there were five soldiers in the vehicle.

"The hood was put back on my head after about 10 minutes," said Holden.

The car stopped and he heard someone say: "We will get out and get the farmhouse fixed."

Holden said he knew where he was being taken as he had been told of a number of assassinations carried out by the Army in the Glencairn Estate area.

"I thought I was going to be assassinated," he said.

"Someone was trying to pull me out of the car. The sergeant was trying to act the hero as if he was going to save me and the SAS man was saying there was no use wasting time."

Holden was taken back to the Army post and was hooded for part of the way. "I was accused of shooting Private Bell and I said yes. I was afraid of being taken to the Glencairn Estate. I was afraid of being assassinated."

The sergeant said he would have to go for his captain and Holden told the officer he had shot the soldier.

"I told him this because of what the soldier had put to me," he said.

Holden, denying he had shot the soldier, said he remembered the day of the shooting as he had been playing cards with his brother and a couple of friends. He knew about it because it was a big incident the only shot in that area".

Said Holden: "There was a lot of talk about it."

The trial continued today.

Death sentence lifted

16 MAY 1973

THE death sentence passed on a 19-year-old chef for the capital murder of a young paratrooper, has been commuted to life imprisonment by Secretary of State, Mr. William Whitelaw.

He is William Gerard Holden, of Westrock Drive, Ballymurphy, who was convicted by a jury at Belfast City Commission on April 19 of the capital murder of Private Frank Bell (18), of the 2nd Parachute Regiment in September last.

Holden is the second man to be reprieved by Mr. Whitelaw on a capital murder charge.

Youth is accused of killing

WILLIAM Holden (19), of Westrock Drive, Belfast, was remanded in custody until October 24 at Belfast to-day accused of murdering Private Frank Bell of the 2nd Parachute Regiment, in Belfast on September 17.

Private Bell (18), from Cheshire, was shot in the head while on foot patrol in Springhill Avenue, Belfast.

17 OCT 1972

Man told of killing Para, says sergeant

A 19-YEAR-OLD chef on trial on a capital murder charge is alleged to have admitted the killing to an Army sergeant, a jury was told at Belfast City Commission to-day.

William Gerald Holden, of Westrock Parade, has denied the capital murder of Private Frank Bell, a member of the 2nd Bn. Parachute Regiment last September. He also denies a charge of possessing a .303 rifle and eight rounds of ammunition with intent to endanger life.

When the third day of the trial commenced this morning an army sergeant—a member of the 1st Bn. Parachute Regiment, alleged Holden had told him during interrogation that he had shot a "Para" on September 17.

"He named him as being Private Bell and said it was on his conscience and he wanted to get it off his chest", the sergeant alleged.

Witnesses Holden had also admitted being a member of D Company Provisional IRA.

Private Bell (18), who came from New Ferry, Cheshire, died in hospital three days after being shot while on patrol in Springhill Avenue, Belfast, on September 17.

Yesterday the court was cleared while an army intelligence officer gave evidence about his training.

An Army captain said Holden had told him in an interview he had shot a British soldier and that the shooting had taken place between two and three o'clock on a Sunday afternoon. Holden also told him of going to the area with some friends when he received word that the soldiers were on their way.

"A soldier was going up Springhill Avenue. He had his back to me and was turning to look behind. I fired as he turned and I think I hit him on the upper part of the body, possibly the neck. Afterwards I left the rifle in long grass by Corry's walliand I cleared off", Holden was alleged to have stated.

Holden told the officer that the gun was collected later by a girl and taken to a house. He was alleged to have give the officer the name of the owner of the house where a .303 rifle had been found a week before the interview.

The captain said Voiden told him that his commanding officer had ordered the shooting. "It was to be done or else I would get shot", he told the officer.

He thought it was wrong to shoot the soldier and he left the IRA a short time afterwards.

At hearing.

Summing up in Para killing case

19 APR 1973

Belfast Telegraph reporter.

A VERDICT is expected later to-day at Belfast City Commission in the capital murder trial of a 19-year-old Ballymurphy chef who denies shooting a member of a Parachute Regiment last September.

William Gerard Holden has been on trial for four days charged with the shooting of 18-year-old Private Frank Bell at Springhill Avenue, on September 17.

Private Bell, from Newferry, Cheshire, died in hospital three days after being shot.

Holden also denies possession of a loaded .303 Lee Enfield rifle which was stated to have been found in a house two weeks after the ambush on a six-man patrol.

This morning the prosecution, led by Mr. Michael Nicholson, QC, began its summing up to the jury and will be followed by Mr. Michael Lavery, QC, who is defending Holden.

Holden in the witness box yesterday told the jury he only confessed to killing Private Bell because he had been beaten up by the Army, taken for a ride in a car with a hood over his head and because he feared he was going to be assassinated.

He said he was playing cards with his brother Patrick and some friends while Private Bell was shot down.

At hearing.
Yesterday's evidence Page 11

Chapter 4

Geordie Boy

Wallsend in the early 1950s was in the heartland of the North East industrial zone. The name Wallsend came from the simplicity of being the end of the Roman Wall. The wall, stretching from Bowness on the west coast to Wallsend in the east, was constructed by the Emperor Hadrian in AD125 to keep out the Jock tribes (Scotsmen). The Roman name was Segadunum but probably for us Geordies, Wallsend sounded better and easier to spell. The Roman Legions must have been gob-smacked to get this tour of duty. From the beaches of Italy, with sun tans and warm conditions, to this area renowned for it cold North East winds, which more than often combined with rain, chilled people to the bone then and now. As an ex-soldier I have been sent on exercise to some remote areas in the world, when you arrive you say to yourself, "For fuck's sake, what a shithole", and where there are sheep even they look pissed off. Otterburn comes to mind in this category, still a training area for the British Army up in the Cheviot Hills of Northumberland. As a Paratrooper plodding along in the same fields as past Roman Legionnaires, I was following my Sergeant Major in a patrol heading for a rendezvous with the rest of the battalion, as possibly a past Legionnaire followed a Centurion. Even with modern military uniforms, nothing stopped the wind driving down your body core temperature. Fine sleet driven by the wind penetrated waterproof layers of clothing, making a shiver down the spine like an icicle being placed on the last remaining warm spot of your body. Water dripped off the end of your nose, your breath turning into a grey cloud as you expelled air and felt miserable. The expression that a man was worth his salt came from the Roman times as they were given a salt ration to preserve their food. I am thinking my wages do not compensate for what I am having to suffer and the Romans were probably thinking something similar, fuck the salt!

In front of me the Sergeant Major stepped on a sheet of ice, unable to support his weight, he disappeared into a small but deep hole full of muddy, freezing, smelly bog water. For a second I was concerned about his safety as only his red beret showed above the water. However, as he scrambled out as fast as he went in choking and spluttering, you could do nothing but laugh and laugh, uncontrollably. Even though he was not amused, it was impossible to stop laughing. Would the Legionnaire have reacted the same if a Centurion had done the same for leading him into this god forsaken shit hole and its inhuman conditions? You certainly remembered the funny side of things when suffering bad conditions in both peace-time and war, to which this book relates.

Scotland had been considered a wild country full of wild people that had nothing and thus not worth fighting for, so the line was drawn and the wall built over the shortest point to divide England and Scotland.

I am sure the local men volunteered to build this formidable wall, with its towers, forts and housing quarters, good tradesmen at least by the time they finished. The local women must have hated to entertain the troops, cleaning and making pasta and the likes. The Romans hung about for 350 years and then left in the 5th century leaving the Toon Army on the dole.

Then we had the Anglo-Saxon (Germanic) tribes take over the roast and they chased out the Celtic Britons to the far north and west to Wales. England was split into kingdoms, ruled by Saxons in Essex, Wessex and Sussex. Jutes ruled Kent and the Angles had the Kingdom of Deira now known as Yorkshire and later after defeating the last Britons. The Kingdom of Bernicia stretched from the river Tees to the River Forth. King Aethelfrith of Bernicia united the Angle kingdoms and called it North Humber Land, so now you know where we got the final name of Northumberland and even England was derived from the Angle name (Angleland). North Humber Land was the most important kingdom; note that the first Christian King Oswald was from our Northumberland. Saint Cuthbert also set up shop in our remote islands of Lindisfarne in response to the King's invitation after he defeated the Celtic tribes at the battle of Heavenfield near Chollerford in 635 AD.

The Vikings started to arrive. For some reason the normal tactic of rape the women, plunder and return in their long ships was not used. Maybe these tall, blond, blueeyed boys did not make it back to their ships as the local women, sick of short-arsed, dark-haired Italians, rough hairy Germans or the thousands of unemployed rough-handed Geordie Britons, local bricklayers, got to grips with them.

Later in 1066 we had our King Harold who defeated the Vikings but then got a bit cocky and tried to fight an invading Norman Army, all in the same week. His next trick was to look up at the same time as a Norman arrow was coming down, so we now all started talking French. Geordie and our women had to entertain the Frogs and learn about making all those sauces and doing it the French way and the likes. So we had our culture, education, history and our women still have an eye for a foreigner.

The history lesson is to establish how I am proud to be a Geordie but could not be a nationalist as I do not know how far you go back in history to say you are ethnically pure. With my father being a Welshman the odds are that I stem from Celtic Britons as they were the original Geordies.

I was born and bred down by the River Tyne, and that made me a Geordie which I am proud of. My family lived at Forth Street, Wallsend in the top flat of a typical terraced council estate. The streets were named after numbers one to twelve as the local council did not have much imagination and could not come up with some thing a little more sophisticated. Hard-working people in my area, down to earth, who in general enjoy life to its full. Geordies in the main are tolerant of all races, religions, political nuts and the imposed English class system.

The twobedroom flat did not have a bathroom. The tin bath hung up on the wall downstairs in the yard next to the netty (toilet) and coalshed (air raid shelter). During the Second World War the coalshed had been given a reinforced concrete roof to protect the people as the River Tyne with all its ship yards and heavy industry, had been a target for the German Air Force.

Once a week we would have a bath which my mother would fill, using kettles of boiling water. It was a living nightmare being first in the bath; you would go in as a dirty little kid and come out like a red lobster. Now every time I cook a lobster, my memory goes back to that tin bath. You were screaming being boiled alive and then my parents would smack my arse leaving white hand prints. Before getting into the bath, I was brothers with the Blackfoot Indian tribe but getting out I had joined the white-hand red-face tribe.

The remains of a Roman cavalry barracks would be later found next to our terraced houses and they had central heating. We Geordies did not need such luxury; we liked to see our breath in the morning and scrabble into our clothes before turning into a brass monkey, the Romans could not have been very tough! I would stand in front of the fire until I got fireside tartan or chillblains, eat my porridge and then get sent outside to play. Running seemed to be the only way to get warm and I seemed to remember running a lot and everywhere. Mind you even that got me into bother. I ran out of the open back gate on one occasion and the coal lorry ran over the top of me but fortunately between the two front tyres and before the back tyres got me, I managed to get into my mate's yard opposite. The driver apparently had a heart attack and when I returned home that night my dad took off his leather belt and nearly beat me to death, I still can not work out the logic of that beating.

The leather belt and beatings I will always remember, they scare you as a child. Come home dirty and get a beating, get my mother upset which was easily done and get a beating, talking in bed with my brother and get a beating. Yes, I remember that happy environment and learned a lesson not to pass onto my children. My brother and I were sent to bed after the evening meal and in the summer months I remember it still being daylight. We were not tired and only talking but that Welsh bastard of a father, did not want to see us or hear us. Even his work mates at the Wallsend shipyard Swan Hunters called him the Welsh bastard, so I was not the only one with that opinion.

The River Tyne used to fascinate me; who did not want to play with water as a young kid? With all day on the streets to kill time, I would often go down to the river. The river was a hive of activity in those days, the shipyards and repair yards were still full of activity. I would sit and watch the sparks made by the welders and the hammering by the platers and riveters, hitting home the white hot-rivets, the noise echoed up and down the river. The ships were higher than our homes, like giants sitting out of the water till the day they were launched. Royalty would travel to our town for the ceremony and proud men and their families would watch with joy as the ship rolled down the slipway and into the water. That industry also contaminated the waters of the River Tyne. Oil of all types, industrial toxic waste, heavy metals and raw sewage flowed into the river, killing all. Dead birds, dogs, cats, seemed to lie bloated with gas, covered in oil and slowly the tide would try and push them to the shore with the driftwood and rubbish of all descriptions. It was funny that the only thing that kept their colours were the white condoms (they did not do colours or flavours in them days) and there seemed to be loads of them floating amongst the debris. The rubber of the condom used to swell to its maximum or there were some hellish big Geordies in those days. I was always tempted to touch the water, make a boat and see if it would float out to the main current, I always wanted to make a raft and go with the river; it just fascinated me as a kid. Going home you could not get the oil stains off your socks or trousers, so I would have a meeting with the leather belt, which would keep me away from my river for at least a few days.

A railway junction and unmanned signal box was another of my play areas. It was on the way down to the river and the safe tunnel crossing would often be ignored by my mates and I. We would cross the lines for the adventure and the excitement in that we were doing wrong and being naughty. Learning about right and wrong starts at an early age and when my mate Jimmy died on the electric line it sank in the hard way. We had been warned about it and could see the danger sign but we were too young to know about electricity and the effects till he burned to death on the line, another hard lesson in life to learn and so early.

My first day at Saint Peters infant school was another one of those days in my life that I would never forget. Miss Burns was my teacher's name, a big fat woman who wanted to know my name and date of birth. How do you spell your name? (Being a teacher I thought she would know). I did not have a clue, that's why I had come to school to learn how to read and write. The class of forty-two and the five or six that could not spell our names were made to be the laughing stock and when I did not know my birthday she had a field day with me. If you talked to me from that day, other than family and close friends, I would instantly blush, till I was beetroot!

I took note of the kids that were the clever shits whose parents had spent time with their children so that they already knew the basics of reading and writing. The ones that had laughed at me, I would later fight. I would never do well at school because Miss Burns kept to her favourite clever children and I turned to fighting maybe out of frustration but I fought.

My name Nigel also turned out to be a problem for

other children (a southern English name). Why my mother inflicted me with a posh name in my area I don't know. Nigger, Nidge but kids like to be cruel. If parents inflict daft, stupid or out of the ordinary names on their children, then the child suffers; you either fight or get bullied. The Glaswegian comedian, Billy Connelly, summed up the problem for children in the song, "What's in a Name?", a song about a young lad in the Gorbals of Glasgow, inflicted with the name, not of the area. His mother comes down the stairs (close), hair in curlers with a head band, a dout in her mouth, wearing a pinny over her dirty dress, stockings rolled down to her ankles, legs covered with fireside tartan and shouts a posh name like Tyrone. I had to fight for my existence as a kid-what parents do to their children!

Into the middle school and with different teachers I started to catch up education-wise; I must have been top of the bottom six in the class! I had no chance passing the exams called the 11-plus which allowed the clever ones to progress to Grammar school and the rest of us to be destined for the mines, shipyards and local industry.

One story my granny told me, led me to think that I might not have been a little angel as a kid! She for the first and last time agreed to look after my brother and I. We had been given cowboy outfits for Christmas, which came with guns and of course no cowboy would be without his rope. She was a lovely and accommodating old woman who had given birth to near on a football team. She allowed us to tie her up to the chair; apparently we had kidded and joked with her that we would release the bonds and we were only playing. Job done and secured, we told her we were going out to play and we would see her later. That was bad enough but she said that one of us little bastards turned on the gas before closing the outside door. I said it must have been my brother as I was the youngest, I always blamed him as I was sure the leather belt did not hurt him as much as me. Fortunately for granny Harris we had not joined the Scouts at this stage and she had managed to escape the gas chamber.

We moved house to Shafto Street, an area called Rosehill. I cannot remember whether the local rubbish tip was there before or after Rosehill got its name, but with the north east wind blowing it certainly did not smell of roses! How wise to put a rubbish tip in a beautiful natural ravine between the grand War Memorial honouring the dead of both World Wars and a brand new council estate, the mind boggles how local politicians think.

Different schools in the area and different gangs and trouble for me. You hit someone in your new area and the next thing gang members are having a go at you.

I got sent by my mother to the local shop cum post office for potatoes. It was pension day so it was full with a queue patiently waiting outside the door. I had waited and was just inside the door when a lad comes straight up to me and asked if my name was Nigel. Well being street-wise I automatically weighed up the situation. I did not know this lad, so I replied "No" to see his reaction. I saw the knife coming out of his pocket, he obviously did know my name but I was running before the first attempt to stab me. The pensioners were moaning, protesting as I pushed my way past them, and then they saw the lad lunging and trying to stab me in the back with the knife. The poor old pensioners turned into potential heart attack victims, the old people started to shout and scream. It was me he was trying to stab but I did not have time to explain the situation, my heart was pounding with the adrenaline rush. I was pushing the pensioners out of my way, in amongst them, up and over the counter, with a storm of protests. I jumped over the counter, and then jumped back over the counter near the exit, out through the door and in full flight down the street, not looking back. In full flight I was fast and felt safe, no one in the area would catch up to me. I said nothing to my mother except that the shop did not have any spuds.

That evening the police arrived at the door wanting to question me and I just knew I would be having a run-in with the belt.

Another fight on waste ground overlooking Haggis Rope Works was about the only time my brother and his friend Eric backed me up in a fight. Normally I would be fighting them. Anyway, four lads from the local Catholic school got a good beating from us and we went our different ways home after the fight. Unknown to my brother and me, a pervert took advantage of one of the beaten foe and tried to shag his arse in the long grass. The police were at the door that evening with the full business, lights and sirens. Again it did not go down well with my dad but he did not beat us that night, which was a pleasant change.

The final crunch came when I challenged the local gang leader to a fight down in the burn."The Battle of the Burn", unfortunately it turned out for me to be more than I had expected. Now this lad Alex Ray and gang were from the local Catholic school but in those days, with my bad education I could not tell you what a Catholic was. At my Church of England Protestant school we had Catholics and I was envious of them as they were the only ones allowed to miss morning prayers. I was also envious of miners' sons as they were given time off school to attend the Miners Gala, pockets of sweets and free entrance to the pictures. The fight had nothing to do with religion or the profession of your father, that is if you had a father!

Alex Ray turned up but not alone, I think it looked like all the lads from the school had come with him. A tribe of Indians coming over the hill and a big tribe. Was this to be my Little Big Horn. Fuck this, with the half dozen lads with me, we started a tactical withdrawal nearer to our school just up the hill from the burn.

I did not want to be seen running as I knew like all bullies they would hound me forever and a day. So I shouted out a challenge, "Do ou need this lot to fight your battles or you man enough to fight me?" sounded good from an 11-year old. He accepted the challenge and I walked back down amongst them, I did not have any fear, how stupid! They made a circle and the fight started, Alex throwing the first punch which only had the strength of a wet fart. My first punch was an upper cut which lifted him in the air; this guy was all mouth and full of wind. His mates also took note things were not going well on his part, I think it was his bloody nose and tears in his eyes that gave them that impression. Some close body work and I realised he was finished, a friendly punch in the ribs and then a kick in the arse from his mates started my brain working, how the fuck am I going to get out of this? They were not going to let me walk away from this fight. I swung Alex round on his feet, taking note of the circle that was getting smaller.

The stream had been altered by men who hated nature; they had dug up the stream bed and laid a concrete one so they could contaminate it with raw sewerage, now the sticklebacks had a more natural habitat, as far as the council could see. The shit had built up over the years and it was hard to estimate the original depth of the concrete base but I was looking at the only "back passage" out of here. I knew I could not jump it, that's why I was thinking of the depth, holy shit. I swung poor Alex again and with another uppercut sent him falling into the circle, I ran over him as he was going down and leaped from the circle. I was running with the pack in full pursuit, no hesitation and I jumped, you know what, I nearly made it! The shit sucked me in, up to my knee but my right foot made the swing to the far bank and with a good sucking sound I pulled my left leg free. "Chicken bastards" I taunted and looked at the gang who had stopped in their tracks and with a two finger salute ran to school, trying to kick the shit off, stuck on my leg.

Now it just happened that my brother was on his way to school and he was never street-wise and is still not! I think that was the day that brotherly love stopped! Well what a fucking nerd thing to say that he was my brother, where the fuck was his common sense? They nearly killed him! Had two men not been going to work at Haggis Rope Works, who stopped them, they would have kicked him to death. The doctor had diagnosed a swollen spleen, besides the obvious cuts and bruises and when he had crawled home he had taken an overdose of pain killers. He was too nice a guy to be my brother, he is now a magistrate, a do-gooder, we have nothing in common, and he does not even look like me, Mother!

We had gangs, school gangs, area gangs but I remember nicking wood from each other before bonfire night the 5th November. It was a typical reason for fighting and throwing stones at each other. Being in a gang was exciting, like the human version of running with a wolf pack. The gang leader is not always the best fighter but the majority conforms to his way of thinking. Someone is always looking to take his place so he is the most daring and starts most aggression against other groups to maintain his position. If you watch a pack of dogs, the leader just has to snap out at a pack member and it normally rolls on its back paws up, tail wagging to show that it is not a threat to his leadership. Then the leader is more generous to the dogs that are a threat to his leadership. How close are our genes to that of dogs?

The police came to the house again with the strong recommendation that if I was not sent away they might be doing it without my parents consent. I was sent to Marton Boarding School, Whitegate, Northwich, Cheshire, a long way from home, my brother had gone voluntarily but I was press-ganged. To say the least it was a strict regime with plenty of teachers who were not slow in the use of corporal punishment, and having in their possession a perverse selection of wooden canes. I was used by a teacher to keep the other kids in my dormitory in line. Yes, a bully, and I was used in the same way as Jews were made to control Jews in their camps. The wooden huts even had a similarity to those at Belsen on the outside but the inside was more like the set-up in an army barracks. Near the end I wised up to the fact I was being used as a bully and fought the teacher in question. It took two teachers to stop me in that fight and I tried to start a mutiny by asking the others to fight the teachers. Funny the teachers never bothered me again and I settled down in the school, I made big improvement in education and loved football, running, long jump which became my passion that stopped my aggression, well a little bit.

I left when I was fifteen and went to college back in Wallsend to do "O" levels. I played football for the Catholic Youth Club, they never asked my religion, maybe they heard I was a good footballer and the priest did confession for letting me play. Catholic girl friends and mates at the club but religion was never mentioned, good times. The priest was a young guy who took me to hospital when I was fouled and broke my collar bone, he cursed like hell, bastard should have been sent off, I am sure he must have done a few Hail Marys that Sunday!

I got a trial for Newcastle United and my dad would not take me to the ground, if I did not get the money for the bus from my mother I had to walk the seven miles to do the training.

Things came to a decisive moment in my life when my dad went to hit my mother, he saved his life by grabbing the blade of the bread knife as I attempted to stick it in his fat belly. Tension was unbearable in the house after that incident and the next time I hit him, the bully had learnt I could no longer be bullied. I had learnt a good lesson: hit the bullies and they think twice about bullying you.

I joined the Army and I think my dad was happy to see me go and signed the consent forms with a smile on his face.

Our shipyards were in decline due to bad management and unions too eager to down tools and-strike. The Tyne was losing its shipyards which had a knock-on effect, closing iron and steel plants, coal mines and hundreds of other associated industrial plants; the great decline was underway. Cutbacks in the number of apprenticeships was one of the first signs of a declining industry. Government in the distant south did nothing to stop the rot and the youth of Tyneside were the first casualties.

I never joined the Army to kill; it never came into my reasoning for joining. I was soon to learn that most lads had similar reasons to join up, family problems or areas of high unemployment. We now had a large family, friendship, comrades and the chance to learn a trade but most of us were young and naive, never thinking we would ever have to fight and kill. I was fifteen years old, just a kid and signed on, taking the Queen's shilling for 22 years.

Chapter 5

We're in the Army now

Boy soldiers served until they were seventeen and were then sent to regular Army units, normally of their personal choice. I had joined the Royal Army Medical Corps, boys unit, stationed at Ash Vale, near Aldershot. Coming from the strict discipline that I encountered at boarding school, I found the Army life quite easy. I was still studying for "O" levels but only managed to pass one, due to a lack of enthusiasm and effort on my part. Now football and sports I really enjoyed and had I tried as hard in education I would have passed degrees at university, but when you are young you do not realise the importance of education. I had the opportunity and blew it, like so many young and immature youths. With a staggering pay packet of three pounds and three shillings, a week, I was enjoying the army life.

Time flies when you're enjoying yourself but I have a few funny memories. I was into canoeing and football and had a group of mates that were a good laugh. We would go to London and hit the town Soho, strip clubs and pubs, rent one single room and seven of us would sleep in it. The snoring, lads getting up to take a piss in the sink, the odd one making the sink to vomit, the jostling for a position to turn in the cramped room made sleep, to say the least, difficult. I have never got drunk without an incredible headache the next day and with little sleep, aches and pains from the cramped sleeping position, I was never good company the next day and envied the lads that did not suffer from a hangover.

I still had a few fights and established I would not be bullied. I think bullies can be found in all walks of life, no-one is totally immune from these people that in the main use their physical strength to dominate weaker people, mentally and physically. As I found at school you can be turned into a bully by your betters so they can maintain discipline without doing the dirty work themselves. If anyone stepped out of line they just pointed the finger. Reading the papers it still goes on within the Army but it is never the Officers that get punished, only the Corporals that do their dirty work. Discipline is important in the Army and it is inevitable that bullies would be promoted with the blessing of some officers to maintain this discipline, which created fear amongst weaker men, sometimes with the devastating consequence that men would commit suicide in extreme cases to escape from this environment of fear that they lived in day and night. I guessed right from the beginning what I would expect in the Army and thus I was not surprised to see these men bully with the consent of their betters who in turn would wash their hands of any knowledge that it was happening under their command. I would stand up and fight for my right to live without being bullied and this attitude does not stop fights but makes the bully think twice about who to pick on. The only time I lost in a fight was when I was asked the time and as I looked at my watch this lad Luis kicked me in the solar plexus. Totally unprovoked, he stated later that he had seen the kick on television and wanted to try it out and I was the first person to come along. A little harder and I am sure he could have killed me as he caught me totally off guard and it took me five minutes to recover from the cowardly kick. I had to learn to keep distance as we had head-bangers in the Army as in all walks of life.

    I was playing football and a guy turned and spat in my face, a good green one. I hit him naturally, but fighting on the sports field was frowned on, not sportsman-like and I ended up on a charge in front of the CO Lt Colonel Davies, obviously a Welshman with a name like that. What would you do if I spat in your face Sir, how would you react? He saw my point of view but had to punish me, from now on you can only play rugby. What a brilliant punishment, I loved the game.

    I met a WRAC, Womens Royal Army Corps and was on

a sure thing for a good time but with three pounds I could not pay for a hotel room. Some would join the Paras in competions drinking beer with all sorts thrown in, e.g. sick, piss, salt, spit you name it and could win on occasion. This bird I had was the more feminine variety and not bad looking, so as a young lad I would do anything to get her knickers off. Trouble was the women's dormitories were guarded, as I was not the only young squaddy to have the same idea and short of money. Sneaking into this girl's bedroom and I got caught, the dog must have been trained to catch blokes with a hard on. In front of Lt. Colonel Davies and the charge was read out. Well it just goes to show I am not queer Sir, but I am guilty that I did not have enough money for a hotel room. I remember him laughing first, then me, then the Sergeant Major, I have to punish you between laughing and I got confined to camp for the week. Trouble was the next week I got caught again and he starts laughing when I walked through the door.

The Queen Mother was the Colonel in Chief of the Royal Army Medical Corps. I had been selected to meet her as I was an accomplished canoeist and was to give her a spiel on one of the many sporting activities that were available to boy soldiers. A few hours before my meeting, a group of senior officers had a run through with the programme, to make sure everything would go well. Even a new toilet had to be made and inspected, fur seat and luxury soft paper; I had thought Royal shit came out wrapped up in silver paper. Anyway, this General was called Niven, he was the actor David Niven's brother, and he had a very nice southern accent that ran in the family. He listened to my speech and within a short time a Scotsman was ordered to teach me English before the Queen Mother arrived! The Scots officer was embarrassed to have to tell me, in a nice Scottish accent, to get rid of my Geordie accent, we were both soon in agreement, that he was proud to be Scottish and I was equally proud to be a Geordie and no attempt would be made to alter my accent.

The first thing I now said to the Queen Mother was, " I hope you can understand my Geordie accent", to which she replied, "I have many fond memories in the North East, especially launching ships on the Tyne", Yes! I instantly loved the lady but she might have liked the party after the launch, plenty of free gin and tonic, which helps you understand Geordie. General Niven was not pleased about my change of script, fucking southern snob!

We had an Arab boy from the Trucial Oman Scouts in the Unit; he was a personality that stood out with his smart Arabic headdress. Being a Muslim got him into trouble, not for the difference in religion but for his shitting habit. Army barracks always had to be in an immaculate condition and part of Army discipline was the endless inspections of the accommodation. It was down to the junior NCOs to organise the cleaning and inspect that the job was done before the senior ranks and officers did their inspection. On a few occasions shit was found all down the back of the toilet and when it's not your own it does not go down well when you have to clean it up. Just before an inspection by the CO, now being a lance corporal, I had to do a pre-inspection before his arrival. Fucking shit all over the back of the seat, I locked the toilet from the inside and slid out of the cubicle near the ceiling. Quickly chalking Out of Order on the door I saved the day as we would have been confined to camp for the weekend. I was determined to find the shitter and my enquiries got it down to three men that had used the bog before the inspection. When it was mentioned one was the Arab boy, it led me to suspect him, as he had different ways, he would never shower naked, he did not drink alcohol or socialise much. I got the lad sleeping next to him to give me a shout the next time he went to the bog. Jumping up to look over the toilet divide I saw him squatting on the seat, no wonder he missed on occasion. He got the job for two weeks cleaning the toilets to see how he liked to clean other peoples shit. Again I never punished him for his religion but obviously it had brought him into conflict. If the authorities want to mix cultures then they should cater for their needs with a Muslim toilet to respect their religious beliefs, as they did not want to sit on a seat used by infidels.

This same boy had the habit of saying yes to every question you asked him, which I noted when I questioned him about his hygiene habits. He was in the NAFFI club down in Aldershot on a Saturday night when I noticed him alone and felt sorry for him so I went over to him and asked him how he was doing and would he like to join the rest of us. "Yes but no thank you, as I am going back to camp after I have eaten". I chatted a little with him and then rejoined the company I was with. I laughed to myself at the number of times he had put yes at the start of a sentence in our conversation. I joined my mates and looked back to see this big drunken guy approach the Arab, Sultan Khamis. The drunk grabbed him and started to hit him, I did not hesitate as I ran and dived in to separate the one-sided fight. "Why are you hitting him?" I said to the big guy, "I asked him if he had stolen my wallet and he said "Yes" so I am going to kill the little thief!" Trying to explain the lad's bad grammar to this guy was a waste of time, I told the Arab to run and report what has happened to the officer in charge of the camp guard. Then I stood my ground as the drunk attacked me for protecting the boy. I was only a boy myself fighting this man and stood no chance, as the power in his punches sent me flying over tables and chairs. My saviour arrived in the form of four military police who arrested the both of us, was I happy and relieved to be arrested! They saved my life as it turned out this was an infantry soldier from the Parachute Regiment that had been kicking the shit out of me. Fortunately the Arab had reported to the duty officer who came to my rescue and smiling, got the police to release me.

I transferred to adult service and joined 4 Company RAMC, stationed at Netley, near Southampton, as a psychiatric nurse. At first I enjoyed it and had a good set of mates, mainly civilians from the town. Then the job gets the better of one lad and he goes and kills himself with an overdose of pills. You would think in a psychiatric unit that someone would have picked up that he was a loner and had problems coping with the job. A lot of people attempt suicide, which in general is a cry for help and with no real intention to kill themselves and normally they leave a message so that they will be saved in time but this lad did a good job. Rigor mortis had set in before he was found and a big enquiry failed to find how he had a set of keys to the DDA box where all the dangerous drugs are kept.

I started to get a lot of night duty, two wards to look after and on my own. I would mix with the patients and have a chat and a laugh with them. This is where I first met Cpl Kevin Walsh, the "airborne wart" which was his nickname, as he was so good looking. He would sit all night and tell me of his adventures in the SAS which enthralled me. His adventures and the excitement in his job made me wonder if I was happy in mine.

A lot of Navy guys, from an Admiral down to Able Seaman ended up in Netley when they stopped the Navy rum ration. Social alcoholics but now with a dry ship they suffered withdrawal symptoms and many had the DTs (delirium tremens) and delusions. As nurses you had to write notes about the patients to say how they had socialised with the other lads and how they slept. So you would chat, play cards in an attempt to find out and write about their problems. A Petty Officer turned on me, "Son I know you are trying to help but what can a kid like you know about life? You have never been married and thus no marriage problems, no kids, no financial problems, don't drink heavy, in fact you know fuck all". Well that was a sting in my tail but I had to agree with him, this job really was not for young people and some of the doctors only related with books and even they did not understand these social problems. They just fed the patients pills or hit them with ECT (electro convulsion therapy) which was a bit excessive when all that was needed in most cases was tender loving care to put their lives in order. When you psycho-analyse mental patients you see many of us are suffering from the same problems but they are the ones that society see with anti0social behaviour and I thought the treatment handed out was more a punishment than a cure.

To buy a car I started doing private nursing at a nursing home in the New Forest, on my days off. I had a nice little affair with the daughter of the owner which did not go down well, so she got sent away and that ended my extra money.

Then a cook starts to chat up a girl I was talking to in the camp bar at Netley and being a bit pissed and pissed off, my heart not in the job and on a downer, I hit him, sorry! In front of the CO the next day and that was the end of my nursing career, kicked out of a nut-house.

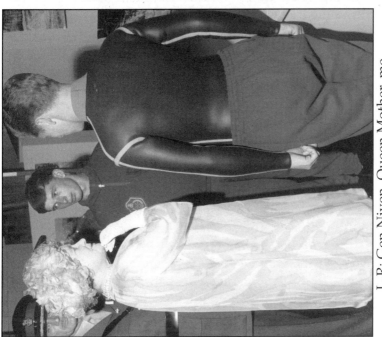

L-R: Gen Niven, Queen Mother, me, RAMC soldier

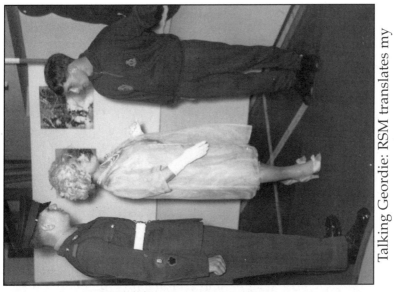

Talking Geordie: RSM translates my responses to her Majesty.

Chapter 6

23rd Parachute Field Ambulance

I was posted to 23rd Parachute Field Ambulance to be a combat medic. I did the training to be a combat medic which was basic first aid and then had to do "P" Company which was the physical test to become a paratrooper. If the course was not hard enough I had a run-in with some infantry that did not think my face fitted in the billet as I was an attached from medics and considered a pansy in their eyes. I came to the conclusion that I had the face that people wanted to hit; I could feel vibes and aggression from some blokes. The Paras had some oddballs that made the inmates at Netley look like little angels and very sane in comparison. My training as a mental nurse had helped me as I could feel negative thought waves, with the ability to weigh people up and normally my instincts were correct. I found it tough passing the Para course, very physical but had the added problem of fighting other potential Paras.

At the NAFFI we were just given 15 minutes for a cup of tea before resuming our very physical activities. I was politely waiting while two women canteen workers were talking a load of woman crap. Myself and the queue behind me must have been invisible to them, excuse me but would one of you ladies do your fucking job and serve me. A fox in a hen house the screams from these two brought all the women staff to identify the man that had asked them to do their job. No tea that morning and by the afternoon I had been identified and put in front of the Regimental Sergeant Major. An English gentleman in the way he spoke but many a man was in the glass house for just coughing on his parade square, am I in the shit thinking to myself, as I double-marched and slammed my feet to a stop in front of him. He was a big man, a fucking giant and someone had beaten the shit out of him as he had a well broken nose and two cauliflower ears, someone told me he had been a sparing partner for Henry Cooper, it had to be someone of that quality to do the damage that had been inflicted on his face. He told me of the complaint from this woman and demanded that I apologise to her. "No Sir, I refuse, I am a soldier and although the lowest I still have my rights and asking these women to stop being ignorant and do the job they are paid for, I do not see a reason to apologise." I did not mention the four-letter word I used! He must have never had anyone say no to him as he was gobsmacked. Then he came up with the fact that this woman was married to a Corporal Paratrooper who would seek satisfaction. "Well if he thinks she is worth the fight I will meet him at the gym." He saw I was not afraid. I must have impressed him, as he now took my side and dismissed me saying that he would have a quiet word with her so the problem did not get out of hand. He was backing me up and I walked back to barracks passing the guardroom prison on the way, a smile of relief on my face.

The problem with the course was that it was a team effort, for example, last but one test, was called the stretcher race. Four men running a run with a stretcher which was weighted with a sixty kilo load strapped to it. You all took your share of the weight for ten minutes while running and then another four lads took over. My problem was the lad opposite was not taking his share of the weight and I nearly did not pass the course because of him, I fell out totally exhausted. Fortunately it was noticed and I was allowed to pass, and then filled in the bastard who caused me so many problems.

I was sent to Abingdon near Oxford to do my parachute training, at the same time the Regimental Sergeant Major got sent there to finish his last year of service as a punishment, as he had verbally abused an officer for having long hair on his parade square.

"Knowledge Dispels Fear" was the motto of the RAF Falcons free fall team that trained us in basic military parachuting. Well after the training and two jumps from a barrage balloon, I still did not have enough knowledge but I certainly had fear from the unnatural act of jumping out only 800 feet from the ground. I had jumped first of the group in my first balloon exit; the instructor said "When you go, look back at me as I like the look of fear." He had seen the fear so often as it seemed ages before the chute opened, your stomach goes up into your throat. If I had not been shouting "Geronimo" I would have been screaming. It took me over twenty jumps and many a night not sleeping before I got the knowledge that dispels fear!

Out on the town Saturday night, in Oxford, with two men from the Marine Commandos who were also doing the parachute course, we went into the first bar that had loud music and loads of women. We got our pints and drank at the bar, eyeing the women, harmlessly being a voyeur, then I noticed a group of lads pointing at us. Yeh trouble, I just knew it, "Drink up mates I think that large group of lads in the corner do not like us looking at the local tarts". We moved out going up a narrow stair case single file, yes they were following. At the top that opened into a courtyard, the gang leader shouts for us to stop and came straight for me, that fucking face again! Then he even said it, "I don't like your face". I hit him with a smacker that nearly parted his head from the rest of his body and as he fell I gave the head a kick that sounded sickening, his whole body spun in the air with the contact. "I don't like your face either pal." The Marine near me shouted "Run." The gang were seeking revenge as the attack on me had not gone to plan. A scene from the Keystone Cops, we were laughing as they could not catch us with us being so fit, but we did not have a clue where we were going on our first visit to Oxford. We did it, one of the reasons I do not like the French, straight into a dead end, cul-de-sac and the three voyeurs had a problem! The wall that had us trapped was high but nothing compared to what we had managed to scramble over on army obstacle courses, so as the hounds closed in for the kill we skilfully overcame the first obstacle. They on the other hand were finding great difficulty to scaling the wall so they started to throw stones that forced us to climb higher and higher up the building. The roof collapsed under our weight, bloody plastic which could not support us; we fell, a long way down but landed on a soft mound of clothing. From the height we fell we were lucky not to be injured but it might have been with all the parachute rolls we had practiced on landing during the week that saved us. Only twenty minutes later, when the police came charging into the room did we find that we had landed on a pile of clothing that had been unclaimed over the years and thrown into this room from the local cinema. Handcuffed, two policemen on each of us, we were frog-marched into waiting police cars. I was smiling because I seemed to be happy every time I am arrested that someone up there was saving my skin! A girl from the crowd said to me "You should not be smiling for being a thief", then I realised we were in trouble with the law. Off to the police station and put in the cells till the early hours, the RSM sent military police to collect us. On parade in the morning double-step and slamming down our feet to a halt in front of him, he recognised me straight away. YOU, explain what happened! By the time I finished, the hostility was gone and he was on our side but said he would not make a final decision on our fate till we had been interviewed by the Oxford CID Unit the following weekend. They took us to every pub in the city centre and a free drink from the owner of each pub; I was definitely happy to be arrested. The last pub and the same one we had the trouble and downstairs the same gang. I said to the CID officer, I hope you can fight as we were out numbered 5 to 1, upstairs and we turned to fight. The CID pointed to a uniformed officer who had been waiting over the road, they will not fight the uniform makes all the difference and he was right. Like sheep they lined up to give their names to the officers, then the gang leader who still had the bruising and swelling on his face, turned out to be the son of the City Mayor, end of story.

On return to 23rd PFA I had my wings and red beret and was proud, as it had not been easy. Standing on parade with the unit, the CO and SGM were inspecting the blokes. If you had not passed the "P" company and not got your wings, they would make you wear a steel helmet with a penguin painted on the side (penguins don't fly). This one penguin, a driver, also had a nervous twitch. As a passenger in his Land Rover you would notice his twitch as every now and then the Land Rover would make a sudden movement to the right, as his whole body moved. We had all got used to him and as everyone in the unit were doctors, nurses, and combat medics, the sympathy angel, to his plight, had to be expected. Most Sergeant Majors were Scotsmen and I think they enjoyed seeking revenge on the English Army by joining and making our life hell. SGM Barker, he lived up to his name and could put the fear of God into any man, he was an evil little Scotsman with a big chip on his shoulder over some King Edward's Army, you know that song them Jocks sing at football matches, that stirs their blood. This poor driver just happened to twitch at the wrong time and was seen by the CSM. "Who told you to move on my parade square, soldier?" he screamed in such a way that made every man cower, even the officers. To the timid reply "It's a nervous twitch sir that I have had all my life". The voice boomed out again, "Well get rid of it by tomorrow morning, you horrible little man". It was spontaneous, everyone, officers included started to laugh and laugh, as if the CSM could cure this lad of his life-long twitch, it would have been a miracle. We knew he had not been joking but when he turned to the OC who was a trauma specialist doctor and tried to kid on to him, that he had been joking, we all started laughing again, as this "Jock" did not joke!

My first parachute jump with 23rd Parachute Field Ambulance was also to be my first night jump and did not go well. The plane had red night-lights on so we could adjust to the dark when we left the plane. I was apprehensive before I jumped, still not confident about this unnatural way of exiting an aeroplane. First the red light at the door exit and then the green which was the order to jump and the men moved to the door and jumped, my turn was soon approaching. The plane had a full load of paratroopers and therefore we did an exit from both doors, with orders from the RAF dispatchers. The Para formation was termed a stick which was formed at the port and starboard sides of the aeroplane. The dispatcher's job was to coordinate the sticks so they jumped in a staggered formation that avoided men colliding at the rear of the plane. I came to the door, a tap on the shoulder and into the blackness I jumped.

    The cold air was the first thing my body encountered as the more than one hundred mile per hour slipstream pulled my parachute from its pack and deployed it as designed. So now I looked up and checked that it was open. Oh shit it had more twists in the rigging lines than I had encountered during training. Pull my reserve or try to kick out as trained. In hindsight I should have pulled the reserve as I was still trying to untangle the parachute when I hit the ground. Someone said to me are you all right and for three days I tried to remember my name and what the fuck was I doing in that field. A total memory loss which was scary, I was transferred to the Cambridge Military Hospital in Aldershot and on my third day was told to lie to attention in bed as a guy called a "general" in charge of the hospital was doing ward rounds with the hospital Matron. He looked at me and I looked at him and he was none other than my CO as a boy soldier then Colonel and now General Davies. He laughed "What you are up to now Nigel?" so we had a chat and my memory came back with the help from my friend.

    The Unit had a good rugby team and I played often, finally being a member of the team winning the Army Cup, all thanks to General Davies. The only problem with this Unit was that the job was boring; the section I was in would spend most of the day drinking tea and counting stores on shelves. When I dared asked if we could do some training for a change, the sergeant had us putting up tents and taking them down, and pointed me out to the lads, as the culprit for the work. I had meant medical training and he knew it.

Moaning paid off as he got me sent to the Southern General Hospital in Glasgow for a month's casualty training and it was that training that helped me save some lives. I also took a fancy to a nurse in the casualty department who I would later marry. We were to go out the day of the Ibrox disaster 2nd January, 1971 when Celtic were playing Rangers (I should have taken it as a bad omen). I heard of the tragedy on the radio and went to help at the hospital. Most of the football supporters brought in by ambulance were dead on arrival and could only be certified and laid out in the corridors, to await identification by family. There were sixty-six people dead and over one hundred injured that were evacuated from the stadium to the local hospitals. I witnessed the tragedy that day, the despair, anxiety and sadness of the people of Glasgow, families coming to the hospital looking for loved ones but little could be done to save the crushed victims, most had been dead on arrival. A day when bitter rivalry in football and religion was forgotten and the true Scotsman came through bigotry to show his compassion, pity it needed a tragedy.

The first three minutes are vital if you want to save someone's life, you have to act and fast. Waiting for an ambulance is not the answer so my job was to be at the sharp end and try to keep people alive before the ambulance arrived.

With my love of the section sergeant got me a job as a combat Medic with the 2nd Battalion the Parachute Regiment and promotion to Corporal. I went on the town, to celebrate my promotion and my transfer to 2nd Battalion Parachute Regiment. In the NAFFI club down in Aldershot, I was dancing with a WRAC and was on a good thing. There were not many women to go round in Aldershot, with thousands of soldiers stationed in and around this garrison town. She was fucking ugly to say the least, but every pint I drank she started to look better and better. Then a guy moves in while I am dancing, a small but stocky character, pint of beer in his hand. No warning, he just throws the pint over the girl. "Hi pal I don't mind you throwing the beer over her but you splashed me", I said. The glass was on the way to my face when I ducked and I followed up with a good couple of punches that staggered him. The table behind him was nearly the length of the dance hall and full of glasses, a dive at him and we were both off balance and hit the table with a force that sent the whole lot flying. This guy was hard, I had given him some of my best punches and he was still fighting with me on the floor. I saw the blokes coming, more than twenty, was it their drinks we had spilt? They dived and jumped on top of us, punching and kicking. I managed to get out from the bottom of the pack, it just looked like a rugby scrum-down, that had collapsed. Again, being street-wise I soon figured they were trying to kill me or the other guy or both of us, as I had to get up in the morning and report to my new unit, so I made a tactical withdrawal.

The Battalion of over seven hundred men was already on parade when I arrived. The Battalion Commander was talking to the troops so I reported, saluted and was told by the Battallion Sergeant Major (BSM) to fall in at the end of the parade. I had to march past the whole battalion, so I did so very smart, to give a good impression on my first day. I heard a soldier say, "That's him from last night", and then I noticed this guy with two black eyes and a few others with cuts and bruises. I am thinking to myself for fuck's sake I am really in the shit now, they are going to kill me. What have I joined?

The Battalion was put on stand-by within 24 hours to move to Northern Ireland, so all preparation for a quick move was to be made and no leave passes. As the CO was giving his pep talk another interruption came, as a woman walked onto the parade square. She was obviously very angry and shouting "Which of you fuckers has got my boot?" "Sergeant Major, who is that woman?" cried the CO, to which the BSM shrugged his shoulders. The lads were laughing, I found out later she was the camp gang-bang that had been fucked for the last few days in the barracks. She had been "B" Company's gang-bang after a night on the town, being supplied with drink to break down her inhibitions but lads from "D" Company had used their initiative and with the help of ladders had stolen her and secreted her away in their barracks. Fed, watered and showered she had not tried to escape till she woke up to find nobody left in the queue as everyone was on the parade square. She had a deformed leg and wore a platform medical boot and this was what was missing when she had put her clothes on! She eventually left the scene after telling the battalion she would not return, cursed them and said fuck you to the BSM as she hobbled away without the boot.

The flustered CO Colonel Hewlit finished his talk and the battalion was dismissed and they all fell out. I saw the large group moving towards me, the lad that I had fought was the first to reach me and he shook my hand, did he see the relief on my face. He apologised, it had been his stag night and was a bit pissed, then they all took turns in shaking my hand, I was now in 2 Para.

We did not waste time preparing for Northern Ireland as the television news and papers had nothing but the problems as the top story. The lads worked hard, physical training every day, weapons practice and live firing down at the ranges.

I was in the billet one morning, changing after a run, when a couple of lads brought in a girl who worked in the NAAFI. The rest of the lads moved in on her and literally in minutes had talked her into getting her clothes off. She knew what she was on and was enjoying every minute of it, trying to act shy, "Oh I shouldn't," she said. Fat was not the word, she could have been called Miss Michelin or Pirelli. The first to jump on her to shag her lifted a couple of layers and made the comment "It must be down there somewhere". She took them all on, getting and giving a good time and there was no shortage of givers as the word got round other Companies. Then she looked at her watch and jumped up,"Oh, I will have to go as I have to make the ham and cheese sandwiches for morning break". She was dripping as she left the barracks and I was put off ham and cheese sandwiches the rest of my life. I think so far in the book we can establish most Paras are male chauvinist pigs and yes I have to acknowledge my bad points.

I started giving first aid lessons to all the ranks and they on the whole took note of what I was saying. Very basic first aid, clearing the air way, mouth to mouth resuscitation, stopping bleeding with pressure bandages and artery pressure points and last how to splint broken limbs, it would all pay off in the tour to Northern Ireland but none of us imagined how as young lads we would have to cope with some horrific incidents that we would soon face. All my training had been in classrooms other than my month at the Southern General Hospital and it had not been sufficient to prepare me for what I would encounter in the front line of Northern Ireland. The books and the training had never changed from the 2nd World War and I was not prepared for what I was to face. I think two weeks in a animal slaughter house is a good start for someone before he wants to be a medic in a war situation, because it was to be blood and guts!

The battalion Catholic Priest and protestant chaplin gave a joint service and everyone was ordered to attend the service even those like myself that did not believe in God. Again I had to question Christian people preparing you to kill people when their home rules say "thou shall not kill."

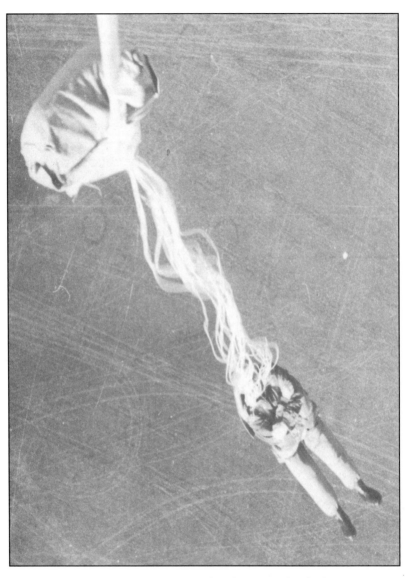
Rigging lines that can twist leading to a bad plane exit

Exit from a C130 Hercules

Posing in front of a C130 Hercules. Me on the left

Chapter 7

The Day of Internment 9th August 1971

The Battalion got sent to Northern Ireland due to the growing problems in the province. The reason given by our officers was to separate the Catholics and Protestants, thereby maintaining law and order in the province. The media had nothing but the growing troubles on the front pages and all television news channels. The first soldiers who had been killed made the front page and were a major story. So many would die in the next few years that the death of a soldier would not make the front page or even get reported.

A journey to Liverpool by coach and then we boarded a ferry over to Belfast. The leaving of Liverpool and England made me wonder how this province called Northern Ireland was part of the United Kingdom. I was totally ignorant about the Province and its history but I would endeavour to find out. We had Irish, Northern and Southern in the Battalion and they seemed to get on well together so at this point in time I could not understand what the current proble was.

This was the second tour for our Battalion so I spoke to men that had been deployed and asked what had been the reception from the locals on the first tour. To my questioning I found that in general they had been received well, especially by the Catholics as they had stopped the Protestants burning them out. The local women were all over them they boasted and some even got married to local girls. The feeling was we would not have many problems and a good few lads were looking forward to meeting up with girls that they had met in the first tour. A Para had been killed in that tour but it had been a bar fight and he had been glassed in the throat. The local yob had gone to jail for manslaughter, this being one of the bad stories from the tour.

Then later, after the official tour of duty, a paratrooper on holiday who had married a local girl was murdered while visiting his in-laws. The story I heard was that his wife asked the local IRA unit if he could safely visit the family without reprisal, to which the request was granted with assurances that he would not be harmed. As soon as he entered the house, unarmed and in civilian clothes, two terrorist burst through the door and executed him in front of his wife as he was sitting on the sofa. They used Thompson machine guns so they made a right mess of him and his hysterical wife witnessed everything. After hearing this I thought to myself that I would not be looking for an Irish girl friend.

I was attached to "B" Company which was a young body of men, most being teenagers, forming a rifle company, as part of the Battalion and I would be with them as the Company medic.

We first went to McGilligan army barracks on the coast up from Londonderry in military 4-ton trucks. Security was minimum as none of us carried rifles or ammunition, all of which was on separate trucks still in boxes, I took this as the Officers saw no threat from the IRA, not even considered that they would or could attack us at this stage of the conflict but I think it was more that from the beginning our officers underestimated the IRA. We were on standby, to be moved to any location within the province that needed the army but in the meantime this camp would be our base. An old 2nd World War camp, wooden Nissen huts which would be our last decent accommodation in a very relaxed beautiful setting by the coast. It even had a NAFFI but the old girl that ran it must have been there when the camp was built and she took ill during our stay. The doctor Captain McCray took me with him to examine her and he then sent me to get our Catholic priest Captain Padre Weston to give her the last rites, she died very calm and relaxed being at peace with her God. In this incident the Paras could not be blamed for her death.

The local news had more details about incidents in the troubles than was being shown to the British outside the Province. Most marches were organised by the "Civil Rights Movement" and these were Catholics protesting that they were not treated fairly. They complained that they were not given the same job prospects or promotion and for example cited the situation at Harland and Wolf shipbuilders in Belfast, who only employed Protestants. Apparently any Catholic employed would find a bullet in his bait box which naturally made them think twice about going to work the following day. Management at the yard dismissed the claim that they were anti-Catholic and would employ Catholics who applied for work. In the staff white-collared dining room, bullets were not on the menu as they were all Protestants.

They complained about housing problems, that they were in ghettos and that it was sub-standard accommodation. They even said that Catholics were not given the right to vote. If all this was true I could not understand how our Government did not know or how they could allow such a situation in the United Kingdom, yes if this was all true, they did have a grievance and the right to protest. The prominent voice in this movement was a woman called Bernadette Devlin (later her married name was McClusky) that encouraged the crowd to protest, which more or less ended in violent rioting. I would meet this future Member of Parliament on two occasions and all I will say at this moment was she was not a fan of the Parachute Regiment but read on to find out why she loved us in the end! When I did get to know the people of Northern Ireland, I thought to myself that if the Catholics were the majority would they do the same discrimination against the Protestants as it was obvious that there was hatred amongst these people that normal Englishmen did not understand.

The camp had a grenade range and a large arsenal of these Mills bombs were stored in the armoury deposit which was fenced in with a pack of killer dogs. The dogs had been trained for the job and even attacked the soldiers sent to feed them, talk about bite the hand that feeds you. So I had a couple of jobs stitching lads who had been sent to feed the beasts, again I must thank the drunks that attended the Southern General for letting me practice on them.

We had been told to report to the range for live firing practice with grenades. I was sent with another medic in the ambulance in case of an accident. I was also being allowed to throw a couple of hand grenades so the whole company was accommodated in one very large concrete bunker to wait our turn and be called out by a Staff Sergeant who was in control of the range detail. We chatted awaiting our turn and the jokes were faster than the queue waiting to throw the grenades. Once you had thrown the grenade you could make your way back to camp over the sand dunes. Few lads had thrown a grenade and you could see some were a bit apprehensive and some visibly nervous, me included, so the jokes calmed you down. A lad before me was literally shaking and his nerves got the better of him, he pulled the pin (no he did not throw the pin if you are jumping the gun) but he did drop the fucking hand grenade which rolled back down and into the bunker. We who were waiting at the exit all noticed this smoking thing roll in and ran at the same time but the bunker was full and we ran into the waiting soldiers who all clicked on that we were all in danger, don't panic Mr Mannering (yes it was like a scene from Dad's Axrmy) but I must admit it was panic. I hate to think of how many men would have died in that bunker if it had exploded. Thank God, the S/Sgt knew what to do, the grenade had an eight-second fuse so when the lad pulled the pin and dropped the grenade he went running after it, counting, picked it up, ran out the bunker and threw it. The lad still had the pin in his hand and was white with shock which was made worse by the verbal abuse from the S/Sgt. When I threw mine I must admit my adrenaline was pumping as you did not want to make a fool of yourself like had just happened and the first time you are a bit tense and hold it too tight. By the time I had thrown the second grenade my fingers were sore with the pressure I had applied making sure I did not accidentally drop the thing. I had held it so tight when released it did not go half the distance I had mentally planned, as if stuck on the palm of my sweaty hand. You don't know what to expect but the first time at anything it is always the worst time, then always a doddle from then on. To top the day, going back in the ambulance via the sand dunes the top high ambulance, a converted Land Rover fell over which made every body have a good laugh, what a day!

The risk of IRA attack was still thought to be low, so we were allowed to go to a local discotheque. Being Paras the only local girl to show any interest in soldiers was an invalid girl who was duly invited back to camp for a gang-bang. The lads said it was good for public relations to show the locals we were sympathetic, she did stay for a few days but I do not know if that was not down to someone nicking the battery from her three-wheeler invalid car.

The Battalion was moved down into Londonderry and into accommodation that was to say the least makeshift. From derelict old mills to shops that had been boarded up we were spread all over the city. I was stationed in a storeroom above a shop in the Diamond Square; from here we patrolled the centre of Londonderry up to the historic city wall that then led into the Bogside, day and night.

It was a relatively quiet time in Londonderry with only one shooting incident and one car bomb. A paratrooper jumped into the car bomb and drove it to where it would not cause damage. I thought to myself what a hero but the officers gave him a right rollicking, stating he had unnecessarily put his and other peoples lives at risk. I was not on the same wavelength with this decision, as my reasoning came to the conclusion that it was the IRA who had done that by placing the bomb in the City.

The trouble with the Paras was that if they had nobody to fight, living in quarters that were sub human, no television and no time off on the town, tension started and aggression followed with the odd fight amongst themselves and I had to treat a Para corporal who had nearly lost his eye in a fight with another Para.

I was allowed to take out a patrol as a Corporal which also gave me a break from that billet; you just had to get out of that confined space. I was the first to admit that everyone in the patrol had more experience than myself and I should not have been in command but fortunately no incident occurred other than a shopping trip, that I had planned. I had a lad called Tich in the patrol, small but one of the best lightweight fighters I have had the privilege to meet and would stand up to any man. I wanted to buy an engagement ring for my girlfriend so I stopped my patrol outside a jewellers shop, put the machine gun outside the door to stop anyone entering and went inside with Tich. I said to the amazed shop keeper "I want an engagement ring that will fit his finger" and immediately explained his finger was about the same size as my girlfriend. The way I said it just did not come out right, everyone in the shop had a laugh at my expense so I did blush a little. When my Catholic girl friend in Glasgow received it by post, the ring fitted exactly. She asked how had I managed to get the right size I replied "Long story I will tell you another day". My future wife was only 5 feet tall and Tich was only a fraction bigger.

Going by the local press and television Belfast was having the worst of the troubles, with rioting and shootings so our Battalion soon got moved there to an area called Ballymurphy. My company was billeted in a local school called the Vere Foster and an adjacent church hall called the Henry Taggart Hall.

Londonderry had been a picnic compared to this new location. I was in a few incidents personally before internment that I will recount, but also the men of "B" company 2nd Battalion Parachute Regiment who were stationed with me in the centre of the hornet's nest were having a daily brush with death. We had replaced a company from the 3rd Parachute Battalion who had had one man killed and warned us to be on our guard. The company Corporals were good and experienced but the lads were very young, not the best educated but not lacking in fibre, proud to be British and proud to be paratroopers.

Corporal Frank Salt was a typical corporal, an excellent patrol leader, a born leader of men, a man's man! He had a few contacts, fire fights with the IRA, as he led his patrol with a determined and professional attitude. His first contact had made him change tactics, an IRA gun man jumped out from an alleyway with a Thompson machine gun, pulled the trigger but the gun jammed Cpl Salt only had a rubber bullet gun which had been designed for riot control, two inch wide, six inch long black bullet (not fitted with vibrator) and was supposed to be fired at the ground in front of a rioter. This bullet had been doctored with an extra charge of gunpowder added to increase the velocity of the bullet and a nail added to the rubber point, when the gunman ran the bullet helped him on his way sticking in his arse. Frank had been lucky that at this stage the IRA were using old Second World War weapons given to them by their American friends or left over from the Irish civil war, but after that contact he changed the rubber dildo weapon for a more lethal variety, a 9mm pistol with an experimental laser sight. He was successful in finding ammunition dumps and some had been well camouflaged by the IRA, for example a washing line turned out to be co-ax cable used in the detonation of bombs. An innocent-looking manhole but he noticed two for the same house and yes another weapons cache. He also arrested a few men on the wanted list passed down by Intelligence Corps. One night a megaphone shouted out his name, the IRA warned him that besides his name, they had his address in England and the name of his wife and children! That was a deep blow to his and our morale; how the fuck did they have that type of information? This made us all feel vulnerable because in Ireland we could not protect our families. The professionalism of Frank and the other corporals was an inspiration to me and the other young men of the company, as they did not shirk from their tasks even though this threat their families existed. The IRA would later attack our barracks. Bombs detonated in Aldershot February 22nd 1972, killing several women employed as civilian cleaners in the officers' mess and our Catholic priest Padre Weston. The IRA knew we were in Ireland.

Raiding a house later in the tour we found a list, naming every man in the company and our addresses. We had a traitor in the Regiment or a security breach in the disposal of office documents. It was later established that indeed the intelligence-gathering of the IRA had been underestimated, as it was discovered even some binmen were members of the IRA, also postal and telephone workers. As some of our men had married young Catholic girls in the first tour of duty, it made you wonder about our security, at all levels, as some mother fuckers were not on the right side!

I was out on night patrol with Frank when I had my first scrape with death. At this moment as I and my comrades approached the planned kill zone, I was ignorant of why these men and women had so much hate in them that they were prepared to kill and murder for their cause. A united Ireland seamed logical for me as I still did not grasp why it was divided in the first place. As a young 20-year old, women, drinking and having a good time were my priorities in life. Little if any space was allocated in my brain for politics or religion which I think was the normal for young people and young soldiers were no different. Northern Ireland was to bring to me the reality of life, open my eyes and form opinions on religion and politics, in my guest to find out the reason why I was putting my life on the line.

Only one street light was left working, they removed the time switches of street lights to use in their car bombs but this one light was to illuminate the soldier they planned to ambush. House lights were all switched off, everyone in the street (Glenalena Road) knew about the plan and were all party to the terrorist plot to kill a soldier. They hid in the dark, watching eyes from windows to witness the killing and I was the target as they identified me as part of the British system.

On the other side of the street, Corporal Frank Salt was in command of the patrol, and I was opposite him so he could keep an eye on me, as I was not combat trained. He saw the danger but our orders were to patrol the streets of Ballymurphy and no matter what, a soldier had to take the risk and cross the illuminated area first. I had always been streetwise and my natural senses put me on guard and I had sensed the danger. Frank knelt down and pointed his gun; he also had his hair standing up at the back of his neck as he also felt something was not right. He covered me from potential fire coming from down the street and my side of the road, a tall garden wall protected him. My eyes were adapting to the light as I was making a run to cross the illuminated area, then an object landed in front of me. A second is a long time, my brain took in the situation, and the short fuse allowed me to see the nails, a good kilo of six inch nails that hid the stick of dynamite, the short fuse sparkled and illuminated the bomb. A metre or a yard it landed in front of me, at the time I still worked in yards but one thing was certain to me it was just out of reach, of my kicking ability, being only a short-arsed paratrooper medic.

The terrorist had missed his vocation in life, if this perfect throw was his natural ability, he could have been a star in most ball games. I had no chance to escape so I shouted "grenade" to save someone else in the patrol and that was my only thought before it exploded, an incredible blast so close, my body lifted into the air and I was thrown back over, like a punch with a glove so big it hit my whole body at the same instant, I landed on my back, the air sucked out of my lungs. Funny but the first thing I checked was that my cock and balls were still with me and with relief a shudder went down my body. I stopped playing with my balls and jumped up, fucking angry! The terrorist was still there and he looked in dumb disbelief that I had survived and he was the witness to a miracle. He was at the corner, at the rear of a house, the opposite side of the garden wall that Frank was taking cover behind; the same street light now exposed him to the blackness behind him. We looked at each other, but my right hand worked the cocking mechanism of my rifle as I put a bullet in the breach and brought the rifle up to the firing position. He reacted to the sound and was now running, he escaped from my sight. I shouted out to the others, "he's in the rear garden behind the wall" and two soldiers jumped over the wall and tried to bring him down with rifle fire. The black of the night saved him but the bullets must have given him the same experience I had just had. I had come close to death and the sad thing was I did not know why!

This was my first direct contact with terrorism but was to be one of many over the next few years. I still remember that incident as if it happened yesterday and ask myself how was it possible that not one nail got me at such close range, was it a miracle, is there a God and why save someone that is not a religious person.

A couple of days later on patrol with Frank again, in broad daylight we were travelling around the estate in two Land Rovers and the incident which occurred got me into a spot of bother. A group of women were making a road block, digging up whole paving stones and laying them in the road. Here they are caught red-handed preparing an ambush against us, then they start pushing and shoving us, screaming insults, they had more cheek and more balls than their men. British fucking bastards and those were the nice words! This big fat cow comes up to me and punched me right in the nose. If you are married and reading this book, ask your wife to stop what she is doing and tell her to hit you in the nose as hard as possible. Now tell me if you would let her do it a second time? I told the bitch,"You do that again and I will hit you back." My eyes were still watering when she hit me again right on the same spot! I brought my rifle down on the top of her head out of instinct and the bayonet connection cut her scalp. Frank to say the least was angry with me for hitting this woman, yes I was wrong but it all happened in a minute of anger! How does your nose feel? The woman was screaming hysterically and all the women rallied round her, she had my beret in her hand somehow after she had given me a head whip with her punch and it had my name in it. We, on Frank's orders jumped into our Land Rovers and returned to base. I was disciplined by being confined to camp for two weeks but the worse punishment was every time the Land Rover went out which I had been riding in, it was pelted with stones and bottles. A young private received a bottle straight in the face; his lip was splade open, with profuse blood loss. When they brought him into me the shell dressing was bright red with his blood and he was suffering from shock. I stitched him up to the best of my ability but felt very guilty with every stitch, twelve in all, to close the wound. The doctor arrived when I had finished and told me that he could not have done a better job. The lad later informed me he got £600 compensation, 50 notes per stitch which helped me get over my guilt, as he was more than happy. He had a permanent fine scar but not a hare lip which could have happened, had I made a bad job with the stitching.

It only turned out that the woman that punched me was nine months pregnant and she had the baby that night. She did not call it Nigel which really was a blessing as I would not like to inflict that name on the poor kid. What the fuck was she doing digging up and laying paving stones in that condition, and attacking me? Was I the guilty party? Only her story hit the newspapers the next day and I was that bastard paratrooper.

Even in camp there were memorable events, some funny, some sad and some sadder! The bedding in the camp had been passed on from one unit to the next and fleas became an itchy problem. Corporal, Mike Harding was the type of guy who showered three times a day and was always smart and immaculate. It's funny how the fleas made a direct line for him being such a clean person; he really got upset about the situation. Being the medic he said it was down to me to get rid of this plague of fleas, which were causing more anger than the IRA. I was given DDT powder to solve the problem which was scattered on beds, and clothing, the long term effect probably did more damage to soldiers' health than the IRA ever inflicted, being now a banned product on health grounds. Mike came into my room, "Geordie look at this", he said he had been searching a Paddy's house and when he came out noted the time. A crack in his watch face and what was now jumping in front of the minute hand, yes a Paddy flea. He taped in that flea to make it suffer every minute for the rest of its life. He had been in the bedroom of a house and moved the bed, to be gobsmacked to find a near mountain of used fanny pads discarded by the woman of the house, dirty bitch. I bet she had been hiding a pistol under them, Mike." "She can keep the pistol to kill the fleas," he replied! I must acknowledge that most of the Paddies houses were like palaces and very clean but like every walk of life you get the dirty bastards. Water, fish piss in it and it does rust battleships but I cannot think of another reason why not to use it when it is free.

On inspecting the barracks, Mike found a dirty soldier who had not been cleaning himself or his kit, and his locker was one of the focal points in this flea outbreak. Mike went berserk, "bad enough the Paddies but not from my own men," he screamed, the lad's kit was burnt, his bedding was burnt and then they carried him to the showers and there things got a little out of hand in the scrubbing of the soldier. The hard bristled brushes were bad enough but someone threw cleaning fluid on him which burnt his raw skin, crying in agony he came to my medical post and told me the story of his plight. Although you could feel sorry for him, his serious injuries were going to bring punishment to all involved in the incident. I had to order his immediate evacuation to hospital and suggested to him to say that he had mixed up the shampoo bottle with one that contained cleaning fluid which would stop the incident going further. How he was going to explain the weals from the scrubbing brushes I did not have a suggestion. I noticed that the lads took an instant effort to improve their personal hygiene, what a way to make a lesson! Pity we could not do the same to the dirty locals!

Some soldiers were new, innocent and these types were always preyed on by the bullies and psychopaths of the unit, fortunately only a small minority fitted this category. One lad stood out as the man, he was a tough bastard and if he was not fully involved with fighting the Paddies, he could turn against anyone. He was a Lance Corporal attached from the Royal Corps of Transport, Para trained, good Land Rover driver but one of the worst forms of a human being! He always had a stray dog in his wagon which he had called "Truck". This was the only good side I saw about him, he fed that dog well, trained it to bite Paddies and in front of the lads in his barracks would often give it a wank, he also called it "Big Truck"! Yes, no wonder the dog liked him. They were on the same wave level, sorry, I take that back because I like dogs and would not like to insult their mentality. A young soldier came to my treatment post and told me that he had been raped by this guy in front of the lads in the barrack room because he had complained about what he was doing with the dog. I was annoyed but the lad pleaded with me to say nothing about the incident. I was also fuming because none of his mates had come to his assistance, some of the bastards sniggered about it, typical cowards as it had not happened to them! To say the least the young soldier was in a state of shock and felt ashamed about what had been done to him. For some weeks, I kept an eye on him, in case he got too depressed and did something stupid.

Had I told the CSM about his plight, I am sure he would have been very sympathetic as he also had a painful experience. He suffered from piles and to say the least he had a bunch of grapes hanging from his arse. The Medical Officer gave them the chop and packed his sore bum with cotton wool which had to be replaced twice a day. I felt that I had once again been part of an English Army taking revenge on the Jocks just as in the days of King Edward. He was so embarrassed that he would only let me change the dressing if he spread his weight against the door of my medical room, I presumed he did not want anybody to take his picture at the moment I was packing the wound but on this occasion I did not keep medical ethics and told the lads so they could have a laugh.

On the Day of Internment the Lance Corporal who had raped the soldier would play a prominent role in the torture inflicted on the poor unfortunate Paddies that he got his hands on.

Like I said he was a good driver and a few nights later on July 13th 1971 he proved that he was also a good fighter, preferably as long he was not against you. Two IRA were waiting in the dark, the evening was cold, so they were well wrapped up with double layers of clothing, two pairs of jeans to keep out the chill lying on a grass bank. The two Land Rovers slowly came down the straight "Whiterock Road" leading to the local cemetery. Not seen by the IRA was that the wagons were empty, the lads were walking behind, only the drivers were near at hand if they needed to adjust the direction of the steering wheel. The wagon's engine was in first gear, low ratio, it went at a slow walking pace. The bombers had set up a device that only needed a wire to be pulled that would make an electrical connection to detonate the bomb. The patrol had been quiet and with the engines just ticking over on the Land Rovers they were closer than expected before the pair of terrorists noticed the patrol in the kill zone. In panic they pulled the trip cable too hard which tilted the bomb down and the shrapnel only impacted a few feet from the detonation point. The lads were shooting at them as they saw them jump up from their hiding position. The explosion had given them the edge to make their escape but Yorky Hill and his patrol had not lost sight of them. In hot pursuit, firing at the fleeing targets, one went to the ground with a scream of agony, his mate kept running. He entered a house and the lads went in shooting, out the lock. Sitting on the settee, trying to act as if he had been watching television, his panting, sweating body could not be hidden. The base radio had been given the sit rep (situation report) by Hill's radio operator I was put on immediate standby to receive casualties and we all anxiously waited the patrol's return to base. Fortunately no soldiers were injured, only the wagons had been nailed and hit by the flying shrapnel but not destroyed. They brought in the wounded terrorist, and then dragged in screaming the one who had claimed he was watching television. I immediately got to work; cutting off the wounded man's jeans, hard work to remove two pairs with a pair of scissors. The bullet had not been a direct entry wound, it must have ricocheted from the ground or a wall as it had entered sideways near his arse hole and it now looked like he had twin arse holes. I turned him, looking for the exit wound but could not see it. Then I saw the bullet just under the skin of his right thigh. The velocity had been reduced being a ricochet; it then hit bone, his pelvis, further slowing the bullet which now rested under the skin of his right thigh. He was not bleeding much from the wound; his pulse and blood pressure were only a little higher than normal. Now being caught in the act of trying to kill my mates, he was not going to get any form of sympathy from me, in fact I told him he was dying and told one of the lads to get the Battalion Priest Captain Weston, both the Priest and the Chaplin were operating from our camp. They did their best to show the Paddies how to live in a Christian way, respecting each other's religion. Padre Weston administered the last rites and I listened to his admissions of guilt being a member of the IRA. His name was Gerrard Fitzgerald, from Ballymurphy Drive, a young man who needed killing. He would have a long career as a member of the IRA, captured, sentenced on numerous occasions for attempted murder, he would be involved in two spectacular escapes from police custody, a real diehard IRA terrorist. The other captured IRA was also admitting his guilt and giving information about the location of weapons caches. He was not getting the last rites but was confessing, he was under no doubt he might need a priest. He was so terrified that he pissed himself, losing all control of his body functions with fear. The driver was involved but I could not see what he was doing to him that was causing him to scream. The ambulance was taking a long time because nobody had phoned for one, wups! This was my first gunshot wound that I treated so I thought it would be a good live demonstration to show the lads the effect of a 7.62 bullet on human flesh, with my officers blessing I showed all the lads, a good demo, nothing brings home the reality of war until you have seen the real thing.

An ambulance was now called to take him to the Royal Belfast Hospital and did not take time in arriving, once it was requested. The Company Sergeant Major took the front of the stretcher and on his command the wounded man was thrown up into the air, hitting the ceiling and then crashing back down to the stretcher. Four or five times he got this treatment in the hope he bled to death before reaching hospital. The information gathered was quickly followed up and numerous weapons were captured. The IRA was forced into drastic and daring action. The next day a group of twelve IRA men overpowered his police escort guarding him in hospital, and escaped with him into Southern Ireland. The other bomber was put on trial and due to a technicality was released without charges being brought against him. The patrol had lost sight of him and the judge had believed the shit that he was innocently watching television (wearing two pairs of jeans).

When I was in the SAS I heard that Fitzgerald had been captured again planting a bomb outside an army barracks, called Silver City. A sentry had spotted him and due to his limp was captured by a foot patrol. In court he gave my name and that of Yorky Hill, stating that we were on the IRA wanted list and accusing us of torture! What a cheek to complain about us when he was caught time and time again trying to blow people to pieces with his bombs.

Londonnerry Diamond Square makeshift barracks above a derelict shop

Me with soldier who nearly lost and Eye (Para fighting Para)

Local school in Ballymurphy

Painted windows to make it harder for IRA snipers

The armoury, Londonderry: Makeshift accommodation for 2 Para

Surveying the aftermath of a bomb against B company

In car park of Henry Tagget Hall, me in centre

16 JUL 1971

GANG SNATCH CK COMRADE RVH WARD

By Martin Lindsay, David Nealy and John Conway

AN IRA GANG armed with sub-machineguns and revolvers forced their way into the Royal Victoria Hospital in Belfast early this morning and carried away a comrade who was shot by the Army three days ago.

They bound and gagged a night porter and clubbed one of two armed policemen who were guarding a dangerously ill patient, 19-year-old Gerard Fitzgerald, of 34 Ballymurphy Drive.

To-day troops and police mounted a fullscale search throughout Ulster for the gunmen who carried out the daring snatch at six am.

The operation was carried out in the best detective novel style. Four of the men strolled up to the door of Ward 10 dressed as doctors—all wearing white coats and one with a face mask.

Detectives were to-day interviewing other patients and night staff in an attempt to build up a description of the gang for circulation to police stations.

Nerve centre of the inquiries is Springfield Road police station, where a maroon coloured Ford Cortina is being examined by forensic experts.

It was found parked—with its doors open—in Sorella Street near the hospital. Police think this vehicle, stolen during the night, was used in some way by the raiders.

A white coat of the type used by doctors was also brought to the Springfield Road station, where a team of detectives under Chief Superintendent Paddy McAndrew is interviewing everyone who can help.

And hours after the

Remand for man on bomb charge

24 NOV 1972

A 20-YEAR-OLD Ballymurphy man was again remanded in custody for a week till November 30 when he appeared at Belfast Magistrates Court yesterday on a charge of possessing a gelignite bomb under suspicious circumstances.

He is Gerard Fitzgerald of Ballymurphy Drive. He is alleged to have had the bomb under suspicious circumstances on July 13 last year. Fitzgerald refused to recognise the court.

Another Belfast man was remanded in custody to the same date when he appeared on charges of possessing over 300 rounds of ammunition, four weapons joining bolts and three ammunition clips under suspicious circumstances on November 17 last at Peel Street.

He is James Christopher McWilliams (27), of Peel Street, Belfast. He was remanded in custody despite an appeal for bail by his solicitor, Mr. Pascal O'Hare.

BAIL FOR FOUR NEWRY ESCAPERS IN DUBLIN

FOUR young men from Northern Ireland against whom extradition orders had been issued appeared before Justice Johnstone in the Dublin District Court yesterday. They are Gerald Fitzgerald, Eugene Fanning, Hugh Clarke and Thomas Joseph McGarry.

They were remanded on bail to April 11.

The warrants for their extradition stated that the men escaped from custody on March 30 at Newry Courthouse.

Detective Sergeant H. Thyne said he arrested the men at the Bridewell station about 1 a.m. yesterday.

Mr. Myles Shevlin, solicitor, for the men, asked the detective did he know the four defendants had been in custody for over 28 hours.

Detective Sgt. Thyne said he was told the men were at the station at 7-30 p.m. on Thursday and went to arrest them.

Mr. Shevlin — I am putting it to you that this was an artificial arrest — an arrest within an arrest, and the High Court has already held that such an arrest is bad in law.

Witness — I know only that they had been in custody on some other charge.

Mr. Shevlin — In connection with a motoring offence?

Witness — I understand they were being charged under Section 13 of the Offences Against the State Act.

Mr. Shevlin said: "It is obvious that these offences are of a political nature and that extradition cannot apply."

Mr. Ivan Duncan, assistant State Solicitor, applied for a remand for a week. Mr. Shevlin asked for bail.

Justice Johnstone fixed bail in independent sureties of £100, which were forthcoming, and the men left the court with their solicitor.

MacCURTAIN HELPS "PROVISIONALS"
Joe Cahill at Cork rally
By Mary Leland

TOMAS MacCURTAIN said in Cork on Saturday night that the battle being fought was "against the same enemy that our fathers and uncles fought here 50 years ago—and, please God, we'll beat them again."

MacCurtain was one of three speakers at a public meeting; the others were Joe Cahill and Sean Mac Stiofain. Later, at a private meeting in the Victoria Hotel, Cahill told local members of Sinn Fein that there was no need for volunteers for the North.

"The North has enough men," he said, "and in a short time we will be victorious." What was wanted, he said, was a "reserve force" in the South, people who would be prepared to obey to the letter directives from the leadership. Sinn Fein itself should develop to become the political movement in the South.

Asked to clarify the situation regarding the Provisionals and any connection with what was described as the "Blaney, Haughey and Boland faction," Sean Mac Stiofain said that it was a lying, base slander to say that Fianna Fail had had anything to do with the split in Sinn Fein or that the Provisionals had anything to do with Blaney, Haughey and Boland. "We have nothing in common with them, they are Free Staters, we are Republicans. We wouldn't touch them with a barge pole."

Mr. MacCurtain said that when he was released from two years' internment in 1959 he found that other men with other ideas and other methods had come to leadership, and had informed him that there was no further use for his services. When he was asked to speak at Saturday's meeting, he had been reluctant, but he felt it was everybody's duty to stand up and be counted in the cause of freedom and truth and justice.

IMPOSSIBLE TO TALK

The peaceful movement had foundered, he said, because it was impossible to talk reason with England. The English were not going to learn in Ireland, except the same way they learned everywhere else.

Sean Mac Stiofain said that to achieve the day when British forces in Ireland would be cleared out, the fight had to become a 32-county fight.

Joe Cahill said the fight in the North was not the fight of the Northern people alone and he appealed to the people of Cork to rally to their cause. "To ensure that no one will block us in our efforts, and that those who raise their hands against us will be struck down by your power. You have that power and you have that right."

Joe Cahill introduced Gerry FitzGerald, who had been taken by the I.R.A. from a Belfast hospital.

Donneadh O Murchu called for a boycott of British goods and for a general demand that the Irish Government would not co-operate with British forces in the North.

Snatched IRA man still in Ulster

THE young man who was snatched from the Royal Victoria Hospital yesterday morning by an armed IRA gang is believed to be in hiding in Ulster. it was learned to-day.

It was earlier thought that 19-year-old Gerard Fitzgerald, of Ballymurphy Drive, had managed to break the security net on the border, but sources were to-day saying that he was still in the province.

The Provisional wing of the IRA has claimed responsibility for the operation. They said that Fitzgerald, a member of their organisation, was "rescued" by comrades.

The hospital authorities have said that Fitzgerald's wound required continuous expert medical care and he is now thought to be getting this from a sympathiser.

He was shot in the thigh by the Army in the early hours of Tuesday morning during a nail bomb attack at the Whiterock Road.

In Dublin to-day a spokesman for the Provisionals said that Fitzgerald was being "looked after" but he would not disclose his whereabouts.

The spokesman added: "My information is that he is not as badly injured as the hospital tried to make out."

Troops saved because mine tilted over, court told

AN ARMY PATROL escaped serious injury because a claymore mine was tilted towards the ground and not towards them, a jury at Belfast City Commission heard to-day.

One soldier was blown over by the blast at Rock Grove, Ballymurphy, in the early hours of July 13, 1971, but the other members of the patrol escaped uninjured, said Mr. John Creaney, QC, prosecuting.

Gerald Fitzgerald (20), unemployed, of Ballymurphy Drive, refused to plead, and Lord Justice Jones directed that pleas of not guilty be entered on his behalf.

Fitzgerald is accused of attempting to murder L-Cpl Joseph Hill and Privates Peter Taylor and Dominic Veigh attempting to cause grievous bodily harm and causing an explosion with intent to endanger life.

When arraigned, Fitzgerald said: "As a volunteer of the Irish Republican Army, I refuse to recognise the jurisdiction of this court until there is a 32-county Irish democratic socialist republic, and Ireland is free."

Outlining the case, Mr. Creaney said that after the explosion, two men were seen running away. A soldier opened fire and shot one of the men in the leg. The other escaped.

A search of the area revealed a crater behind houses at Rock Grove and equipment used for detonating a claymore mine.

Mr. Creaney added: "This particular explosion could very well have killed members of the patrol. But the device was tilted over and the blast precipitated into the ground, rather than towards the soldiers."

An explosives expert said that had the mine not fallen over he would not have given much for the chances of the soldiers in line of fire. "I would not like to be within 25 ft of it. It would be lethal," he added.

In a statement read to the court by a detective sergeant, Fitzgerald said that he had been taken to Rock Grove by another man who showed him a box and a line and told him to pull the line as an Army patrol passed.

"I was surprised by the soldiers. They were almost on top of me," the statement went on. "Between panic and surprise I got up to run and doing so pulled the string."

Fitzgerald, in a statement made from the dock, accused the Paratroopers of leaving him on the road for over 20 minutes. he claimed he had been brutally treated, beaten, spat on and abused before being taken to the Royal Victoria Hospital.

He added that three days later he was rescued by his comrades and the "black British" issued a statement saying he had only three hours to live.

"These men have charged me with attempting to murder them when in fact they did their best to murder me," said Fitzgerald. "The fight will go on until we are free of these men."

Chapter 8

Ballymurphy

A few days passed without incident, but then a simple fall from the top bunk bed and a friend Lance Corporal Pete T, broke his leg. We were all laughing in the barracks as I fixed a plastic blow up splint and organized him to be lifted onto a stretcher. "You will soon have your plaster on and be back at home with the little missus, what some guys will do to get out of here," I jibed. The armoured Saladin ambulance arrived down outside the Taggart Hall so we walked from the school and in front of the Hall to the waiting ambulance. The big red cross on the ambulance could not be mistaken, four men carrying a stretcher was to be the snipers target. Crack, crack, crack, the bullets flew close over our heads and we all instinctively hit the deck. The shooting started again as he had us in open ground. We made a dash and took cover behind the protection of the armoured ambulance but we all forgot Pete T stuck on the stretcher with his broken leg. Fucking bastards he retorted as he got up from the stretcher and miraculously ran for cover. Talk about Lazarus, take up thy bed and walk. We could not stop laughing as he hit the deck with us behind the ambulance; even he started laughing through the pain of his broken leg. I was the only one with a gun, a 9mm Browning pistol so I tried to fire a round to frighten off the sniper but the gun was broken and would not fire, so we started laughing again when I said I had been carrying this fucking thing three months and it did not work.

Corporal Harding was talking to the local Catholic priest from the Ballymurphy estate, he was complaining that we were all trigger-happy and anti-Catholic but Mike was trying to reassure him that was not the case. One of his soldiers at that moment accidentally fired his rifle. He had been resting the long rifle barrel on his boot which was a common practice with the lads. The British Army regular issue rifle (SLR) was long and most Paras were short guys, so carrying it for four hours, you either cradled it in your arms or rested the muzzle on your boot when standing still. The priest walked away cursing God or something like that. The soldier was carried back to camp, Mike had found it very embarrassing and still in a bad mood about his fleas. Arguing the case that we are not trigger-happy and then this private soldier blows a hole in his toe. He was in the process of giving the soldier now in a state of shock, a bit of verbal abuse, saying it was probably his brain in his big toe. The Sergeant Major came on the scene and questioned the soldier, as this would be a military trial and at least 28 days in prison for the lad. The soldier said he had not touched the trigger; the safety catch was on, it had just gone off on its own, well no one, even his mates did not believe that story. I managed to remove the lad's boot and was apprehensive as to what I would find, being at such a close range when the bullet had fired into his boot.

Not much blood had spilled from the boot but his sock was well soaked with congealed blood. His big toe had a neat 7.62 hole going in from the top and the same on the exit and I was surprised, as I was contemplating a more blood and guts effect at such close range. The toe was waxy white with a black ridge around the hole and particles of sock sucked into the centre by the velocity of the bullet.

The CSM inspected the weapon and unloaded the bullets from the magazine onto a bed; nearly every bullet had a strike in the base which meant the soldier could be right. He got the rest of the patrol to unload their magazines and found more than 50% of the bullets with strike marks. The bullets had been passed down from unit to unit and the act of putting one up the breach from old, well-used rifles, had the mechanism striking the rounds, all the ammo had to be replaced. From this incident we were not allowed to put one up the breach from then on, so that gave the IRA a second advantage. Had I had a bullet up the breach in my incident with the IRA I am sure I would have managed to get a shot at him but being the medic and not combat trained I had not put one up the spout.

The IRA were in the process at this time of getting new American Armalite rifles, and here were our rifles worn out and dangerous. The soldier in question never returned to duty and was given a medical discharge from the Army, his toe had to be amputated and you cannot walk well without your big toe.

The traffic was being stopped by a crowd of lads on Springfield Road and Lt John Easton was ordered to take out his platoon and make arrests. When something like this happened we found it was more than likely a "come on" organised by the IRA so that they could set us up for an ambush. John was a good officer and briefed us well in case an incident developed; I was to go along just in case it was a set-up. The lads were so fast in making contact with the group causing the problem that they were taken by surprise and a pitched battle ensued. Every other soldier had been carrying a pickaxe handle and they were used without mercy. The quality of the handles was brought into dispute as some broke smashing down on heads. A sport that I had never played, curling (like a hockey stick) was popular in Ireland gave the local lads a stick weapon that they also used against us. I ran to help one soldier who had five lads on top of him as they were trying to get his rifle. In a fight like this the rifle was a hindrance as we could not use lead in a stick-and-fist fight. Fortunately, in his other hand he held a rubber bullet gun and as he feared loosing his rifle which was the objective of this group, he fire at close range with the rubber bullet gun. It hit one of his assailants in the mouth ripping open the bloke's cheek. Did he scream as he was helped away by his mates, his face torn open. One civilian went to pick up the rifle, I pointed my pistol,"pick up the rifle and I will shoot". He backed off, as he could see I meant it, but would the pistol work was ticking in the back of my mind.

I went to the assistance of another Para in trouble, who had been hit in the back while he was holding one of the Paddies. "I don't know what I was hit with but I cannot feel my legs", he told me. I knew that this could be serious if his back was fractured so I called for assistance from John, who then sent me three lads who had done well with the first aid training back in Aldershot. An ambulance was called for and I reminded the lads that we would be doing a blanket lift so that a stretcher could be slid underneath him. The lads rolled the soldier so I could slide the blanket under him, half was tightly rolled and he was rolled over this part so it could be unrolled on the other side. Now in the centre of the blanket both edges were tightly rolled so that they could be gripped. Two more men joined us so we had three men either side, crossing arms we firmly grasped the blanket and lifted sufficiently so the ambulance driver could slide under the stretcher. They worked as we had done in practice and I was pleased and sure that we had done a good job in not causing any further damage to his spine. The ambulance sped off and we smashed some more pickaxe handles.

The Day of Internment was a well-guarded secret, even we did not know about it till a few hours before the operation was to be carried out. The company was stood-to, with pre-orders to get your rifle cleaned and ready for some form of action. An Officers' briefing was followed by NCOs briefing and then the individual patrols were briefed in their mission. I could feel a sense of excitement from the lads and the camp was buzzing, the thought of getting a bit of revenge against the IRA was in the back of most soldier's minds. I did not need to be told to get my medical kit sorted; I knew it would be needed!

All had been organised down to the finest detail, 2 am and the patrols moved out to the targets. There was an inward hope that some might have weapons and resist, which added to the excitement. The hour had been well chosen, if you have ever done night duty in what ever capacity, 2 am to 4 am is the most difficult to stay awake and alert. Thus in the military this is a good time to carry out any surprise attack against the enemy. The local dogs sensed something was up, dogs could be heard from one end of the Ballymurphy Estate to the other as the men moved to the houses to be raided. The IRA dogs were slower to react, the doors of the houses were demolished in unison and the soldiers rushed into their objectives. Most were in a state of waking up in a nightmare, as they were grabbed and dragged out of bed, their women screamed thinking their men were going to get shot on the spot. Some were naked, some were in pyjamas, some in underpants as they were dragged down stairs and frog-marched back to the Henry Taggart Hall.

Mission almost complete, the lads started to joke as they brought in the prisoners; did you see that fucker's wife starkers just standing there in her full glory? "This fucker's wife was a right dog, I think we rescued him", was another comment, I overheard.

The prisoners had their heads covered with an empty sand-bag and their hands tied behind their backs. Yes, they were mistreated, pushed and shoved, punched and kicked. Some were made to think they were going to be pushed off a table and hung, but in the main the torture was only psychological. When later I joined the SAS, I was tortured for three days and three nights as part of the entrance test and that was a lot harder than anything done to the IRA on the Day of Internment. The fear amongst them was very real, some lost control of their bladders; literally pissing themselves with fear. They were interrogated; name, age and the names of next to kin and some gave more information to save their necks from more punching and kicking. The officers were there; even the Battalion Commander Colonel Hewlit. They stopped the lads going too far, but allowed and encouraged most of the treatment. It was in my opinion, that not all were IRA, some were too young, others too old, but British Intelligence and the Police don't get things wrong. (Intelligence, could they spell the word?).

Like all bullies, the IRA amongst the prisoners did not like being on the receiving end of what they had been inflicting on others. The IRA had taken over the role of the police against local petty criminals and showed what it would be like if the IRA took over in Ireland, knee-capping (shooting with a pistol into the back of your leg blowing the knee-cap off), public beating of children and even some kids were knee-capped, tar and feathers to women, hair shaved and then tied naked to lamp posts, just for speaking to soldiers. Well, it certainly put them on par with what the Muslim terrorists are doing in these days. Remember at this point if you have sympathy for the IRA, they never took British soldiers prisoner, they were either executed on the spot or taken away, tortured then executed! One SAS officer, Captain Nirack was captured, tortured and then his body put into a mincing machine. What the lads were doing was kid's play in comparison to what they were prepared to do to us, in the name of the cause. Most soldiers did not respect the IRA, shooting us was OK and part of the job but the indiscriminate bombings and killing of women and children did not go down well with us. You had to be a low life to carry out such a crime against humanity. When you have to pick up the bits of meat that only moments ago was a child or a woman or a mate, we were only human, yes we started to hate the IRA and their supporters. Yes, some soldiers had killed kids and women but never had they gone out to intentionally do it and that was the difference, we would be prosecuted for our mistakes. Then the IRA propaganda would use our accidents to justify their indiscrimate bomb.

Even in peacetime you get soldiers dying by accidental friendly fire, but in conflict with a bullet up the spout, young soldiers, tense and tired; you're going to have more accidents than on a normal exercise. In Germany there is a monument to

NATO soldiers who have died in training preparing for war against the Soviet Block. A death rate was allowed for before a major exercise would be cancelled.

A young man about 18 was sent to me to check him out. He was so scared that he was in a state of shock. His pulse was so fast, I thought he could have a heart attack at any moment; so I stopped any more mistreatment against him. I had him sent by ambulance to hospital; I could not believe he was IRA. Those who had been sleeping starkers were given trousers. As the wagons came into camp, they were taken out and thrown into the back with all the respect due to such terrorist scum.

At first light a crowd appeared with the rising sun, chickens without heads started to gather in large numbers. Insults were followed by stone-throwing. "Fucking British bastards" shouted the crowd, nothing original in their insults. In front of the Hall was a car-parking area and to the front of the Hall a look-out post had been built on scaffolding some five metres high. Two Paras were in the post that was well sand-bagged and they were in contact via a telephone land line to the ops room, giving a constant update about the gathering crowd and individuals who were now controlling them. The stone-throwing intensified and the principal target was the two lads in the post. What we did not see was that the constant barrage,was causing holes in the sandbags and the sand was running out like an egg-timer. The lost sand was underpinning the structure and it was becoming unbalanced and top-heavy. Petrol bombs were now being used and were landing in the car park. The CO saw the danger, the Henry Taggart Hall was three foot red brick but the rest was (creosoted) treated wood, highly inflammable.

He gave the warning, over the loud speaker system, that petrol bombers would be shot and he was not kidding. The Catholics also got the message, so now they only allowed young kids to throw the bombs, they knew the British Army would not purposely shoot kids! Fortunately the kids could not throw them far and could not reach the Hall. Then the first nail bomb landed in the court yard, boom, and shrapnel went flying in all directions. The order was given to shoot dead any person seen throwing nail bombs but you could not pinpoint the bomb throwers amongst the never-ending barrage of stones. The amount of stones was such that you could now not see the tarmac of the car park. Then without warning the lookout post started to topple and the lads had to dive out to save themselves. A great cheer came from the crowd as they saw the tower topple in slow motion. The lads managed to scramble over the rocks and into the Hall; both were cut and bruised but fortunately nothing more serious.

It came into my head to shout at the crowd, "Up with the IRA", now that made the crowd go completely quiet and all the soldiers looked at me and then I followed up the first message with "by the fucking neck." The crowd mumbled and started throwing the rocks with a new intensity. The lads laughed but the Sergeant Major and the OC did not see the funny side. When a break came in the stone-throwing I was sent out to move stones, fucking hundreds of stones.

When you get a lull in a riot situation, I found out the hard way, that it was not for our benefit. Regrouped and more organized, a constant bombardment carried on all day. A few lads made up some catapult slings and managed to get some rocks into the crowd, they did not like their own medicine. Rubber bullets were used to move the crowd back and some of them now took injuries which were a welcome sight, doctored bullets with six inch nails imbedded into the point, the lads chuckled as they got nailed. The hours seemed to pass so quickly and none of us managed to get any sleep, plus I had my stone-picking duty!

I was out moving stones again when the major attack started, near last light. Not stones but bullets hitting the barbed wire fence in front of me and such a heavy fusillade, the few of us outside dived for cover behind some armoured vehicles.

From the relative safety behind the vehicles, I could see the situation develop. The gunmen were using Thompson machine guns, Armalites and other weapons such as shotguns and pistols but from the range they were engaging us they were not powerful enough to penetrate the Hall and most of our men had taken cover under the brick level. I could see a large group break cover and start running towards the front gate. The sentry at the gate was on the telephone land line giving a running commentary to the CO and was now informing him of the attack on his position. Well one thing was obvious, the guy in charge of the IRA and organising this attack did not have a clue, to think they could overrun 120 well armed paratroopers in a defensive position, was to say the least suicidal. The CO ordered soldiers out to the car park with orders "shoot to kill". The combined fire-power of these men stopped the group of locals in their tracks; I saw at least six were hit and went down wounded or dead. The rest scattered and ran for cover, wounded shouting for help. I was amazed to see that they had organised stretcher bearers with white overalls, clearly marked with a red cross. After the killing was over we found that they had prepared a school as a makeshift hospital, the attack on our position must have been planned well in advance. We had respected the Red Cross and had not engaged the wounded being evacuated. The IRA had blocked and barricaded the roads into Ballymurphy, manned by IRA gunmen whose task was to stop reinforcements reaching our position. They honestly thought they could take us out and this was them separating us from reinforcements. From our position anything or any body that moved was a target; if you were innocent you should not have been there. For all the rounds that had been fired at the Henry Tagget Hall and the Vere Foster School, at this stage we had still not taken any casualties. I fired a couple of rounds with my pistol and went inside the Hall. I did not want to be outdone and at least the pistol now worked! Most of the lads were on the floor, sitting or lying, some even managing to get some sleep. The television was on and I remember News at Ten started with dramatic headlines and it was us, a camera crew had taken up a position looking down into Ballymurphy from the Black Mountain area and you could see all the tracer rounds and hear the explosions. We did not have any tracer ammunition which was a bullet tipped with phosphorus that glowed when fired. We are on tele and everyone woke up with the commotion and watched the News, some lads were shouting "Hello Mum" and the rest started laughing.

The OC had ordered an ammunition count and was preoccupied with the amount we had fired and we had no reserves. A tank had been brought in by the high command to cover our position from the dominating position of Spring Martin estate, a Protestant enclave overlooking the Murph. Shooting carried on till the early hours and then the OC ordered two patrols out in Saracen armoured cars to attack the houses to our front and recover any wounded. As the cars moved out, the tank on the hill engaged a group of people moving position, with its heavy 30 calibre machine gun. The OC quickly demanded that they stopped firing as it was getting obvious that the IRA had been beaten and were withdrawing from their positions. The patrols moved out and the lads deployed some shooting at fleeing targets, the OC was not there to stop them. The wounded were collected and thrown into the back of the armoured vehicles and returned to camp. When doors opened, my eyes met a moaning, groaning mass of bodies which I quickly had emptied and helped onto beds so I could administer first aid.

The worst injured was a man called Daniel Taggart. How could I forget his name, I did not ask him if Henry was his brother. When I saw his wounds, all I said was "for fuck sake!" Both his lungs were hanging out of his back, going up and down like two frothy balloons. The impact of two bullets into the front of his chest had sucked out the lungs from the two much bigger holes in his back. "How was he still alive?" I said to myself. I used the waterproof airtight covers of the shell dressings to seal the wounds after pushing his lungs back into his chest wall. As I cut off his clothing I found another few bullet holes in his arms and then more holes in his legs. Fourteen bullet wounds and he was still alive! The blood was filling his lungs so I sat him up in bed to help his breathing and shouted to one lad, "get Padre Weston" this guy needed our Catholic priest. I left the priest with him and went to the next casualty.

Gunshot wound to the thigh, with no exit wound so it must have hit bone; I applied a shell dressing and raised the leg on pillows. Shock had set in from internal bleeding; he needed an ambulance and a surgeon and now!

Next man, a young guy early twenties and the bullet had got him in the neck, in one side and out the other with no external bleeding. I said to him "Are you all right?" to which he replied "Yes". I asked his name and a few other questions. I was damned if I knew what was the best way to treat him. Well, I could not put a shell dressing round his neck and he was not bleeding externally from the wounds anyway. He was not paralysed or in a state of shock. "Look mate I will come back to see how you are later, Lie still and don't move your neck," and on to the next man! Being honest, I just did not know what to do!

I asked an old fellow, "What are you doing getting mixed up in these troubles at your age?" He told me that he had ignored the fighting and was walking to work in the middle of all this shooting when he had been hit and to confirm his story he still had in his hand a plastic bag with his bait and flask. I finished dressing his gunshot wound to the arm, and then I was informed that we had received our first Para down, up at the school.

A fighting patrol from Support Company arrived into camp bringing more ammunition and a medic, Cpl Fraser. He came with me to the pathway leading to the school. The pathway was about 100 yards long and was floodlit with a brilliant beam focused down from the school. I thought someone would have the sense to turn it off but nobody was on the same wavelength. I said to Cpl Fraser "It's pointless us both taking the risk of getting shot, so I will run for it and you cover me, here is my pistol (9mm Browning)". If some one had had a watch, I am sure I did an Olympic qualifying time for the hundred yard sprint, and uphill!

The OC actually met me at the door when I arrived, "That was hairy running up the path", I said. He took me to the wounded soldier who was holding his arm and in some pain. Top right arm and a lump of metal fragment had penetrated under the skin. Shell dressing, sling and some dressings used as straps to stop any arm movement. I gave him a morphine injection and wrote it on his head, that he had been given morphine. His pulse was a little fast so I gave a first aid-trained Para the task to monitor the situation by keeping regular checks on his pulse and told him to pass on the information to the ambulance people who would evacuate him. I told the soldier he was in no danger of dying but would need an operation, so don't drink or eat anything. An officer lent me his rifle Lt Big John Eastern (one of the best) so I could do the run back down to the Hall. I had given the CO a quick briefing about the state of the wounded down in the Taggart Hall, that in my opinion if an ambulance does not arrive soon we would have a few dead men to account for. He informed me that the IRA had fired on civilian ambulances trying to come into the area but the Battalion doctor had been ordered to move his team in and evacuate the wounded.

Back at the Hall the priest called me to look at the lad with the bullet in the neck, he had stopped breathing, his eyes were dilated and the priest did his bit for the dead, I did my best to bring him back and upset the priest, heart massage and mouth-to-mouth for five minutes, but the priest was more experienced with the dead. One of the lads watching said "if you will do that for the enemy, you can't be a bad bloke Geordie!" Fucked if I would kiss him, then more laughter and jokes from the lads.

Another fighting patrol had gone out and this time retrieved the body of a woman and another wounded man. She must have been in her 40,s but you had to guess as a bullet had entered her left eye and taken off the whole side of her head. Another Para turned and said "I bet you can't resuscitate her, cos she's got no fucking mouth"! Besides the head wound, a bullet had taken her in the thigh ripping the muscle from the bone. Yet another bullet in the hand but I don't think that was the one that killed her. Rigor mortis had set in and the white skin glistened with dew. If her picture had been taken and shown on TV it might have stopped a lot of people joining this war, I never forgot her death mask! I think it must be just British mentality to make fun and jokes about death and tragedy. No matter what disasters happen in Britain you are sure to hear jokes about it within a few days and these lads were no exception. Maybe British mentality to get rid of grief and depression, but it was a fact that I found in most killings of our mates or the enemy.

The next to die was the lad shot in the leg and then shortly after Daniel Taggart passed away, the Hall was turning into a morgue and I could do nothing as my training was not good enough. I don't think the top Brass ever thought that we could get a situation were we could not evacuate the wounded and yet the hospital was only a mile away. Why update the training from the Second World War, terrorism was a different ball game with no rules and no respect for the Red Cross!

A battalion attack by the 1st Battalion Parachute Regiment ended the Day of Internment for us but more IRA would die. An armoured personnel carrier crashed the first barricade; the corporal sitting next to him said I think you ran over one of the bastards. The driver put the wagon in reverse to make sure.

Mrs Taggart came to the front gate the next day, I assumed she wanted to know how her husband had died, and I was thinking of ways to console her."Did you find in my husband's pocket the family allowance book?" "No" I replied, "Fucking hell, I'll have to go down to the Social and report it missing", then she was gone. I looked up to heaven, you married her Daniel, I said to myself.

I had treated several people with numerous gun shot wounds that night, going from basic training to that situation was a test that I would not wish on anyone but I know I did my best for all the casualties. The number carried away and treated by the IRA was unknown but going by the blood in their casualty centre they had a few men down. One grave in the local cemetery was unearthed as the workers stated it had not been them that made the grave; two fresh bodies were found inside.

Ballymurphy never forgot the Day of Internment and celebrate it every year with the slamming of bin lids on the ground. Hatred of Paras could not be higher but the Brass still sent Paras back into the area and I would also do another tour in Ballymurphy in the near future but this time as a Para and not a medic.

I received letters from the GOC Northern Ireland, Harry Tuzso, the Para Brigade Commander, Fara the Para and the General in charge of the Medical Corps, giving me a pat on the back. I felt ashamed that the training in the Parachute Ambulance had not prepared me better to deal with the situation. I had spent more time drinking tea and packing shelves than being taught how to be a good combat medic that was needed to save lives-most of my patients had died. The training books had been pre-war and had not kept up with changes in medicine or warfare, and most of the teachers at the time would have been put in the same category. I was not a stupid person and I could have been trained better. Being honest the sight of all the blood, the horrific nature of the wounds, I felt like passing out on one occasion and I thought I was tough. I would recommend to all people who would like to learn first aid not to get dropped in it when the shit hits the fan, but to work in an abbatoir or butchers for a month, so that you get the smell of death, the ripping up of guts and the warm stickiness of fresh spilt blood. My only training that had benefitted me was the month I had been sent to work in the Southern General hospital in Glasgow and I think the few lives I saved was down to the professional nurses and doctors at this hospital. I was better at killing people, so I set out to join the Parachute Regiment.

The Brass tried to help morale by giving us day trips out from Ballymurphy, not that morale was bad, and now with what we had been through comradeship was at a height unknown in the company.

The first excursion was considered a joke by us, but not by the Brass. They organised a day trip out to a cake/bread making factory at Omar Bakery, we could not stop laughing but were ordered to show we enjoyed it. Can we fuck the staff, a Para asked the CO, expecting a load of women but in the end it turned out to be mostly blokes, we all had pissed-off faces on return to camp, it was more exciting in the Murph.

The next trip out was to the fishing village of Newcastle and its then one and only bar by the quayside. Free drinks at the bar, permission to get pissed, now that raised morale. Now when Paras get pissed something is sure to happen as it was never done quietly. The local fishing men could be seen just out of the harbour and soon returned with their boats full of fresh mackrel still jumping about at the bottom of the boat. Geordie Nicholas went up to a tray and picked out one still alive and kicking, he then held it in both hands and ripped out its brown guts with his teeth. He turned to the lads and asked if anyone else wanted one as they were dead fresh, guts down his chin and the front of his shirt. The lads could not stop laughing which only egged him on to do it again. Then they wondered why the local girls did not fancy them?

Yet another piss-up, this time to a secure camp at Lisbon, so we were allowed to go to the NAAFI and get pissed. Three women WRACS sitting at a table and ten of us moved in on them like flies around shit. The beer was flowing and the chance of a gang-bang increased, as the girls got steadily pissed and were enjoying the dirty jokes. Then I saw Dave Manion, going down in his seat, then a red face. This guy did not blush so I knew he was up to no good. He sat up and put a pint mug in the centre of the table that was steamed up. Oh fuck, I said to myself, and then one of the girls picks up the jug being too inquisitive for her own good and lets out a scream, she dropped the glass and the turd tipped onto the table in front of her, the three girls ran away screaming shouting something like dirty bastards and we nearly pissed ourselves laughing at their reaction.

I came to the conclusion that the only women that loved Paras were their mothers and many did not have fathers, but if you have to be in a conflict, I would rather be fighting with them than against them.

Internment showed the IRA that they could not take on the British Army without a lot of losses to their own, trying to fight Army against Army. Their main tactic in the future would be to shoot a soldier in the back and run away, so they got known as the "I Run Away men". Propaganda and intelligence- gathering; making capital from every British Army accident would get big news in the world to promote their cause. Our British system just could not understand the situation on the ground and instead of the stiff upper lip they should have had a propaganda campaign to destroy the image of the IRA. So- called freedom fighters.

Ruthless young men filled the gap of the old guard IRA, and the criminal element of the area could see the financial benefit of being a member. The people would be fed on hatred and fear, blinkers would be provided for all the people with an ounce of intelligence. The main problem with the British is that they could not keep up with the evolution of the IRA.

The IRA was jumping on the bandwagon of the Civil Rights movement which as an organisation was bringing to light the obvious discrimination against Catholics. Without bloodshed, they were getting the British Government to change the laws and give proportional representation to the minority. The IRA wanted a united Ireland with their leaders in control (goodbye democracy) and they had to turn the Catholics into their camp even if it meant killing Catholics. This intimidation of prominent Catholic politicians of the SDLP party I would witness first hand in my next tour of duty.

If the history books had been read they could have seen the IRA leaders were using the ideology of Michael Collins to stir up the natural inbred Catholic hatred against the mainly Protestant British. Speaking to one nationalist, he wanted the Protestants kicked out and all their houses and land signed over to the Catholics in a united, Catholic Ireland. I could not believe what he was saying as he was a well-educated person. To me this Irish Nationalism had the same ideas and elements of the German Nazi Party and seeing what the IRA were doing they would not be short of volunteers for the extermination camps. The Protestants were there in Ireland before they discovered America. I could just imagine the Red Indians saying the same, it is just not practical to deport every white man from America and equally every Protestant from Ireland. Then I thought if in England we deported every man with Catholic Irish connections we would have millions of empty houses to re-house the deported Irish Protestants, then I stopped my brain as I did not want to get on the Irish wave level. I was getting confused and frustrated trying to find out what these people wanted but would increasingly come to the conclusion that these nationalists had something missing between the ears. Not wanting to discriminate, I drew the same conclusion about the Protestant nationalists who claimed to be

British.

They did the intelligence-gathering better than the British and infiltrated every government department, the Prison Service and even the British Army, all done so easily because we did not discriminate against the Irish living in England and even the Southern Irish could join the British Army. Our politicians and civil service had turned a blind eye in Northern Ireland to what was going on. How had they allowed the discrimination by the Protestants against the Catholics which was one of the main reasons for the conflict? Most British soldiers, myself included, were amazed by the open hatred between Catholic and Protestant that we had never seen in England. We did not comprehend how the situation had developed or the history of Ireland which had led to this inbred hatred. The Battle of the Boyne was never mentioned in my history lessons and when was that you would ask? "1690" the reply, and shit you are still fighting about it, what fucking idiots are we separating here, were my thoughts. So the Army had replaced the Protestant police but a lot of direction and tactics came from that corrupt, biased, perverse, bigoted, direction and the Army were the fall guys that were more dispensable.

It was also my thought at the time to use Paratroopers was not going to help public relations, not the right lads to keep the peace but good to fight a war!

We left Ireland to return to our families and I was returning to marry my Catholic girl friend in Glasgow.

LIEUTENANT GENERAL SIR HARRY TUZO, KCB, OBE, MC.
GENERAL OFFICER COMMANDING
NORTHERN IRELAND
LISBURN, CO ANTRIM
LISBURN 5111

30 December 1971

Private N J Mumford RAMC
2nd Battalion
The Parachute Regiment
Normandy Barracks
Aldershot, Hants.

Dear Private Mumford

I am delighted to be able to award you my
Certificate of Commendation for your fine work
during the evening of 9th August 1971 when you
treated your patients, both civilian and
military, in a calm and competent manner under
extremely difficult circumstances.

You carried out your duties in an exemplary
manner and are indeed a credit to your Corps.

Well done!

Yours sincerely,

Harry T.

Wedding Day, Glasgow.

Chapter 9

New Lodge and another Tour

After my wedding in Glasgow I began to understand the sick minds of so called "Christians" as my wife told me about her problems arranging our wedding. She was a good devoted Catholic, had attended her local church once and sometimes twice a week. Catholic school, communion the lot and now she was a trained nurse in the Southern General Hospital working in the casualty department where we met. She had gone to the Priest and yes he was Irish, she asked for a dispensation and permission to marry in the church she had supported and attended all her life. The Priest responded by saying, "I suppose he is a Protestant, well I can tell you I will not marry you in my church; I would rather see you dead," and that coming from the mouth of a Christian, a love thy neighbour, thou shall not kill, bigot. She left in tears and told her family who rallied in support and confronted the priest. She must be confused, the Priest would never say a thing like that but they all got the whip from his sick tongue when they met him. To the Jesuit priests you must go was the opinion of the family, they will marry you and yet another rebuke for trying to marry a Protestant. Saying I was Protestant was a title put on me by my parents who were non-church going, I never in my life attended church voluntarily as I did not believe in God! I told Irene my feeling about religion but also note I told her I respect anything that she or anybody else wants to believe in. They had to also respect that a lot of people do not believe and I am one. I would go through the ceremony, sign a paper that said I would bring my children up in the Catholic church, it did not bother or mean anything to me, as I was only respecting the beliefs of others. Again I said to Irene I will not put a stigma on our children but when they were old enough they could decide for themselves, Muslim, Jew, Catholic, or

Protestant, what ever they wanted, to which she also agreed. A little back street, small Catholic church where the priest was hard up, was the final solution. He would not marry us while Celtic football team was playing, we would have to wait till the match was finished, later in the afternoon. The funny thing at the wedding was the 70-year old altar boy, who must have volunteered so he could drink the Holy wine. He swayed back and forward and when he fell forward both our families and friends could not stop laughing, it just made a final joke to the whole religion bit.

  Had I known the problems she was having earlier, I could have gone to Captain Padre Weston MBE (the Battalion priest) to marry us. We had had a few discussions about religion when he was stationed with us in Ballymurphy. As we had worked together with the wounded and dying. A man I admired because he acted like a Christian and I respected he believed in his God and he did not try to convert me. He did his best to show the true meaning of his faith by walking the streets of Ballymurphy unarmed, with the Protestant father, trying to get them to recognise the ten commandments which are Catholic and Protestant law and even laws that a non-Christian like myself can accept because some very wise man realised we all had to live with a set of rules. He admitted to me that even as a priest he found it difficult to understand the hatred forged into the minds of the Irish. He was in the front row when porno films were shown at the camp and assured me he would attend confession, the Protestant father sat next to him so they both had something in common besides religion. Then here in Glasgow we were coming across the same hatred amongst "Christians" which I found in, had its roots from the Irish community. I was surprised because in the North East of England we respect each others different views and religions. To us Geordies friendship is first, we would not even ask what your faith was, as it is irrelevant in friendship. If it turns out there is a God, I am sure I have got possibly more points to get past the Pearly Gates than many who profess they are Christians, as the rules were cast in stone and not bent to suit the individual. Heaven, I hope it does exist as everyone fears death and the fate that it beholds. I see different religions work on this fear to attract vulnerable people and to me that is sad. If Ian Paisley and the Pope are in heaven I could not visualise it as a peaceful environment. If it does exist it might be full of Geordies because of our tolerance and respect for the beliefs of others.

My wife's belief had been shaken to the core by her spiritual leaders so I decided to cheer her up by telling her that we were going on honeymoon with the best man and twelve other paratroopers. True, we had organised a canoeing expedition down the river Tay. The blow-up igloo tents did not stay up long enough by the end of the nightly drinking sessions at local pubs, so being pissed we found a second use for a canoe paddle. The planned early start never happened till the hangover wore off. Then the CO, Lt Colonel Hewlitt paid a visit with his wife so they could wangle a free Scottish holiday out of Battalion funds. We were eating when they arrived and the Colonel's wife asked my wife if she had been doing the cooking, to which she replied that it was the first thing she had put her foot down about by telling them that they had better not think she was doing the cooking or cleaning, taking her on her honeymoon with twelve men. Then she pointed to the pears and custard in a soldiers mess tin and asked, "What was the brown stuff around the custard?", to which he replied "gravy" from the first course. They did not stay for a meal and we got on with our holiday which we all enjoyed.

My wife still attended church with her mother when I was sent back to Ireland; they were with the ones that did not walk out when the priest let loose his verbal whip after Bloody Sunday 30th January 1972 and I was in Ireland. Just imagine what he would have said to my wife if he knew I was a Paratrooper. She made her own mind up to pray at home, as the priest was more in need of confession! We moved to Aldershot, a place called Haig Lines, a renovated army Nissen Hut which was our first home. We loved each other so; we endured without complaint the conditions we had to live in which as a class 3 married quarter can only be described as the pits. Just weeks had gone by when I was ordered back to Ireland with the Battalion and my wife went back with her family in Glasgow and resumed her job at the Southern General Hospital.

Back to Ireland but this time I was with Support Company, as the Company medic, commanded by a Major Burke who would live up to his name. The men were older than the lads of "B" Company, technically more qualified and supported the Rifle Company in a time of war with 81mm mortars, GPMG machine guns used in the SF roll (six guns on tripods that would rain down bullets on an area the size of a football pitch), also Land Rover-mounted anti tank guns. In Ireland their technical skills were unusable, they would be just another figure 11 target patrolling the streets as this was not conventional warfare but urban terrorism, still in its infancy.

The first day on duty in the New Lodge area of Belfast and a sniper from a flats complex took out a Sergeant with a shot that entered his thigh. He had been in command of a patrol deployed in two open Land Rovers, the wagons returned to camp but I turned them round with one look at the shattered thigh, get him to hospital now, that would be the only way to save his life and that was the first day.

I was assigned to go out on patrol with Burke when he or his 2nd in command Captain Idiot wanted to check out the men on patrol. The open-backed Land Rovers gave us no protection from snipers and I never yet saw the bullet-proof vest we wore to stop a bullet, true. On the ranges I was inquisitive to find out if this flak jacket would give me any protection against a bullet so I fired my 9mm Browning into my jacket, straight through the front and out the back and my pistol was not a high powered weapon so I could only surmise we were wearing them to stop stones. I changed my pistol for a rifle as this was becoming more a battlefield with incidents on a daily basis. Shooting was nearly daily in the Battalion area and still the lads were sent out without protection, to show the IRA we were not afraid or that our officers did not respect their lives. Armoured vehicles were the only answer to stop casualties, we had a couple of them but for some reason they were seldom used. The powers to be had not felt it necessary, maybe the officers did not ask for them, maybe the cost of fuel was too high but I am sure our wounded and families of the dead would like to know the reason we mainly used the open Land Rovers and body armour that did not stop bullets. That cost-cutting attitude of British civil servants and politicians have put soldiers lives at risk in most conflicts and theatres of war. It was obvious to me from the start of this tour that the IRA were better organised, had new weapons and our tactics' of driving around in open Land Rovers was an unnecessary risk. On foot patrol you could use doorways, hedges, run, duck and dive to give the enemy a harder target but in open vehicles you could only hope that it was a wanker on the other end of the rifle. I thought at the time if they wanted to save money, cut out the bullshit in the Army e.g. the band and its instruments, the fancy household cavalry, the dress uniforms but the brass tacks are bullets and armour, you can not cut on them as we would always need them at the sharp end.

    The order came that the CO wanted us ready to go out on patrol. We in the patrol never got briefed, where we were going or what was going down, we just waited till he was ready and we would follow like sheep. Night-time and we jumped out the Land Rovers and again like sheep followed Burke the black sheep. We end up in a scrap-yard with all the obstacles you could imagine, a new moon the only light and then to my left a guy with a gun jumps on top of a wall. Talk about being frightened of the dark and a bogeyman jumps out what a start he give me, a bogeyman with a gun. I cocked my rifle to fire and then Burke screams "don't shoot you idiot he is one of ours." Which idiot was not briefing us, we were being treated like mushrooms, fed on shit and kept in the dark and that is what causes accidents and being shot by friendly fire! I was a bit shaken that I had nearly killed one of our own. A briefing is so important before going out into the field so you know the position of friendly forces and every time that these officers took us out without a briefing they broke every basic rule about warfare.

Out with the 2 I/C (second in command) was to prove worse for me, night time again, the Land Rovers going slow, no lights and making little noise. Bang, a shot fired and very close, we jumped out from the Land Rovers and I moved to the alleyway where the shot was fired, the rest of my Land Rover group behind me. I quickly took in the situation, a man on the ground with a placard round his neck, holding his knee where the now fleeing gunmen had knee-capped him, (the form of punishment given to petty criminals in the IRA-controlled areas not collecting for the cause), IRA doing their version of community service. Three gunmen less than a hundred yards and about to enter a getaway car on the New Lodge Road. Women always were important in the IRA, and here a group now took the iniative and protected the fleeing gunmen by standing in the line of fire. I fired a shot over their heads so they would dive out the way and give me a shot at the gunmen. The second I pressed the trigger the 2I/C Captain Idiot came round the corner into the alleyway to my left, the wounded man between us. He had a SMG machine gun that fired automatic or semi (single shots). He dived to the floor and fired the whole magazine of 28 rounds on automatic from less than ten yards from me. I was screaming for him to stop firing, but fear kept his finger on the trigger. Even the wounded man who was also in the line of fire screamed for him to stop, bullet holes all around us, covered us with wall plaster and brick dust where the bullets impacted. Our 2 I/C stopped when he had used the last round and then opened his eyes to see who he was shooting at. He got up and ran back to his Land Rover and drove it into the walkway, where I was. We had a metal vertical bar welded to the front of the Land Rover so that the nice Irish people would not decapitate us if they put a length of fine wire across the road. This was called the cheese cutter, and driving into the covered walk way, it hit the covered way and buckled the Land Rover body, the 2 I/C also wedged it between two walls, he was still in a state of shock and his brain still not working. He managed to reverse the vehicle, I told him to report the car with the gunmen going up New Lodge Road which he did and started to calm down. He was now thinking about all the bullets he had fired and how under the law, he was going to account for them, and you could never fire automatic as every bullet had to be aimed. We drove to the local Catholic hospital next to Crumlin Road jail and took the knee-capped thief into casualty. I could understand the wounded man being in a state of shock, as I did not feel too good myself after the ordeal we had gone through. Back at camp I filled in my form stating why I had fired one bullet. The 2 I/C had to account for his bullets, but being an Officer things were covered up to protect him and even the lads covered for his story. He never apologised for nearly killing me and the knee-capped thief lived to steal another day but with a limp!

A few days later out with Burke, for some reason a soldier was climbing over a bombed-out ruin when he lost his footing. His 9mm sub machine gun hit the ground and fired accidentally. Nobody hurt but he got 28 days prison and loss of wages as punishment. No cover up for a soldier, different rule book.

The same officer Captain Idiot tried to kill me again during a riot. The stone-throwing crowd was on New Lodge Road and we were taking cover from the bricks and petrol bombs on the corner of Crumlin Road. Suddenly the crowd quickly disappeared and everything went quiet. A warning bell was ringing in my head. Why me I don't know as I was still only the medic and not a trained rifleman, "follow me" he ordered. "Sir before we walk round that corner, let me or someone else look over the wall to see what is going on". It was so obvious to me what was going to happen next, but he ordered me to shut up and follow him. He was fortunately three paces in front of me and the gunmen chose him as the target. Three gunmen using automatic fire opened up, it was like slow motion, the bullets landed all about us, but mainly at him and he looked like he was dancing; his long lanky body was like a puppet on a string I grabbed his arm and dragged him back into cover. I then went back round the corner and fired six rounds at a man with a Thompson machine gun. I did not have time to go into the aimed position, I fired from the hip and he had to dive for cover. The 2/IC shouted "stop shooting you are not firing aimed shots, shooting from the hip". I showed him where the gunman had been and that I may have wounded him but I still got a rollicking for not firing from the shoulder. The lads later took the piss by calling me Audi Mumford, but I was sure I may have got the bastard. I was starting to be more worried about British officers (Ruperts) than the IRA.

Bombings and shootings could be heard from our camp on a daily basis . The IRA were at the height of the conflict, the bombing was mainly in the city centre and commercial areas, killing innocent civilians, mainly women and children. The lads were doing roadblocks and searching cars in an attempt to reduce the car bombs. Cpl Bill Cotton stopped a taxi and searched the passenger, he was carrying a loaded pistol, so the road-blocks stopped at least one killing that day.

The lads were doing well against the IRA. One Sergeant had one of those memories, that he could look at a wanted photo and pick the man out in a crowd days later. The IRA were making false identification, dole cards, driving licences, rates bills, using people that actually worked in these government offices to provide cover for their men. This Sergeant, once he picked up a suspect, asked them one simple question, "What is the name of your next door neighbour?" That was the name he checked out via the radio and twenty five IRA men did not come up with the right answer.

Most of the houses were terraced, so the lads would enter via a derelict house, go into the loft spaces of occupied houses and listen to the conversations of suspects. The lofts often had a glass skylight and these also provided good observation points. A man carrying a rifle was seen entering a house from just such an observation point. The house was searched and racks of rifles were in nearly every room, pistols in drawers and loads of ammunition. The owner was arrested. The next day the owner was back home, he had told the police that the IRA forced him to store the weapons and he was released by a judge. This type of justice was beginning to piss us off and this poor innocent man could not tip off the police to his plight, that his house was full of guns and ammunition.

On a road-block a Para comrade was searching the boot of a car when another car, waiting to be searched, accelerated and crushed his legs between the two cars. The lads beat shit out of the driver; they knew he had done it deliberately. Then again, the man was freed the next day, the police saying it was a traffic accident. We were beginning to wonder whose side the police were on!

The Company Sergeant Major stopped a woman in Belfast City centre acting suspiciously and asked to look in her bag. She hit him with it, kicked him and then tried to scratch his eyes out; we had to come to the rescue but not too quickly. "Get this fucking woman off me," he shouted so we overpowered her. She kept on fighting and struggling, it took four of us to hold her down and put her in the back of the Land Rover. On the way to the police station we started to grope her tits and look up her skirt, just to make sure she was not carrying explosives, you had to get some entertainment! We were still writing statements to the police when she was released. Oh she is a paid informer we were told but it turned out she was a prostitute who paid her protection to the police. We even witnessed police taking money from prostitutes and offering us a free fuck in the back of their Land Rovers. Who was the pimp?

Cpl Bill Cotton was the next to take a sniper's bullet as he and his patrol in two Land Rovers travelled along Crumlin Road towards the Divis Flats. The sniper had fired from the Flats and the lads had taken cover and trained their rifles on them, but with a thousand windows it was impossible to see from which one the rifle was fired. Nobody got Bill out of the Land Rover, he was slumped forward on the dash board, it was fortunate we were minutes away and had heard the shot, I got Bill out of his seat. I could see the bullet had gone through the metal frame of the front windscreen and still it had penetrated the so-called bullet proof vest we had to wear. I took him to an alleyway, pushed open a front door that was not locked and then laid him down in the hall. He was in pain, "I feel I've been hit with a sledge hammer" he said. The bullet had entered his chest and I had to expose the wound to fix a shell dressing. Bill was a big heavy lad and I tell you, what a job to get to the wound, bullet proof vest, Para smock, army jumper, shirt and a vest but I got to the wound and applied the magic shell dressing. The woman of the house being a good Catholic brought a bottle of "Holy Water" on the scene and insisted Bill drank it. As he would be having surgery on arrival to hospital I was polite and said so, nothing by mouth but thanks for the offer. The next thing she does is open the bottle and start throwing it over the both of us which started us both to laugh. Anyway Bill did not die and later became an officer. Was it the "Holy Water"? I asked myself.

Another night patrol and another killing, we almost ran over the body lying in the road. A local Catholic businessman who had objected paying into the IRA family benevolent fund and this was a warning which had them queuing to pay. One of my Irish Catholic friends told me his family had owned a discotheque in Londonderry and a group of men had refused to pay the admission fee on the door. "Do you not know who we are and you are asking us to pay for admission?" they said. They were informed that everyone pays without exception so they coughed up the entrance money. A bomb blew up the building a few days later and the Catholic family had to leave Ireland. They were becoming a law unto themselves and every criminal was jumping on the band wagon, collecting money for the IRA. Certainly it beat working for a living and all entertainment free, or the business would get destroyed for not being sympathetic to the cause. Who wanted this gravy train to end? Certainly not the IRA nor the Protestant criminal element whose gangs of thugs all jumped on this lucrative bandwagon. Every criminal act was being put down to collecting funds for the armed campaign of both communities. The British public had to pay criminal compensation to all the businesses destroyed by the terrorists of both sides and it did not take a blind man and his dog to see that this was also lucrative for all parties. We checked a bombed-out warehouse supposed to be full of televisions but could not find any sign of them, not even broken glass.

    Out again and I witnessed the evil of the women's contingent of the IRA; they were responsible for stripping naked a young woman, cutting off her hair, then tar and feathering her body. Her placard read, "Do not befriend British soldiers." She sobbed and shivered, her body covered in cuts and scratches. We took her to hospital to recover from the injuries inflicted by her once friends and neighbours.

    In a message received into camp from another area, a wounded Marine Commando was being evacuated to hospital in an ambulance, when women and children formed a line and blocked the ambulance trying to take the soldier to hospital.

They were waiting for two gunmen that now were going to kill the wounded soldier, making their way to the back of the ambulance. The women made way for the killers to do the job and murder what they thought a defenceless wounded soldier. Fortunately a fellow Marine was travelling with his comrade and saw what was about to happen. You can see out of an ambulance but not into it. He fired through the glass, killed one and wounded the other. YES. Justice done! It did not stop the women complaining that the shooting from the ambulance had put their lives and that of their young children at risk. What?

Two bombs were planted in the large Co-op store just out of our allocated area, but we responded to the incident. The police and fire service were at the scene, but up to that moment nobody had entered the building. A small explosion and the fire brigade went into action with their ladders to the window of the first floor. They were passing down the ladder loads of fur coats, sheepskin jackets, jewellery; everything they could carry went into the fire engine. They made no attempt to extinguish the fire! Another engine arrived so the one that was now full left the scene. At least the next crew pretended to fight the fire putting their hose pipes up the ladder but the theft continued. The fire took hold, gutting the building and then it later collapsed, no evidence of theft and all lost in the fire. The British tax payer would foot the bill, £7 million on this occasion. This type of fraud and theft was on a grand scale. I was convinced these people, Catholic and Protestant, did not want an end to the troubles as they were all making money out of it. Bad enough the different groups of terrorists but when the police and fire brigade are jumping on the band wagon it made us wonder are these people worth dying for! The police at the scene of the Co-op building later had the cheek to arrest people for looting from the burnt-out rubble.

The indiscriminate bombs of the IRA were a crime against humanity. On the 4th March, one bomb in a café "The Abercorn" exploded without warning. When the lads got to the scene they were shocked at the horror and devastation. A child's leg was in the doorway, the bomb was like a scythe and under the solid fixed tables. It had the devastating effect of blowing legs off the mainly women and children that were in the café. Two dead and over one hundred wounded, mainly women and children, nothing could justify this pure act of terror. The men and women who did this crime wanted a united Ireland but how could you allow sick minded people to take power of a nation? On the news that day, it was the first time I witnessed a reporter break down and cr, when trying to describe what he had witnessed. It had the same heart-wrenching effect on the soldiers that evacuated the wounded. Many cried that day and it made us all work all that harder to get the bastards.

An Army bomb disposal unit was billeted in our camp and they had managed to defuse some of the bombs. The IRA had within their ranks, engineers, electronic experts, and they soon made life difficult for the bomb team by making the bombs more and more sophisticated. The bombs now came with booby traps, mercury tilt switches and other devices designed to kill the bomb disposal team. The flag in the camp was soon at half mast with the killing of the first disposal sergeant. A few days later a replacement was brought in from England and within two weeks he was also dead. These killings made the bomb teams go high tech with the use of the first robots which are now common throughout the world. A camera and a rifle on four wheels saved a lot of good, brave men. Trying to shoot the bomb apart often deactivated the device but also there were a lot of dead robots. You could do nothing but respect the bomb disposal teams and we were still receiving letters addressed to them from friends and family weeks after they had died, which did not help morale.

A car-bomb was placed near the camp in front of a car show room and the CO wanted to be on the scene. I was a hundred yards from the car bomb and watched first hand as a police officer ran up and ran away as soon he had confirmed it was a bomb. Lord Gerry Lynch, lived in a terraced house close to the bomb and he was on the IRA death list for not being supportive to the IRA. Not all supported their ideas of nationalism or the armed struggle, but to speak out put your life at risk even if you were Catholic. The bomb team had been in another part of the city, occupied with yet another bomb, so we all waited for them to turn up. The bomb did not wait, it exploded with an incredible force and the shockwave was like rolling thunder and sent everyone diving for cover. If in slow motion, I watched a large piece of metal that turned out to be the car's engine rise into the sky and then start its descent, "For fuck sake", I shouted a warning as the engine whistled down landing in the street where we were taking cover. The force, the shock wave, the disintegration of the car making every piece of metal a lethal fragment to anyone who was nearby and these sick bastards in the name of a cause were using them all over Northern Ireland.

As the devices became more sophisticated, they also took a toll on the IRA planting and activating the bombs. The designers were not the guys that normally placed the device. A simple ramp on the road and a bomb exploded, killing the three IRA occupants carrying it. It was with great pleasure to us and true justice when we received the news. One of the lads at the scene asked the crowd, "Is this one of yours?", as he picked up a head by the hair and showed it to the Catholic population. Nice for them to see first hand what they were doing to others. Ramps soon became a weapon against the terrorists and their car bombs. When an IRA bomb accidentally went off we called it a "home goal" and we felt this was real justice for the crime they were committing!

A meeting by the INLA, a breakaway from the provisionals was to be held in our area and the main speaker was to be Bernadette Devlin MP. To great applause she walked onto a stage that had been erected on New Lodge Road. I was interested to hear what they wanted and how they were going to do it, coming from a democratically elected Member of the British Parliament. The venom in her tongue, this bird was a sick mother fucker. She pointed to us and cursed and cursed and cursed, "She really likes us" was one comment from a soldier, "she needs a good fucking" was another. Then I heard her say "once we have got these bastards out of Northern Ireland", pointing at us, we will then sort out the Southern Irish." What did I just hear her say "Sort out the Southern Irish people". Where are the reporters, why was nobody taking note of what she was saying she was to start a war against the Southern Irish!!

This gave me the incentive to read more about the Irish, the fight for independence and its civil war. The history of Ireland and trying to understand what these Paddies were about was now a priority in my life. The civil war started because the treaty signed by Michael Collins with the British was not accepted by all the Irish. It went to a democratic vote and was only just approved. Unfortunately two thirds of the IRA fighters were against it and they had the guns, even though the majority of Irish now in their own democratic country accepted the treaty. Collins now asked for help from the British and with the supply of weapons started the civil war. Collins men were called the Regulars and later the Free Staters and the IRA opposing the treaty were called the Republicans. The Irish do not like to talk about what they did to each other, but whatever the British had done in the past it would be a Sunday picnic in comparison. The Irish were more brutal to each other than the English or the Black and Tans had ever been. All civil wars, brother, fighting brother tend to be nasty, as this was. I watched a series on the BBC about the history of Ireland which was a must if you wanted to understand the conflict. A group of brothers captured nine of the opposition; they tied their feet together in a circle, then placed a land mine in the centre and detonated it, one survivor, the only one who was blown over a fence by the blast, lived to tell the tale.

Collins decided to execute in jail two Republicans for every official soldier who was killed, plus many summary executions of captured prisoners on the battlefield that never even made a trial or prison. Under an Emergency Powers Bill, 77 executions of prisoners were carried out by the Free State. Collins was using his terror tactics but protected by State law (State Terrorism). This brutal policy proved to be the only way to stop the civil war and the Republicans were ordered to hide their weapons by the future President Delavere. Michael Collins, who had drawn up the agreement with the British was ambushed and killed. A lot of Republicans took shelter in America, Northern Ireland and Britain, as there was much bad blood and many debts to be settled.

I assumed this was the grudge Bernadette Devlin had her knickers in a twist over with the Southern Irish. She wanted to restart the civil war and get revenge.

It was obvious that all Paras were hated by most Catholics as we were a heavy-handed unit. Even in our home station at Aldershot we were not generally liked by the civilian population. I will go into more detail why, but I would like to remind people that it was the Paras that stopped the Protestants burning out the Catholics in 1969 when the troubles re-started.

Beradette Devlin later married and is now called Mrs McClusky. A group of seven Protestant terrorists shot the couple several times in their lonely border farm house. A patrol of Paras from 2 Para, who had been given the job of observing the house from a distance, captured the terrorists and gave first aid to the Mccluskys, which saved their lives. This was a perfect example of the professionalism of the Paras and proved we would fight against both sides, Catholic or Protestant and also show compassion to our enemy.

It had to happen. With the amount of sniping against our lads, a 2 Para soldier was killed on Saturday the 29th

January 1972, and the Catholic population made it abundantly clear they were happy. They painted the walls with the Irish flag and had the slogan," Belfast one"and underneath "Up with the Pope." We were angry about the killing of our friend and comrade. The gloating, rejoicing, smiling to our faces from the local populace was hard to accept, added to our growing hatred towards these bastards who called themselves Christians. How can you be nice to people when they are trying to kill you, it had fuck all to do with religion as these were not Christians doing these crimes, more like Satan's recruits hiding behind the religious groups.

Then on Sunday the 30th, now known as "Bloody Sunday", men from the 1st Battalion Parachute Regiment shot dead thirteen Catholics in Londonderry. This being a demonstration by the Civil Rights movement and led by our Miss Bernadette Devlin. The massive crowd knew this was not going to be a peaceful demonstration, as rioting had followed most of these protests. Shooting from the crowd and buildings led the soldiers to return fire, a decision made on the ground by individual soldiers who had to decide whether these people were worth dying for or protect yourself. The IRA wanted this reaction from the soldiers to turn the people from the civil rights campaign into that of a campaign for a united Ireland. The whole thing was a success for the IRA who were the winners on the day and got what they wanted, even though it cost the lives of 13 Catholic people.

In Belfast, our lads got out the paintbrushes and where the IRA wrote their evil we countered it with ours. Under "Belfast one," we wrote "Londonderry thirteen" and crossed out "up" and put "Fuck the Pope". A good riot followed in most of the Catholic areas and the hatred got deeper between the Paras and those that supported the IRA. We were the wrong unit now to use in Northern Ireland as we were starting to hate the Irish in general and again our Officers could not read the situation and see the growing anger amongst the soldiers.

Would bloody Sunday have happened if the IRA had not fired on the young soldiers? What would have been the death count had it been another army in the same position? The Americans would have called in a napalm air strike. As if the Israelis, well, you can imagine if they had been Arabs. Would there have been an inquiry if they had done the shooting or would they have backed up their soldiers, even if it was an over reaction?

The bomb planted in our officers' mess in Aldershot was the IRA'S revenge for Bloody Sunday, but the bomb was planted in 2nd Battalion mess, not the 1st Battalion who had taken part in Bloody Sunday. It was an unguarded easy target as the IRA knew we were still in Ireland, so they purposely killed the women cleaners who were civilian workers and my friend, the Battalion Catholic priest, Padre Weston. The building had a lot of glass in the structure with the effect against human flesh that it tore these innocent people to pieces. The soldiers who had lost friends were taken back to Aldershot but the professionalism of the Paras was incredible. How many Regiments in the world would have just carried on with their jobs just like any other day's work? No demand for an inquiry for killing our innocent people!

No matter how good the soldiers are, you will still have accidents, especially with the younger lads. A private soldier on sentry duty ran into the office that was manned by a sergeant called Mariharty, who happened to be the battalion sniper, and shouted that he had been shot at. The sergeant grabbed his rifle and returned to the look-out post, "that van down the road" the lad pointed to the sergeant. He aimed and fired two shots that entered the back of the van, hit the driver in his head, the bullets splattered his face against the wind screen. The van had only back-fired as it passed the young lad who was only 18 years old and the van had stopped at a traffic light which a terrorist would not have done. So quick, so fast and a stupid accident that had taken the driver's life, but this was down to the situation caused by the IRA and a young soldier making a human error. A Cpl H from "B" company stopped at the scene later in the day and went to see what was causing the traffic hold up.

A group of Catholics and a priest were setting up a shrine, in the road to the local dead Catholic van driver. The candles were blown out and the corporal started to sing happy birthday, now that caused another riot that lasted three days! No action was taken against the soldier or the sergeant as it had been an accident, the shoot-to-kill policy had not been in place at this time in the conflict and there was no need to arrest soldiers for public opinion or foreign policy!

Our tour was at the height of the IRA terrorist activity in Northern Ireland with over 10,600 shooting incidents and 1,380 bombings. The politicians did not have an idea how to get us out of this situation. Willie Whitelaw MP came to visit the camp and I was one of about ten soldiers selected to meet him. What a fucking nerd, he did not have a clue what the problem was about, thus he was given the name Willie Whitewash by the Catholics and most of the lads were in agreement with his new nick name. One of the lads asked why we did not pull out and let them get on with it, as we are just in the middle. It turned out we were protecting the Catholics from the majority Protestants, well someone was not getting the message over to the Catholics.

One Company working in a Protestant area, had a gun fight with armed Protestant terrorists and captured them. Three days non-stop rioting followed, these people who claim to be British hit us with some very heavy fire power. Machine guns and rifle fire against the Company had a few men badly wounded. Support company and a battalion of reserve troops was needed to restore control. At one road cordon we were facing a few hundred British flag-waving Protestants, burned out cars and trucks were in every street making barricades to stop us entering the area. Stones and petrol bombs rained down, then I witnessed them bringing up a heavy commercial vehicle, they jammed down the throttle and sent it down towards us, we were forced to run or be killed. We had gun battles in every street during the night and they went back to their houses before first light. We recovered many weapons but by the amount of fire power used against us we only found the tip of an iceberg. No wonder our government was taking sides against the Catholics as there were not enough men in the British Army to fight the Protestants, if they took up an armed struggle against us.

This tour of duty we found that we were working seven days a week, 12 hours a day and during riots we would work on occasion 72 hours non stop.

One evening a show was organised by the forces entertainment group and I must admit it was top class and thoroughly enjoyed by all. Some men were brought in from other companies so they too could be entertained. A female singer, a comedian and a guy that played a penny whistle gave a show lasting an hour. About a hundred Paras got the opportunity to relax but then shooting could be heard close by and a soldier came in to inform the CO of the gun fight, so a few men had to leave and go on duty. The man with the penny whistle started to play "Amazing Grace" and I think because of the atmosphere thinking of friends who had been killed and wounded, being in a hostile environment and missing our families in England the lads started to gently hum to the music being played. With perfect harmony, everyone joining in with the music, it was beautiful to the ear, especially as it was unrehearsed perfection. Even the acts that had been on stage and their helpers came from dressing rooms to listen, as this sound was a one-off from the heart.

Major Burke was given permission to flush out the snipers from the New Lodge as a new weapon was being used against us, rifles fitted with silencers. To us it meant you did not hear the bullet coming so it was a more peaceful way to die. The officers got excited to find bullet holes appearing in Land

Rovers on return from patrol and especially in the Major's wagon, the same as I sat in.

We had grouped on Springfield Road at last light, so the IRA had been notified by telephone from their numerous supporters. They let us move 50 yards before they fired bursts of automatic fire at us. No officer thought of getting the street lighting turned off before the advance, so all the men could be seen under the street lights as they moved down through the estate. Almost the first bullet hit a Sergeant Neilson, in the wrist. He ran back to Burke and reported that he had been hit. I went into action. I took out a shell dressing and led the sergeant into an alleyway out of danger. As I took his hand away from the wound blood spurted out. The bullet had burst every main blood vessel, as it had completely shattered his wrist. Not just a simple little wound as the major had surmised, as he had been able to run back and report to him. The sergeant had seen the blood spurt as he had taken his hand away from the wound, so I got him to lie down flat and raised the arm to reduce the blood loss. I firmly bandaged the wound but the blood soon soaked the dressing so I had to apply pressure to control the bleeding. With the loss of blood, shock was setting in, white, sweating skin which was the brain's ways to reserve the blood supply to the vital organs. I could not let go of his arm so I looked back for assistance from someone else in the patrol and to my surprise the street was empty. They had moved on and nobody had passed on any order to tell me what was happening. Where was the ambulance, had it been called for on the radio? I banged on a door in the alleyway and a woman came and opened the door. I demanded she give me a blanket for the wounded soldier, she quickly returned and handed me a blanket and closed the door, as she did not want to risk her life for helping a wounded soldier. I saw a soldier moving down the street so I shouted to him "Where is the ambulance? I have a wounded man here." The ambulance was just round the next corner, Burke had not given the exact location of the wounded sergeant. They came round with the armoured ambulance and the doctor and medical assistants lifted the sergeant onto a stretcher and into the ambulance. I asked them where had they been, and they stated they had not been given the right location of the casualty.

Once the ambulance had left the scene, I asked the radio op to inform Major Burke that I was with them and wanted his location so I could join back up to the patrol. An odd reply, "Tell him he has been noticed by his absence and to stay with the patrol." That had me baffled at the time to what was he meaning. The shooting was very heavy in the Lodge and I envisaged it would not be long till I was called for. Thousands of rounds were being fired and the main reason was that the patrols under fire were silhouetted. They started to shoot out the street-lights to save themselves. Shooting in the dark is not easy, the snipers were not hitting the Para targets and the lads were making heavy work shooting out the lights. With the lights out, they could now see the gun flashes and engage the snipers, which they did. The patrol I was with was ordered to get into an armoured car that had now been requested and we moved down to the flats. The "Pig" was hit with a couple of rounds as we moved into a street near the flats, but with the armour protection we were safe from the bullets. Eventually we dismounted and I met up with the Major at the base of the flats. "You have been noticed by your absence," he shouted to me. I thought it would be better not to say anything at this stage as he looked stressed out. He now started shouting orders to the rest of the unit. The flats were occupied and being searched on every floor, lots of rounds had been fired down at the company and this I presumed was the reason for the Major's state. The lads could not find anyone wounded or dead even though thousands of rounds had been fired and had to be accounted for and at this stage no weapons had been found either. Search again; search again, were his orders, the weapons have to be in the flats. Hours went by and no weapons found, then by luck a soldier used his brain and searched the containers at the base of the rubbish chute. The IRA had dropped them down the chute as the lads moved into the flats and not being caught in possession of a weapon we could do nothing to the suspected IRA men. The operation was terminated and everybody was ordered back to camp. A de-briefing in the ops room which all NCOs and officers were ordered to attend which included me. The first thing he said was "Cpl Mumford had been noticed by his absence and I will make a note of his behaviour on his army records." He was calling me a coward for not staying with his patrol, even though no one had passed down the order that they were moving out. And I was doing my job looking after the sergeant, I was the Company Medic. He stopped me saying anything in my defence. I was being used as a scapegoat for his total incompetence in controlling the situation on the ground . Then he ordered me from the room. Never in my life have I been so devastated and insulted and upset and not given the chance to reply to such a totally unfounded accusation. I went straight to the doctor who technically was my boss and informed him of what the Major was accusing me of. "Where had you been, why did you not come sooner to the wounded Sergeant?" I stated I could not leave him. If he had bled to death, it would have been my fault and the Doctor was in agreement. He went to have a word and smooth things out with the Major, but returned in ten minutes also annoyed that the Major would not listen to him either.

    The next day the Major, myself and a driver went to visit the sergeant in hospital, but only the Major and I entered the room. Two drips were being fed into the sergeant; he was sedated and heavily bandaged. "Oh, I thought your injury was not that bad," said the Major. "Sergeant, can you remember last night and what happened?", I said. "Yes and thanks for saving my life", he said in reply. "Did at any time I look nervous or frightened or did I do my job professionally looking after you till you were evacuated in the ambulance?" As I said thank you for saving my life. On return to camp I asked the Major if he would apologise to me in front of the men but he did not reply and never apologised. Who was the coward I ask!!!!!!!!!!!!!

We captured more weapons, explosives but still the Police seemed to be releasing the IRA as soon as we captured them. How can you fight terrorists under conventional rules and law? We had our hands tied and had to play the system. The IRA were winning the world opinion with their propaganda as freedom fighters, and our civil service, government were being outwitted and caught with their thumbs up their bums. We returned to Aldershot with our wounded and dead and the memories of the IRA atrocities, especially the Aldershot bomb.

I personally found it hard to live with the insulting remarks of my Commanding Officer, slapping his face with a pair of gloves and asking him to duel with pistols is what I wanted but I think that was only between officers. Punching him in the face was what I wanted to do, but against an officer I would be in jail for a long time. I thought the truth would come out with Sgt Nielson but he did not return to the Unit. Looking back, he stressed me out I was still a young lad and I was to find that even though I was totally innocent, mud sticks, as the true facts were not stated in public like the insults.

Patrols in open Land Rovers and approaching a major riot.

Lookout post at the top of New Lodge Road.

Me in the camp near the Crumlin Road prison from where we operated into the New Lodge area

Sole guard on a Polling Station on Crossmaglen

Chapter 10

Life as a Para

Death and injury never seemed far away, even in training as a paratrooper. A soldier doing combat training on the military ranges dropped unconscious. It was a very warm summer's day and we were carrying full kit, rifle and ammunition. Training to the extreme, "Only mad dogs and Englishmen go out in the midday sun" a saying passed down from our days as an Empire when the class system was at its peak by observers from native countries that knew and respected the elements. To a British officer, the elements were a challenge that under their command a soldier could fight in extreme conditions with or without the right equipment. Every man is different and suffered in different ways fighting the elements. Some could withstand extremes of cold, and others extremes of heat which varied with a dry heat or hot humid heat. Basically it was down to officers showing off to other officers how fit his men were and what hardship he could inflict on his soldiers without them complaining. "My men can do it" was typical of one Officer talking to another. The men did as they were told as you can not disobey an order from an officer in the British Army. To sustain the physical energy needed to run with full equipment. You had to be fit, but this one lad's heart could not meet the extra stress caused by the temperature being so high, that his heart literally burst. Was it so necessary to make the men fight the elements? I was called out to try and give him first aid, but the lads had left him on his back with a mouth full of sick, after 10 minutes like that, he had no chance. I turned him over and got the sick out with my fingers, "that is what you should have done," I told the rest of his comrades. I had not given up trying to perform a miracle, so I slammed down on his heart and gave him mouth-to-mouth resuscitation. The smell from his stomach had me retching, so I decided to try the bottle of oxygen I brought with me. It was not this lad's lucky day. I found more holes in the rubber pipes than a sieve and had to turn it off straight away. On return to camp I informed the sergeant who was responsible for maintaining the medical centre equipment, a wanker, that had known the rubber was perished and had left the oxygen bottle with the emergency equipment. The Battalion flag flew at half-mast for the dead soldier, but had his death been necessary? The men would fight in extreme elements but was it necessary to practice under training? I personally thought it was not and I would see many more deaths due to this totally irresponsible attitude from Officers.

I transferred to the Parachute Regiment more to prove that I could do the job and show I could be a good infantry corporal. Most of the lads trained hard, played hard and I enjoyed the lifestyle of an infantry soldier which was more exciting compared to that I had experienced with the medics. I transferred and joined "B" Company as a Lance Corporal under the command of a new officer Major Patton.

One of my first ventures with the Parachute Regiment was to Malaya to do jungle training you would think this was a good posting, like a holiday, but two men from the battalion would die within a month. In the jungle you could often hear old or diseased trees crash to the ground which was nature in its basic form. One soldier was too late to dive out of the way, as in the dense undergrowth you could not see the direction that it was falling. The chances of getting hit by an old dying tree must have been long odds against and after this incident I was coming to the conclusion in life, that if a bullet had your name on it or a tree in this case there was nothing going to change your fate.

There were a couple of funny incidents during the training. Our commanding officer, Major Patton, who did not have much of a clue about anything, a born Rupert, trying to live up to a big name, decided he was a jungle expert, Tarzan, but half the size. Our company moved from the base camp in Singapore to the jungle training area in Malaya, an area called Jahor Baru or (something like that). The CO wanted us to work as a company moving through the jungle so for some reason my patrol was given the lead position to enter the jungle and navigate the company, to a clearing within the jungle marked on the map. We had transport to the edge of a rubber tree plantation and then form up in line to enter the plantation, thousands of trees with cuts draining the white sap called latex into a bowl. The plantation workers had removed the undergrowth, so moving and navigation was no problem to me as I led the company. Then we hit pure native jungle and what a difference. A wall of green, a botanist's paradise with every plant imaginable, that hid every insect and animal within its dense foliage. I had a compass and a bearing to my objective, but if I could have been like Doctor Doolittle and talked to and listened to the animals I was sure they would have been saying "Where the fuck are you going?" The noise of the jungle was incredible with all these creatures making a constant noise, day and night. I pointed the way for my men to cut a path with their machetes and the hard work began in the stifling heat that was an experience you do not want to volunteer for. Within minutes we had sweaty bollocks and dripped sweat as if someone had opened a tap, the humidity level was over 90%. I replaced my men with fresh lads and we moved slowly forward, this was a shit job at the front. My radio operator received a message that we had to move faster so I kicked arse to get the men working harder, I took my turn cutting and slashing at this wall. Many plants came with thorns and one in particular the "waitawhile plant" was awesome. The thorns were razor sharp. If you pushed against them they cut you to pieces. You had to stop and back out, picking the thorns from your clothing. This was a plant to be respected and avoided with a wide berth. These problems all led to a slow advance and a CO that could not understand what we had to deal with as point patrol. "Faster, faster" were his constant radio orders. The lads were fucked and then we hit elephant grass which was even harder to penetrate, over two metres high with an incredible density. In desperation I held my rifle above my head and fell forward, I got the next lad to walk over the top of me and do the same, and this proved the only way to advance and the fucking Rupert jungle fighter was still on the radio, demanding we go faster. We literally fell into the clearing on top of a hill, exhausted! The next company passed us theirs been a stroll as the pathway had been cleared for them. The CO arrived and could see my men and I were spent and fucked. Why had I not asked for another patrol to relieve us at the point? I was speechless. Who was the fucker in command and the expert in jungle warfare? We took time to recover and drank water with salt to replace the body fluids. Cramp in our muscles had us very weak to carry on but even in our exhausted state we caught up to the rest of the company with another patrol finding the green wall.

The next brainwave for our company was a night march with no lights of any description; it was hard enough during the day. He also decided that so not to lose anyone it would be better if everyone was tied to each other, with a toggle rope (a small length of rope with a piece of wood at one end and a loop at the other). When one lad fell over, a fallen tree, all the lads near fell with him, with a knock-on, domino effect. We seemed to be falling more than walking, the whole idea was stupid but the officer did not want to lose face and agree he was a "Wally". Then some of the lads started to make animal sounds (baa, baa, as in black sheep) then (moo, moo, as in cow) then donkey noises, the lads were now falling over with laughter. The Rupert could not see the funny side and tried to get the NCOs to report offenders, but it was mostly them taking the piss out of the officer.

Back to the drawing board and our CO decided to test

our patrol tactics while he organised the activity from a base camp. I had an army officer, a helicopter pilot from the Air Corps attached to my patrol as an observer. Each patrol was given a route to march through the jungle. Travelling miles through the thick jungle was an experience and hard physical work but without an officer in command it was less dangerous as we often stopped to rest and drink.

Mosquitoes, ants and leeches all seemed to welcome you to the jungle as part of the food chain and the insect repellent supplied only attracted them more. We came to a deep ravine with a fallen tree across it. The tree was so wide that it was simple to cross. The officer, a helicopter pilot, refused to cross frightened of heights! I had to go back and get his kit, and then he climbed down and up the other side of the ravine. The stream beds gave us our fresh water and travelling in them you covered more distance if they were on your route. Stop for a tea break and remove the boots to find out what was irritating and then you discover what a bull leech was, what had been a thin worm had now sucked so much blood from you that now looked like a big fat slug. Drop your pants and more of the buggers; one was so big I thought my dick had gone black! Then the shirt, they were everywhere and you never even felt them bite you. If you pulled them off it left it's head in your skin which would then get infected. The only way to remove them was to pour salt on them or borrow a fag from a smoker. I have only tried smoking two cigarettes in my life but I have found a few good points about being a smoker, removing leeches was one and I will point out some other good points as the book develops. Sit on the ground and the ants started to bite but you felt them, as they had a good nip that made your arse muscles contract. The buzzing around your ear was the mosquitoes telling you that they were going to inject you with parasites and suck your blood, the ones you managed to hit were the ones a bit slow and had just finished eating you, full of red blood. I found the odd pathway in the jungle and in them some big turds, nobody had told me about wild elephants but the insects of all descriptions were having a field day. As long as I did not step on a turd or meet the thing that dropped it, I was also going to be happy. Then it rained every day but you were so wet anyway with sweat, it just washed your clothes and help get rid of some of your body odour. Sleeping in the jungle, you put up your mosquito net and tucked the ends under your waterproof poncho. The jungle noises were at a even higher pitch with the news of fresh meat trying to sleep If they found a hole in the net, then forget the sleeping. I rested my head on my belt which had pouches of water, food and ammunition attached, not soft, but stopped the crick in your neck. One morning after a restless night I found that some animal had eaten its way through a tough webbed pouch and a tin can of food, I thought thank God I had not disturbed it whatever it had been, it must have had teeth and a jaw with some incredible power.

    We passed a tree that day that had a wooden scaffold around. It wasa real primitive job but it had my head thinking, why in the middle of the jungle a tree with man-made bamboo scaffold? Then, later on moving down a stream giving more food to the bull leeches, a fucking real live native, standing there looking at me with a blow pipe in his hand. My rifle only had blank rounds so I was hoping he was friendly, and then he smiled, much to my relief. Around his waist was a load of dead tree rats which he had just finished cleaning in the stream. He waved his hand and then he disappeared, two and two became four and I knew which tree he was using to get the poison for his darts. Not one hundred miles from the hustle and bustle of Singapore and here are native tribes living and hunting in the jungle like prehistoric times, gob-smacked.

    Out of the jungle and on to Singapore, with all the nightlife and fucking you could imagine. Bogy Street and the women were not women but men with a sex change. I had my photo taken with two kities as they were called, dresses down to the waist and a tit in each hand and I sent it to the wife with a caption that I was out with the boys. As a nurse at the Army mental hospital, I remembered a marine commando that was sent there for marrying a "kiti", now I understood him as some of them looked beautiful and the more you drank, say no more.

We went to the Singapore Hilton Hotel and to the bar on the roof. We ordered drinks meaning to pay but the waiter asked for our room number, so with a good guess, we drank all night and someone else picked up the tab.

At the Royal Singapore Sailing Club a few of us did a course in learning to sail in the Straights between Singapore and Malaysia. After seeing a few deadly water-snakes I soon learnt not to capsize the dingy and enjoyed the sailing experience. Others went to the beach for a swim and sadly we lost another comrade. Lads with him tried to save him but they even had trouble getting out of the deadly current just yards from a beautiful "postcard setting" beach. They found his body a few days later, at least what the fish had not eaten.

We just got on with life, and forgot about men dying, by getting pissed and painting the town red, then flew back to England. Nothing else could go wrong, thirty thousand feet in a C130 and the pilot's window cracked. Another episode from Dad's Army, the plane goes into a dive and we are all given the feeling that someone is trying to pack you in a tin of sardines. The RAF crewman is now shouting that he has a bottle of oxygen but he is taking big sniffs of it and the funny part was how long it took to get out the sentence as after every word he took a sniff of oxygen. I sniff, have, sniff, got, sniff, a, sniff, bottle, sniff, of, sniff, oxygen, sniff and we all started to laugh as he was in such a state of panic. If you, sniff, need it, sniff, raise your, sniff, hand, sniff, you would have to cut his hand off to get your sniff. The pilot levelled out less than 10,000 feet and we turned back to Singapore for another glass window and to refill the oxygen bottle for the crewman. A long flight in a C130 was not recommended, it was noisy, smelly and no fucking toilet.

Then we got flown to Turkey, to an air base in the south, to take part in the biggest airborne drop since the 2nd World War. The American 81st Airborne, a Turkish airborne brigade and 2 Para, to parachute into Turkish Thes. We did not have the whole Brigade because the 1st and 3rd Battalions were deployed in Northern Ireland. Also because of cutbacks we did not have enough C130 aircraft to deploy the whole Brigade unit with attached support units so we were a paper Brigade hoping the Americans would give us the planes if the shit ever did hit the fan, and we went to war, sounds familiar with our past history. This was as part of a NATO exercise to reinforce the Turks against an invasion from the cold war enemy, the Soviet Block.

The Yanks could get food from the Mess 24 hours a day, no wonder they looked a bit overweight. Every morning they would line up as a unit with flags to the front and do a two mile run, singing and shouting. It was so funny to watch, as the Yanks were soon spread out, with the fat lads looking like they were going to burst a blood vessel. In the evening they had a caravan, used as a bar and they were all lined up waiting to buy a few cans of Budweiser. We did not have any money on exercise so we just watched the Yanks enjoy the drink. Some enterprising Paras told the Americans that our berets were handed down from the 2nd World War, so they were selling them to get beer money. You had to wonder if these Americans were knitting with one needle to believe the lies the blokes were telling them!

Then a couple of 2 Para started to hand out cans of warm Bud, they had used tin-openers to open the caravan at the rear: initiative. There was soon a line passing out the crates of Bud only to leave one stack that hid us from the Turkish bar staff. I do not recommend getting pissed on warm Bud, most of us suffered the next day as we entered the planes for the jump. The sight was impressive: 100 aircraft, C130s, lined up ready to roll, an incredible noise and pollution of exhaust fumes. I was sitting next to my apartment neighbour Cpl Pete Bedford and our plane was the first to taxi onto the runway. "Did you hear what happened to Paddy McClay?" No" I replied, "He fell into the shit pit". I could not stop laughing at the thought of it. The Yanks had made the most basic of toilet, two poles over a deep ditch and all the thousands of Paras had to use this one and only shit house! I was glad I was not sitting next to him, then Pete pointed to him sitting across from us, we both started to laugh again. The plane motors reach maximum and it started down the runway, just as it was about to take off it braked and braked, the tyres locked. We were all violently thrown forward, my head was forced next to Pete,"Just think, two widows in the same block of flats", he said, "should be some funeral" I replied. The pilot had nearly passed the point of no return! He managed to control the plane but we were lucky as he had run off the end of the tarmac and was now on grass. He taxied to the end of the 100 planes and the engineers came on to fix the plane. Now we were the last plane to take off which we eventually did. The pilot then tells us we are going to land again as we have a problem, "For fuck's sake, let us jump out" was the wish of most of us, that was one of the problems no windspeed indicator, so you cannot jump! The plane dumped its fuel and we landed like in the movies with all the ambulances and fire trucks doing their thing.

Back at the drop site a stand had been built for the VIPs and a young Lance Corporal screamed all the way down tangled in his chute. He died instantly, breaking every bone in his body, right in front of the VIPs. It must have put them off their lunch. We had jumped at 800 feet and the American and Turkish paratroopers at over 1,200 feet which gave a better safety margin when you have a problem. Who were our officers trying to impress? Jumping so low, 400 feet could have made all the difference to trying to open his chute, pulling his reserve or give a longer time to scream!

The Lance Corporal was the only one to die, but we had

some casualties that had the ambulances working. The drop zone had been surveyed when it had been full of sunflowers that were just getting harvested. The stems had dried out in the harsh sun and were like millions of bayonets waiting for paratroopers to land on, a prickly situation. The exercise lasted a few days and then in the middle of a lightening storm we got onto transport for a nine hour drive to an army base just outside Istanbul. The air was full of static electricity that made our hair stand on end, and then bolts of lightning came down in a display that impressed mortal man; glad to get on the wagon, get the rifle out of my hands and out of there, awesome!

We stayed in barracks that had 50 showers and a 10-gallon tank to feed them all, one drip per person per minute and that was only the showers nearest the feed tank. Still a bit smelly, we put on our civvies and went on the town. Istanbul, painted the town red, we had a ball and I ended up fighting the one-eyed taxi driver. Take us to the night "life" I noticed him give us a tour of the city and stopping at the street next to where he had picked us up, no wonder he only had one eye.

The local brothels were in a street that was partitioned off from public view; we had found the door that led to the Street of a Thousand Arseholes. Outside each door were a group of local Turks, looking at the merchandise on display inside and for the price of a coffee you could have one of these women. They liked their women fat, rolls of fat, wrapped in a black bra and knickers, and then my eyes noticed the varicose veins that led down to their black ankle socks, then a roll of fat that seemed to be part of the small, high-heeled shoes. No, no, I am going to buy the coffee instead.

We went from sweating our bollocks off in 30+ degrees dressed in smock and denims, to freezing our bollocks off in temperatures -20 degrees in the same uniform. We had to do a NATO exercise in Denmark, yes to reinforce the Danish bacon in case the Soviet Block wanted it. This time we were told the drop zone had over 60 small but deep ponds and we would have to wear life jackets. Not that the life jacket was capable of holding you above water, a Para with all his kit. That was to be proved in the disaster jump at the Kiel Canal in Germany when several Paras became anchors on the bottom. The RAF would fly in formations of three and drop us off at different heights on the smallest possible area. As I jumped and was going down in the freezing cold air, I'm thinking was that an aeroplane that just went under me or was I seeing things. Fortunately nobody was killed on the drop, even though the RAF did their best and only one man fell into a pond and he was the Colonel of the Battalion so he was quickly rescued. Kids started to run on the drop zone, give us your parachute and we will give you some porn books, so now a lot of the lads were carrying books! Talk about cold, if you touched the metal on your rifle your fingers stuck to it. We shivered in groups to keep warm, cut-backs in military spending and no proper uniform for fighting in the cold. To keep the Parachute Brigade was an uphill struggle with the civil service who were wanting to cut the defence budget as normal, so asking for better clothing was a non-starter. The cut-backs always seemed to be looking at us and the marines and as was proved in the Falklands, without us, the regular Army does not get a foothold on occupied territory.

When the exercise was over we were taken to Danish barracks for a hot meal, could we believe it, prunes in gravy. A near mutiny, as the Danish cooks were pelted with the shit food. We all started to laugh at the hundreds of prunes being fired, almost stoning to death the cooks trying to hide in their clean and open kitchen.

Danish people are very honest, leaving their coats hung up in discos where anyone a little dishonest could nick one. A few blokes now had nice warm coats! The price of everything compared to England was really expensive. I don't know if that was the reason two drunken Paras tried to rob a bank, but they soon got caught, being too drunk to run. Mind you, they had stolen a pistol from the armoury, so you could not blame it all on the drink, the intention was there. They were handed back to the Battalion when we flew back to England. Discipline and punishment was tough in the Paras as you had a few lads on the borderline of being crooks and real animals. In my couple of years with the Paras I witnessed two attempts by blokes trying to commit armed robbery, after stealing pistols from the armoury, we did have lousy wages!

My flat neighbour in Aldershot, Pete, was a lad for the women but when pissed turned out to be a failure. As you walked round Copenhagen guys would try to sell tickets to a live sex show, so as to get out the cold a hundred odd-men and myself were watching the show. Now on the ticket it said you could join in, so after all the stripping and fucking, Pete shouts out that he wanted to participate, "come on down" was the reply from the two girl stars. They take off all his clothes and start giving him a gobble but he was having great difficulty in getting a hard on, a bit of a let down, or brewer's droop. The girls tied a pink ribbon around his dick, slapped his arse and sent him packing with his clothes. He said to me after "I didnt think it would be so difficult but with all you lot watching I could not rise to the occasion". His wife Brenda, who was beautiful, was very forgiving and every time I went over two ramps in the road I thought about Brenda!

A battalion drop on Salisbury Plain and as we had just had a pay rise they were lowering the drop heights, only a second to decide when to use the reserve. What was the point of carrying it? In combat we would jump at four hundred feet if necessary but why train at stupidly low heights and risk men's lives for nothing? It took the "Ruperts" several deaths before the obvious unnecessary danger sank in, or was it that the last to die was a Rupert Colonel from the reserves?

The drop was on a nice day with only a little wind and I jumped number1 in the starboard stick. It was impressive to see the 30 planes and the several hundred men in such a very small area. The advantage of jumping first was the lessened chance of getting tangled up in someone else's parachute which was the biggest problem with everyone so close in the air. For such a nice day it was amazing to find that several men had accidents. I landed without problem and got to my Company RV (rendezvous point). A Cpl from HQ Company was near the "B" Company RV and calling for a medic, so I dumped my gear and went to his assistance. The broken leg was obvious with his foot lying at a right angle flat on the ground. He was in pain and I felt down the leg to find the break. The femur was broken and he was in a state of shock. I knew this was life threatening if an artery had been damaged, so I shouted to a radio op that this was a priority casavac and to inform "Starlight" which was the radio code name for the doctor. The CO Major Patton now calls to me, "Mumford, you're not a medic any more but a patrol commander, join your patrol". I ignored his order as I knew better than him that this soldier's life, was in danger. He gave me the order three times and was going to have me put in jail, had I not seen the ambulance coming I would have refused. Not allowing medical treatment to a wounded soldier was a crime against the Geneva Convention, this was a fucking exercise with no real enemy and this "Rupert " was prepared to risk a soldier's life on exercise. I could not serve under this man; I vowed that if he ever got shot I would never treat the cunt. Bad word to describe him as a cunt is useful!

After exercises, parachute training, weapons training, marching and running they had to finish, the lads went on the town. Abroad it was the married men that were the wildest but back in Aldershot it was normally the single men letting rip. There were certainly some characters that stood out and the more they drank they became colourful, funny, loud, extrovert and you had to be diplomatic with them when you wanted to stop the enjoyment, especially at closing time. Men would take their dirty laundry to the laundrette, set things spinning and go to the bar. Most Para underpants and vests would be white when issued but every thing used to get thrown into the same machine including red T-shirts so the clothes going into the drying machine had a pink colour, so pink was the unavoidable favourite colour, nice boys. The men would fill their bergans and go back to camp at closing time, sleep things off and be back down for the evening session. One sunny day that I remembered, a large group of men were sleeping it off in the local park on the grass, taking in the sun. Let sleeping dogs lie is a good old saying, but not known by a couple of mounted military policemen that started hitting sleeping men with big long truncheons. It did not go down well and soon un-mounted policemen were calling for assistance and a riot developed that started bad feelings amongst the police both local and military. Then one day a drunken para was put into the cells where brave policemen then took turns in kicking shit out of him. More than fifty men from the unit went down to the police station the police had to barricade themselves in to avoid justice and see how brave they were. These incidents led to a duty for a Paratrooper Corporal to have to go on patrol with the military police to name men causing trouble. Judas patrol but under orders to protect the police. I reported for one such duty and in a Land Rover. We headed up Queens Avenue that led into town. A straight road and the military policeman hit the curb twice; I looked at him, not blind but under the influence for sure. Going round the town and I had to mention he was going the wrong way down a one-way street, in case he met another vehicle head on. Then later he stopped when a man in civilian clothes flagged him down. "You fucking Paras are nothing but shit that live on past glory," again he was also pissed and on duty. The driver called him Staff which was two ranks higher than mine, so I held my tongue and took the abuse. I said to the driver that I had left my ID card in the 2 Para guard room and he obligingly took me back to camp. I informed the duty officer about my patrol and both policemen were arrested. If you don't want to obey the law, then don't be a copper! Crap hats anyway and I did my duty but it did not go down well with the police who would take their revenge framing drunk Paras.

Paddy McClay was a big Irish lad that would often be in trouble with his missus; going home drunk she was not impressed and then would not drop her knickers. He killed her budgie, not a wife-beater but more a budgie-killer. Next day he was kicked out of the house had to spend a few days in the barracks, he ended up buying a look-a-like budgie and pleading for forgiveness.

Dave Mannion was King Rat, the things he got up to would fill a book. A married man who was totally different under the control of his wife, unfortunately his wife did not always keep him under control. Paddy McClay dropped his trousers in the middle of a bar and, yes, had a shit right there in the middle amongst everyone. The soldiers laughed but the civilians, men and women, cringed and complained. The men even became aggressive, then Mannion takes control of the situation, picks up the turd in his right hand and asks what all the fuss is about and more cringing. He then stuffs it in his mouth with cries of horror! His two eye teeth are missing so in a spin he squeezes out the shit with his tongue, and that brought the house down. I don't know if they purposely went out to shock people but there was never a dull moment with the Paras.

Trucial Oman States was our next exercise in the desert and yes still with the same uniform. A couple of long marches and some men went down with dehydration, one of the officers tests to see if you could manage with only a little water in the desert. The answer was no as all men need a good supply in the desert, did these officers have brains or was there something lacking in their schooling? I started to worry about what these officers were going to do next. Who needs an enemy to kill you when our own officers were experts at getting men killed and injured? I did not lose anyone in my patrol to heat exhaustion but I did have to punch a guy washing his dixie with water when I had told everyone to use sand to clean cooking equipment. I did hit him only once but he had two black eyes and I broke my hand. How else do you maintain discipline in the middle of a desert? Heat exhaustion was bad enough for some men, but sunstroke is the killer and a few men had to be evacuated by helicopter to save their lives.

We did one fantastic march in patrols from the Gulf across a peninsular to the Indian Ocean, more mountain than desert so we found fresh water on route and rested on the beach after finishing the march. We went swimming and there were sea horses in the shallows and fish of all colours and descriptions, fantastic. I dressed and strolled round the shore line with a couple of mates. A shelf a couple of metres deep with crystal clear water and we stepped back in unison when we saw two big sharks. We started shouting to the lads in the water, sharks, sharks, they must have thought we were joking as no one paid any notice to our warning and it turned out even sharks do not like Paras as they did not fancy eating any of them. The evening was something that I had never seen before, the waves were full of a form of plankton that glowed in the dark like millions of small electric bulbs. The only other thing I had witnessed that compared was in the jungle, a fly called a "Fire Fly" also glowed in the dark. Travelling was an experience that I enjoyed with the Army that gave me the opportunity to see magic things, weird and wonderful, the only downside was training to kill people!

The class system was maintained in the Army by the Officers Mess. Officers that came through Mons Officer school tended to be from your normal English working background but Sandhurst officers were more from the private school, dad was a general, a top civil servant or elements of the colonial past. The fact that these officers had fathers who had spent fortunes on educating their sons only to get the minimum qualification to join the army as an officer, was evidence of the calibre we had in the army, literally the dregs of the class system. The Paras was not a Regiment that attracted the snobs as it was not a Royal Regiment, with little prestige, physically hard and thus not rated by the class system. The Officers Mess fees were payable from the normal rate of officers pay but your Guards Regiment kept out the men from normal families by making the Mess fees higher than an officers' wages. Put it this way, not many Para officers had a string of polo ponies or an estate to keep them on. Soldiers who worked as waiters in the Officers' Mess were normally volunteers and paid extra for the job. It was only on one occasion that we were ordered to work in the Mess as the officers were having a big celebration for Airborne Forces Day and had invited Generals and dignitaries from far and wide. I am not a servant to any man, nobody is better or inferior and being ordered to work in this class system did not go down well with me or the other lads. On the officers table I only had respect for a handful of these men who had proved they were leaders of men and up to the job. The soup was the first to be served; the solid chewy green things were the best we could get up from our lungs and pickings from our nose. The lad that pissed in it gave it the real flavour but he overdid it as half the soup came back. Suspicion of sabotage was evident as we never got ordered to do the job again!

    Then from all these exercises we were put on standby for another tour in Northern Ireland.

Jungle Training 2 Para

Lt, Easting (right) and me at the Yacht Club

Chapter 11

South Armagh - Bandit Country

This is where I had intended to put the first chapter but because of its importance I thought it had to be read first. So this chapter relates to the events after that tour of operation in Ireland and the death of of Pte Francis Bell.

We returned to Aldershot and one month's holiday with our families to help us wind down from the anger within us and try to forget what we had just experienced. I had planned to travel to Glasgow to visit my wife's family and then to Newcastle to see my family but first I had to hand over my wooden rabbit-hutch of a house in Crook, moving to a nearly-new flat in Aldershot with all mod cons. So in comes the civil house manager to check the quarter and then for me to hand over the keys. I had previously improved the property by painting and decorating, as when we had moved in the place made a slum look good in comparison. I was also told at the time do not worry about the state of the furniture as it was class 3 quality over twenty years old, everything stained, marked and well worn. Not the same nice guy signing us out, marks and stains on nearly all furniture, garden grass needs cut, 30 pounds to pay out of my wages. The third of an acre field had grass one metre high and nothing but a pair of rusty old garden shears to cut it with, what did they expect after being away from home for four months, did they expect my wife to get down on her hands and knees? I lost my bottle and shouted at the bastard, so he reported me to the Housing Officer who defended the civilian giving me two weeks punishment reporting to the guardroom twice a day with my best uniform and to top that a fifty pound fine. That ended our holidays, as I also had to cut the grass and all my savings gone. Feeling pissed off and angry was an understatement after spending four months in Ireland and this was the treatment meted out to me.

Going to the new apartment in Aldershot and I only get conned once. A nice housing manager wanted me to sign for everything without me inspecting the furniture and contents, up yours Jimmy. I found marks and stains on everything as it had been used and not cleaned, some other squaddie had paid for cleaning the stains which had not been done, so in the end he had to write in the inventory that every thing was marked and stained. It turned out that this was the fiddle, fraud on a grand scale against married soldiers. They were charging for cleaning the marks and stains but it never happened, the money was going into their own pockets and even the officers were taking a cut. When I moved out of this apartment to join the SAS at Hereford I got the same nasty, robbing bastard who took great pleasure in marking and noting the marks and stains, then the pure disappointment on his face, as he read the last sentence written in the inventory book. I would love to know how many soldiers were robbed in this way!

Fortunately our neighbours were nice and we had some good times to make up for the bad ones remembered. Young families and most of the married soldiers had to get jobs with civilian firms during holidays just to make ends meet at the end of the month. Most worked through an agency called "Man Power Services" and I ended working in a Coca Cola Plant, then in a store belonging to a big supermarket chain and finally a freezer food store. Soldiers were badly treated and poorly paid but we had our comradeship and friends and would party at home or take turns baby-sitting kids so we could take our wives out.

You had to laugh at the things the lads got up to. A publican bought a fish tank and put a couple of piranha fish in it, so the first drunken Para that comes along loses the end of his finger.

Two lads did their washing at the laundry, got drunk at

a bar, went to the Chinese for a meal, then decided to do a run-out without paying. Doing a run out in style, straight through the restaurant front window and back to camp, leaving the Chinese in an initial state of shock, but they had left their laundry with every item having a name tag.

Drunken Paras gave the military police plenty of work and this did not create any friendship between us. They did not see that soldiers had to let off steam. Instead of calming a situation they just had an attitude that aggravated it.

My wife was now pregnant but also had to work so we could manage to get some savings for the extras you need to raise a family. She worked in Boots the chemist till she was nearly due to have the baby.

Then the Battalion got sent back to Ireland again but I got sent to Brecon to do a Non-Commissioned Officers (NCO) course with about 80 men from the rest of the Parachute Brigade. The course was, at the time, the only one in the army for NCOs to be given special training and tested in all the skills necessary for a soldier to be an NCO. Weapon training and how to teach soldiers, physical training to the extreme, patrol, platoon, company attacks and the command organisation of the battalion from top to bottom. We all had a go at being patrol leader, then a few of the best got to be platoon leader as the Officer and then Company Commander. I was given CO position twice and coped so well that on the end of the course I was given a "B" grade and besides an SAS trooper we had the highest grade amongst the entire cadre. Independent Officers and senior NCOs who examined our performance made a report on each soldier's performance under very tough conditions. Basic soldiering is very important to learn as lessons have been learnt in past conflicts and wars that the deaths of many soldiers need not be repeated if the basics are applied. Generals in the first and second World Wars could calculate how many men they would lose, killed or wounded, taking out any enemy defended position. This knowledge helped with how many men would be needed from fresh reserve troops to fill the gaps. How many ambulances needed and where to set up field hospitals before the attack started, food, ammunition re-supplies all had to be calculated. We were told you could expect to lose three men for every enemy soldier in a defended position. Things that helped to reduce the losses would be the timing of an attack and this was found that at first light just before dawn as soldiers were still awaking, morning mist and the enemy not fully alert would reduce losses. Last light was also a good attack time as it was harder for the enemy to bring in aircraft or artillery support, especially if your side did not have that type of assistance. So if you were the defender it was important that near last light and first light you have every soldier under your command alert and ready to fire their weapons The reason soldiers carry a digging tool is that when you come under fire a simple shallow trench can make the difference of life or death. Most artillery and mortar ammunition explodes on the surface, artillery shells throw the shrapnel forward at a 40-degree radius and the more deadly round is from a mortar that has a 360-degree killing area. A good camouflaged position and personal camouflage also breaks up the silhouette of a human form. Showing us how to detect the position of a sniper by the crack and thump from his rifle. We stood there while a sniper put some shots over our heads. We were told the rules of the Geneva convention in the treatment of prisoners and what information you had to give the enemy if you were captured, army ID number, name, rank date of birth and religion. So all this information should be known by professional soldiers and taught by their experienced non-commissioned officers.

Brecon is another place in the world where the sheep look depressed as the climatical conditions are severe most of the year round, cold wind and more often than not accompanied by rain. The British Army must have bought all these sheep-rearing areas as a job lot, as no one liked living in those bleak exposed areas.

A company of men from the Royal Irish Rangers was used as our enemy in the exercises and were permanently based at the Brecon barracks. It did not take a genius to establish that there was no love between us Paras and the Irish Unit. The Royal Irish Rangers. The training for riot situations was real, they went overboard with stones and petrol bombs, and in return we kicked so much shit out of them, Officers and NCOs had to intervene. That night after riot training a Para went round to their barracks and hit everyone with a hammer as they slept. We knew who did it but with our love for the Irish, we were not going to shop him. The Irish Regiments got all the good postings abroad as the rest of the British Army were back and forward to Northern Ireland. They were exempt from that duty as their alliance was in question with Irishmen put against Irishmen. So to keep their loyalty they were given the best postings abroad but this one company got the wrong posting and a big headache acting as the enemy to the Parachute Regiment

I returned to my unit in Ireland with a fellow Cpl who had scraped in with a low "C" grade. Patton got me to one side and said he was giving the other man promotion, making him full Corporal, as he was liked better by the men. Arse-licking was not a qualification on the course and I knew my liking for the CO, Major Patton, was zero so this made me think it was time to move on. I also had to think, had Major Burke put an end to my career in the Paras, as I said "mud sticks" even when proven innocent and I was learning this first hand. I would finish this tour in Ireland and try to join the SAS in a last attempt to make the Army, my career.

South Armagh was known as "bandit country" by the Army. The Army had heavy losses on the border, with big bombs packed in milk churns, placed under the road in drainage ditches. Some units would do very little patrolling on their tour of duty and their Officer would be praised and given medals that under their command very few incidents had occurred. The next replacement battalion who secured the area and did the job properly would run into the booby traps that the IRA had carefully prepared and camouflaged. Often the wire from the bomb led to the detonation point, just across the border, all the IRA had to do was to wait and press the button. The tactics had forced the Army to increase the use of helicopters.

Searching roads to clear them of booby traps was a dangerous job and when on a couple of occasions I noticed things not right I asked for the bomb squad, to be given the message, "You cannot call the bomb team every time you see something suspicious." (What?)! Men died unnecessarily because of these stupid remarks from officers that still underestimated the capability of the enemy. A sergeant major from another company flew by helicopter to a suspected object reported by another patrol. The Cpl had not wanted to risk his men and die for the Paddies and for what! The Cpl pointed to the unusual bump at the side of the road and the CSM set out and walked straight up to it, as if to prove we were being over-cautious and should not waste the time of the bomb squad. The Cpl said later that the CSM had turned round and his face cringed, knowing the Cpl had been right. The blast left a 10-foot hole in the road and all that could be found of the big CSM was enough bits of meat to fill a 24-can Fanta box. Now the bomb team came out escorted by the Lancers in armoured vehicles and a driver found the command wire then started to pull it. He and another soldier died as the wire led to a dry stone wall which was also booby trapped. One was decapitated by a large boulder and the other cut in half. They were another statistic in the conflict and officers were still not getting the message that the IRA were getting good at their evil job.

Road clearing was the most dangerous job and Patton gave me a good share of the work, was I getting a message from this man. I arranged my men in a "V" formation, well spread out. I and another man were at the point on the road checking the culverts, drains and any mounds. We could only hope the men in front either side, would find a detonation command wire before we found any culvert bomb. I checked the hundreds of places a bomb could be concealed and finally reached the end of the road which could now be used by army transport, orders completed. One man did crack on route but I did not report him because I understood the pressure and stress put on us all.

I got sent to mount a static patrol on the M1 motorway border leading to the South and had a run-in with the Little John brothers. These were two blokes built like brick shithouses they were members of the IRA, specialising in clearing the route for cars carrying bombs, weapons or important IRA members. I unfortunately stopped them as they travelled south but at that time I did not know about them or their activities. I asked them for identification to which they gave me a scrap of paper with their names written on! "Pull over and turn off the engine," I ordered because these two were up to something. "Get out of the car" I ordered and they first refused. I called over a few lads, they then said to me" put down your rifles and we will fight you all". They got out of the car, fucking giants, was Robin Hood in the boot with Will Scarlet and the rest of his merry men I was thinking when I saw these two monsters. They had obviously been in a fight or two, looking at the scars on their faces. I looked at my young lads and back at them, I came to the conclusion they might win the fight if I allowed my men to try and over-power them. How do you maintain order in a situation like this, they knew we were not allowed to shoot them and we did not carry rubber bullets or truncheons at the check point. It might have been extreme but I went for it and shouted "I suspect these men are carrying guns put a bullet up the spout and shoot to kill if they make any false move or refuse my orders". I looked and sounded that I was not bluffing and an order is an order which they also knew. I kicked their legs open and made them spread their legs and hands on the car. Then I searched them and the car and found nothing. The mouthy one was at it again so I hit him with my rifle over the head. The guy did not flinch and I broke the hand grip and wooden stock of my rifle. A car then passed and they smiled at the occupants, then they became nice as pie. I sussed what had happened straight away, they had removed my patrol to allow terrorists to pass the check point so I arrested them putting on plastic handcuffs. I had my radio operator ask for a back up so I could bring them into HQ. After twenty minutes an officer arrived full of hell, he had been dragged out to duty because of me and ordered I explain why? You hit these men, you have no right to do that and give me a right rollicking that every body heard, even the smiling brothers. As he went to talk to them, his Sergeant said to me he was out of order not backing me up in front of the Micks. The officer ordered my whole patrol back to HQ and it was me in the shit and not the Little John brothers.

At base the sergeant did a check on the brothers and found their past form which implicated them in terrorist activity. They had taken on a patrol from "C" Company in similar circumstances and had kicked shit out of them, so now the officer backed down seeing that I had been correct in my assumption of the situation. The Mick lover realised I was telling the truth and ordered the two brothers charged, but I thought how many other patrols would fall for this tactic before the "Ruperts" passed the information to the men on the ground of how the IRA were getting through check points. The two brothers snapped off the hand cuffs just to prove the strength they had. How would you have coped with such a situation?

Many soldiers were killed in the same circumstances as intelligence briefings were given to the men in the ops room, mainly Ruperts, and not enough to those on the ground. A need-to-know basis covered up most stupidity by not passing down the information. It was the men on the ground that could only win this terrorist war and soldiers walked into the same type of ambush tour after tour, dying for nothing and caused by lack of information, again basics learnt should be passed on to stop fellow comrades dying.

Bessbroke Mill was the base camp for my Company and a helicopter was permanently based there. The pilot was a Staff Sergeant who was a little mad to say the least. It was unusual a pilot not being an officer but out with this guy you soon realised he was a little crazy. A dolly-bird hitching a lift on the slipway to the M1 motorway and he hovers over her offering a lift. Then he goes up to the maximum a helicopter can fly, gradual circles, up to ten thousand feet and I am standing out side on the pod with another soldier with only a webbing strap holding us. He then turns off the engine with a loud warning buzzer sounding. For a few seconds we had negative gravity and started to float, my feet lifted off the pod, I nearly dropped my rifle as I clung on to the webbing and this guy is laughing. Later he tells me pilots practice twice a year, bringing down the chopper safely without the engine, I still do not know if he was telling the truth but he managed to restart the engine before landing. Autogiration was the term he used similar to a Cycamore leaf as it spins and slowly falls to the ground.

He also had a thing about collecting IRA flags off chimneys. He would hover on the apex of the roof and get me to jump out and collect the flag.

Never a dull moment with this guy, hiding behind hills, hovering and then swooping down on cars crossing illegal roads over the border. Then one day he was flying very low going down Carlingford Lough towards the south. I am sitting next to him and suddenly I thought his brains had been splattered over the chopper. Whack! Blood was everywhere, you could not see out of the front glass, blood covered the whole front. I turned and saw with relief he was OK but fighting to control the chopper. I prepared to jump as I had a chance to survive hitting the water I waited for his reaction. He pulled up and revved the engine, turning on the front wipers and with great professionalism I witnessed him control the situation. We had hit one or two seagulls but fortunately they had not entered the engine air intake vents but the sudden impact had rattled his feathers it was a close shave with us flying so low. I met the mad man again when I joined the SAS, a fitting unit for this guy.

Another bomb and another dead sergeant: he had been ordered to search a house on the border which did not appear to be occupied. He had approached it carefully and noticed all the windows were drawn with curtains; he could not see or hear anyone. The front door was the obvious booby trap, so he decided to enter via a window. He broke the glass with the butt of his rifle and pulled open the curtain to see inside. At that moment the house blew up and proved to the IRA that their new photo sensitive detonator worked. When we were told of his death and how sophisticated the IRA were becoming; Paddies were not so thick as the officers thought, we wondered who was giving them this technology.

The CO Patton goes and orders me to search a disused house the next day. Is this Rupert taking the piss or does he want rid of me, it had to be one or the other. Mind you I could not hide the fact that I had a personality clash with him so I was just as much to blame for him giving me these shit jobs. The house appeared unoccupied, heavy curtains closed. What would you be thinking; well I came to the same conclusion. I shouted loud enough for anyone inside to hear me but no-one opened the door. I ordered my men to back off and asked by radio that the owner be found and asked to open the house. We waited hours, so in the end I said sod it. I had my men withdraw to a safe distance and from a small mound I had a few stones and threw them at a window. I dived behind the mound while the stone was still in flight. Third time lucky and the stone shattered glass and slightly opened the curtain. I waited another five minutes before approaching the broken window, as I sent in one of the lads a car pulls up and out gets a priest. "BeJesus what the hell are you doing?" in a fine Irish accent. I told him that I was ordered to search the house and had waited for the owner. I told him of the death of a fellow soldier in similar circumstances. "I wish it had been a bomb and had blown you to Hell", he shouted in my face. Fuck you, I had him on the ground and searched him. Then had his car emptied and then went through the house with a fine tooth comb. Five double beds with a crucifix above each, "Is this where you bring the nuns to fuck or is it the little boys' arses from the choir, "No more being polite to religious nuts. Any car with a priest or a nun I gave them fucking stick, evil, sick, bastards, what was the Pope recruiting?

On a lighter note I was guard commander in charge of camp security at Bessbrook Mill when the guard on the front gate phoned in and reported that there was a woman across the road from him having a piss in the gutter. "She might have been desperate and caught short", I replied."She must have been cos she forgot to take her knickers down". I laughed and told him to keep me informed. Next thing he is on the phone again, she is at the gate and wants to come into your guard room. Why, I asked. She says she comes every Saturday night to give the soldiers a good time. Send her in I will have a look at her, she knew the way and staggered in the door. Next thing she starts taking off her clothes without even a remark between us. Now this was not a pretty sight she had to be 60-plus, if a day, not that I have anything against older people. Her dress off exposed her soaking wet-knickers, her perfume, a mixture of alcohol, cigarettes and piss. She did not have a bra, as it was not needed to hold the two flat dried out prunes and the skin could do with good ironing. "You come here every Saturday", "yes" she replies. "Now hold on, you can give me a gobble but I do not want a fuck", I had my principles and the thought of fucking her, no way. She stunk of piss but I suppose her missing front teeth would be better than a wank. "No, no, I don't give gobbles" she protested, this woman had principles and I liked women with principles. "Hold on then, let me go to the barracks and find your friends." The lights were off and most of the lads were either sleeping or wanking. "Any of you lot fucking this old bird in the guard room?" I could not stop laughing as three of them jumped out of bed and made a beeline straight for the guard room. The last out was a Lance Corporal SH, you have to finish my duty in the guard room to which he agreed, so I let them get on with it.

The same guard duty a few days later and the Colonel came into camp with his men to have a briefing with our officers. A corporal doing escort with the Colonel's patrol came into my guardroom and starts to have a conversation with me, I presumed to be friendly and kill time while waiting for the Colonel. I made him a coffee and he took off his Para smock and we talked about how the battalion was doing and showed me on a wall map how we were well spread out trying to secure the area. He finally left when the CO was ready for departure. I finished my duty an hour later and put on my smock that was hanging on the back of a chair. I realised straight away that it was not mine. My wallet, my watch and two magazines complete with forty rounds of ammunition were in my smock. I managed to get a lift in a patrol that was going to headquarters and found the man that had my jacket. To my surprise he denied that he had my jacket and showed that the pockets were empty. What was going down? He was the only one who could have taken my jacket and I had assumed by mistake! Then I saw my watch on his shelf, a couple of punches in the face and I recovered my possessions. I reported him but the officer put it down to a mistake on his part taking the wrong jacket. I was not of the same opinion and later I found he had a Irish wife, I just wonder was he another traitor as nothing was secure in Northern Ireland in or out of barracks.

Talking to my wife on the phone she was telling me that she was due to have our baby at any moment, then a voice interrupts our conversation shouting "Up with the IRA". Even the fucking phone was tapped by the IRA and so blatant that they interrupt my conversation. This whole Northern Ireland involvement by the Army was becoming a political error that the Army could not win as the grass roots of the IRA was now taking advantage of the long-drawn out conflict. The Army changed every four months but the IRA and its support grew in strength militarily and politically, with better propaganda and more sophisticated weapons.

    I read a book about the Irish famine to pass the time and learn about why this hatred existed, and later a press cutting that the Irish wanted an apology from the English for not helping feed the starving people. The reason the English class system did not help was that the potato blight also affected England and Germany and they did not want to give a hand out to our working class either. Do you think women and children working down coal mines on a twelve-hour shift knew about, could read, or had time to give a damn about the Irish famine? What I do not understand was why the Irish had a staple diet that was so dependent on potatoes as they had been brought back from the Americas by Sir Walter Raleigh? In the British class system only the few ruled and the majority suffered just as much as any Irishman. How can we be responsible for our history? We can not rewrite the past nor be responsible for all the wrongs in the world! The British are responsible for many good and great things that have helped the world more than the bad things in our history. Tell me which country has been perfect in its evolution? Are the Americans proud of what they did to the native Americans or their black Americans? We can not turn back the clock and can not be held guilty for our forefathers!

    My son was born at the Cambridge Military Hospital and thanks to a comrade's wife I got the good news that both were in good health. Major Patton gave me a day off duty to celebrate with the comment that because I had missed time serving in Ireland while on the NCO course at Brecon that he was not giving me leave to see my wife and son. Naturally they were constantly on my mind the last few weeks of the tour. Passing the one and only public telephone used by over two hundred men and their families, it started to ring. Nothing had been arranged as I still thought my wife was in hospital but for some reason I knew it was her. I picked up the phone and said "Hello Irene how are you and the baby"?"How did you know it was me? I've just been released from hospital", even I could not explain how I knew it was her!

More men were now being killed and wounded by these expert terrorists with incidents on a daily basis. They operated from just over the border but the Irish regular Army did nothing to stop them and they were always there to stop us going after them. Thirty years later and I still never buy anything with an Irish label. Was I getting the "inbred hatred" illness?

The mad pilot and his helicopter, working South Armagh

Para dispatching from a C130 aircraft

Chapter 12

The 22nd SA.S Regiment

I applied to join the SAS and was accepted to do the course in January 1974. An effort was made by my Officers to talk me out of the idea but when someone says to me you will never pass or be able to do a thing, it is like showing a red flag to a bull. So off to Hereford City having a Cathedral, rural setting in the Wye Valley, market place, local hospital, teachers training college, abundance of girls, what a place for a small Army Unit. The local girls did not hate the army like in Aldershot and the lads were not jealous as there seemed too many beautiful girls to go round. We were told fight a local lad and you would be RTU'd (Returned to Unit) so little fighting took place in the 70s and if anything the locals even seemed to like us.

Some soldiers who arrived never even got the opportunity to see the city. When we turned up, a nice little Scottish Sgt Major told us that there were not enough beds for all the volunteers that had arrived. Put down your kit, holdalls, suitcases and start running around that parade square. Only when enough men had dropped out did the nice SGM send us to our barracks to rest while he gave return rail tickets to the men that never even passed the first day! I had prepared myself for the course by running at least 10 miles a day and gradually built up the amount of weight I carried in my bergan so the training had paid off as I made the first obstacle and got a nighs sleep in Hereford. I introduced myself to fellow volunteers who seemed to be from every Regiment and Corps in the British Army I was surprised even to meet two Royal Marines and a man from the RAF Regiment but the majority were Paratroopers from my Brigade. Unlike "P" Company the selection course to get in the Paras, the SAS was up to the individual and you could rap in, throw in the towel any time you wanted, if the going got too tough for you. Looking back you needed your brain examined to volunteer, allowing people to torture you both physically and mentally, for one month. Most people have read books on the SAS and the training, so I will only write about the hardship and pain that stuck in my mind.

I am no superman; I don't look like one and like most volunteers who attempted the SAS selection found it very hard. I was physically fit but in the Paras I knew a lot of men fitter than myself. Navigation, common sense and a little grey matter were to play the most important elements in passing the SAS. If you mark point "A" and point "B" on a map, draw a straight line, then that is the shortest route as a bird will fly. Now with the ability to read a map you can pick out the best route, that contours round mountains, bypass bogs, dense forest, safe places to cross rivers and that was the difference in passing the course and failing. Going in a direct line was for supermen without much of a brain and doing it the superman way, most ended up failing. Physical injury, fatigue, unable to go through the pain barrier would send most men back to their mother units, so you had to pace yourself every day, pull a muscle, break a leg and in some cases die, you never made the next day's test and you were RTU'd. The clocktower in the centre of the SAS camp at Hereford had the names of the dead, in battle and training within the SAS and looking at the list more had died in training than in battle. You never made the clock if you died trying to get into the Regiment.

The first couple of weeks on the course was called "The Sickener" and that was designed to get rid of the men not mentally or physically prepared for the hardship that was about to follow. The best example that I remember, was running up a Welsh mountain in the Black Mountains with full kit, rifle, bergan and inside for some reason we had been told to carry, an empty jerry-can! Head down looking at the green,

green grass of home, arse up, running up a mountain that seemed to have no end. Then the SAS instructors (torturers) stopped us at the stage where your lungs are about to burst, steam was rising from everyone in the group, we had a man-made cloud above us. "Look down there at that stream", commanded an instructor! We had been running up a ridge that had been getting narrower. Both sides were now steep sides and a long way down in any direction."What stream asked a volunteer?" as it was impossible to see any stream! Don't worry I assure you, you will find a stream down there. Right, he commands, "everybody run down find the stream and fill up your jerry-can with water." Running down was another set of muscles and a knee jerking experience, down, down and down, diving to the left and right to stop your legs running away from your body. Where is that fucking stream? Then we found the trickle of water, so shallow that you could not dip in the can. The can on its side half filled it, and then we had to use the mug from our kit to fill the can. Running back up with the now full jerry-can was a pure physical torture. You had to use your free hand to stop you falling back down the steep slope. If the first time up had been hard, it was now a doddle compared to this second time up this fucking Welsh mountain. Yes you started to hate Welsh mountains. The instructor was shouting down,"Hurry up I'm getting cold waiting for you, move your fucking arses". On reaching the top I could not talk, my lungs ached as I gasped for breath. "Get the can out and take the top off" ordered the SAS corporal,"I told you to fill it and I can get a tot of whisky in it so it's not full is it?" Empty the can and this time fill it to the top." You stare in disbelief but argue or refuse an order and you were out and RTU'd. I was running back down like most of the men but a few had refused and the instructor was happy that he had achieved his objective to thin out the men from the boys. The third time up that fucking Welsh mountain and I find it impossible to describe the physical pain. Again the corporal was not happy about the amount of water in the can but it was now obvious to any arse-hole you could not get a tot of whisky in the can. "Empty the can and down again", Jesus, this was the mental torture side of the course, he knew we were exhausted and had no intention to send us all the way back down. He got another few men to refuse the order and now he and his mate had rested enough doing their Grand old Duke of York routine. He shouted down for us to return. What a relief, as most of us, myself included, had reached our breaking point, physically. The lads who had refused were sent back to the starting point and a waiting vehicle. "You lot up and follow me", again running up the remainder of the mountain, and now at least the jerry-can was empty! At the top you could straighten your body which was in itself a physical relief, but we now stopped again, at the edge of a frozen ice-covered lake. What perversion were they dreaming up? No, no, I hoped it would not be swimming lessons! This lake-cum-natural reservoir was so wind-swept that no bushes or trees had managed to take root. "You all look a bit hot to me; into the reservoir up to your necks and walk round in a circle", This was his next torture, I had read their sick minds. The saying about brass monkeys must have been thought up in this situation. Breaking the ice to get deep enough, the shock to your body, guys heads were still steaming but your body quickly started to freeze. This was a test for your heart and the lump in your throat was your balls that had shrivelled up. My teeth were chattering so much I thought I would chew on my balls. The SAS man was shouting "Don't get your weapons wet and hurry up", Again he managed his job with a few more lads getting out of the water before completing the circle. My head had gone under, talk about pissing on embers to put out a fire, the steam stopped rising from my head. Then the freezing cold took my breath away and gave me an instant migraine attack. I finished the circle; I did not show emotion or jump up and down in case anything fell off my frozen body.

He apologised to lads that had refused the ordeal, "You will have to complete the run as the lorry is down at the other side of the mountain", and we were off again running down a gentler slope but a longer distance. We all ran faster than the instructors trying to get warm again, and they now found it hard to keep up with us. The lorry took away the RTU´d but our torture was not finished! "You will make your meal and sleep the night in this field"; we dug away the snow and shivered making our meal with army field rations, shivered eating it and shivered all night trying to sleep in our wet kit. Remember I said a cigarette is the best way to get rid of leaches, well I now found another reason for a cigarette. A fellow volunteer offered me a fag and I used it cupping in my hands to try and get the blood circulating in my frozen fingers. It certainly helped so I found the first advantage on health grounds for being a smoker! If your sleeping bag had been dry, it absorbed the water from your wet clothes by the morning but was also wet and smelly. I had removed my boots and socks to empty the water and wring out the socks, but I slept in my wet clothes, in the morning my socks were solid lumps of ice. Can you imagine trying to get them on in the morning? It had been impossible to sleep that night, the longest night of my life and by morning everyone looked like zombies and was still shivering. Lorries arrived and took us back to camp. So went by the first two weeks of hell until the course was reduced to less than half of the original 110 volunteers.

The next two weeks saw individual navigation testing which got harder each day, with more weight to be carried and longer distance to run and march! Marching up mountains and running down, you soon got to dislike, even hate the Black mountains of Wales, it was only liked by sheep and sheep shagging Welshmen who must have shagged the sheep to keep warm. With an 8-figure grid reference you would have to find a tin can with the next grid reference, very much like orienteering but the tins or an instructor were five to ten miles apart. If you met an instructor at a check point he would weigh your bergan, to check you were not cheating by dumping your kit and then tell you to hurry up, as your pace was too slow.

I experienced my first white-out on one day's test, which is snow on the ground, snow falling from white cloud and everything white, the wind blowing the fallen snow and the still falling snow, it was quite an incredible experience, you could imagine you were in heaven but reality made it more like hell. Up a mountain with sheer cliffs on either side is not the ideal situation to come across this climatic condition. Nothing to take a bearing, scary with cliffs to the side of you! I had been sweating and like the rest only wearing army uniform-not the protection needed in these extreme conditions! Now I could only advance slowly and my sweat was starting to freeze. It was not hard to see how men had died on the course. If you stop when you have been sweating and exhausted you could just freeze to death in minutes, and this is where you have to have true grit, bite the bullet and keep moving. My life was now in danger and the only thing I had to rely on was my compass. I literally bumped into another volunteer in the same predicament and another bumped into us two. I shouted: "We will have to work together, we know we are in danger, move forward and I will shout left or right to keep on the bearing and then stop every 10 yards and we will move up to you". This worked and we reached the summit and the descending slope did not have the same dangers with the cliff face, the snow stopped and visibility improved. We had put our lives on the line to pass the SAS course.

You could say not enough safety was provided with shorter check points needed in extreme conditions! A waste of life, men's lives needlessly put at risk as I witnessed with the Paras jumping at the lowest heights possible. In battle I could understand taking the risk, but in training, you had to question the mentality of officers.

The last day was the hardest test and embedded into the

memory of all SAS volunteers. A 60-mile march over ankle-breaking clods of grass, up hills, down hills, round hills, sixty pounds of kit in your bergan, your emergency kit on your belt and your rifle! This was to be down to good map reading, using your brain and finding your tin can with the next reference. Most carried water to make up the weight so you dumped the water out of the check point and filled up before the next check point, just in case an instructor was there. Again the supermen did not need to use the brain and carried the full sixty pounds all the way on the test. Anywhere possible you ran, elsewhere you marched head down, arse up. Yomping was the army expression for this activity, the wind, the rain and cold just added to your discomfort. The bergan rubbed your skin so that it turned into a red weal and then by the end blood seeped from the wound. You do all the check points and on the last one they tell you that the lorry has had to stop five miles down the road and you have to run to catch it before it goes back to Hereford. At this point men jacked in and refused to go on, only to find the lorry around the next corner, they tested you right up to the last final hurdle.

When working with other men under extreme conditions a comradeship develops and respect for each other, as we all knew how tough the course was and how much every individual suffered. The bond stayed even if you got sent to different troops or squadrons. Later when some of these men were wounded or killed, it felt like losing a member of your own family. At weekends we had time to recover. Having a car, I travelled back to Aldershot for a weekend with my wife and child. I soon met a fellow paratrooper, Watty Graham, who also wanted to travel back to Aldershot, so we shared the petrol expenses. I am not normally superstitious but on the way to Aldershot a black cat ran in front of the car. With no chance to avoid it, the car wheels made that bedum bedump sound as I squashed it. After having a good weekend with our families we set out for Hereford and the return journey on Sunday afternoon, the same stretch of road and another black cat, yes, bedum bedump, it had to be a warning!

On my course, the SAS Company sergeant major in charge of selection had been diagnosed with a fatal illness unknown to us on the course. I take my hat off to the man, he did his job till the end, never moaned, never mentioned he was ill and shortly after I finished my course, he died. Most of the men in the SAS had bottle like the SGM and would do anything asked of them, without question, until the end. Unfortunately this type of man can be manipulated by unscrupulous officers and politicians. The dedication would lead to exploitation and that was what I would witness, and I should have taken more as a warning the killing of the black cats!

The escape and evasion course training would be our next test but now the hard part was over, we were now only about to be starved and tortured which was easy compared to what we had just done.

We trained with a mixed bunch, pilots, navy, marines and foreign soldiers doing the escape and evasion course- lectures on how to survive and escape from the enemy! There were personal stories from men that had been captured by an enemy force, men that had escaped from the Germans, the Chinese in the Korean conflict and an American Green Beret officer, who had been one of the longest surviving prisoners in Vietnam. We learned how to read the stars and navigate by them, how to use the sun for navigation, make a compass, make a radio from a razor blade and length of wire: what plants, berries and fungus you could eat, from a sweet old dear that lived just out of Hereford. At the end you were captured and had to endure seventy-two hours of torture to finally pass and get the SAS beret. The same torture given to the IRA, who were awarded money from the criminal compensation board and we volunteered for the same torture! You could only give as under the Geneva Convention your name, rank, date of birth and religion, any more and you failed. The torture was from a special group of men whose identity was not given but to a few, on a need-to-know basis, civilians we were told but I suspected police officers, MI5/MI6. The pilots and other service men only had to withstand twenty-four hours but SAS, seventy-two. The technique used was to take your senses, e.g. a hood to take your sight, ear phones that only transmitted mush from a radio, incoherent sound that deprived you of your normal sense of hearing, cold, hungry, (you were fed slops of waste potato peelings every six hours and a slice of bread), no sleep, placed in physically uncomfortable positions, touching your toes for six hours, leaning spread eagled against a wall, on your knees with your hands behind your head, all for six-hour stints. Then you were interrogated by these men specialised into making you talk and giving information to the enemy! Some men turned into old wives and could not stop gibbering and giving information to the interrogators, the technique worked on most men but not the SAS volunteers. The 'before and after' photos speak for themselves!

Although you were taught a lot on the course, the exercises that followed to put into practice the theory, was a bit of a disappointment and brought doubt into my mind about the professionalism of the organisation. We were put into a wood a few miles from Hereford and told to feed off the land. Now to put us all in the same wood, it was impossible to find enough food so I could not see the merit of the exercise. Thus a few men had stolen some piglets from a local farm and it did not take the farmer much imagination to whom was the guilty party. The exercise was terminated and the farmer was demanding compensation for the most expensive pigs in England. Now the men who stole the pigs did not share the spoil and they ate all in front of us, mouth-watering roasted pig stuffed with apple and mushrooms. When it came to paying, everyone was asked to pay, some of the men were officers on a lot more wages than I earned. Most lads were single but I was married with a young child and I did not agree with everyone paying an equal part. I suggested those that ate the pigs pay for them and I refused to pay a share on principle. A bit of a fall-out with some lads but I would have RTU'd at this stage voluntarily on principle.

We had been told once we had our beret, that parades, bullshit would be in the past. The officers and NCOs would not be pulling rank but would lead by knowledge and experience. I had my beret and was very proud at that stage in my life.

I soon noticed not all the men had the same knowledge as they came from all different units within the Army and were now advancing in a specialised unit, but some had not been taught the basics of infantry work. I can say without prejudice that men, who had done the Para NCO course, had a better understanding than some of the lads in the SAS and I am not just saying that because I had done the course.

Only eight men achieved the SAS Wings from my course of the one hundred and ten volunteers. We returned to our parent units and handed in our kit wearing our SAS wings and grey beret, to end a phase in our careers. We returned to Hereford, with our families, full of expectation on how we would be taught to be one of the best units in the world.

Before the torture: Mixed bag of Special Forces from all over the world at the SAS barracks in Hereford

After the torture: The men who passed the test

'B' Squadron 22 SAS. I am 5th from left back row. With only four Sabre Squadrons in the Regiment you can see we were really under strength, only 47 of these men are SAS.

Chapter 13

South Oman - first combat mission

My wife and I explored the City of Hereford and liked everything about this area of rural England, but it is always hard to move away from friends and in Aldershot we had good friends and neighbours. She soon found that in Hereford even the wives did not talk about what their husbands did and the first question asked from one wife to another was were whether your husband was Regiment attached which was a barrier in making friends. Unfortunately, like the class system, soldiers such as signallers, cooks and drivers were attached to the Regiment and outnumbered actual SAS; they were looked down on and not treated the same.

    The pubs in Hereford did a good trade and the Grapes Bar at the time was the most popular with SAS soldiers, thus a guard was on the door carrying a 9mm Browning pistol. The Irish troubles, the bombings in Aldershot, Guilford and Birmingham, etc heightened security concerns that the IRA would have a go at bombing our camp, even though we were not active in Ireland as an official posting. If you had an Irish accent, asked a local "Where are the SAS barracks?" parked your car in the wrong place, you would be noted and a phone call would soon alert the Ministry of Defence police who protected the camp. Within our camp was a restricted area that was guarded by SAS and even we could not walk about in that area. Nobody talked, they just got on with their jobs and you did not ask questions. It had a bunker that was a communication centre. MI5 and MI6 did there training within the inner circle, so to a new boy like me the security seemed impressive.

    Most Paratroopers would remember well in Aldershot a young woman reporter who seemed to do nothing but sleep with anyone who could tell her a story. Well, drinking down in Hereford and who is there but Mata Hari. I and most ex-Paras instantly recognised her and then pointed her out to other SAS soldiers, not that the lads talked about the job in pubs or in bed. I am sure she managed to fuck a few SAS, but I doubt if she managed to break them into telling about secret missions. There was a formal dance at the barracks, and the lads brought their wives and girlfriends, as did the officers. All heads turned when the Camp security officer walks in and introduces his new girl friend, none other than Mata Hari. The officer did not know why the lads had started to laugh, until the "airborne wart" went over to him and put him in the picture. So you could say we had a crack in security, and women taking their knickers off could beat the best security!

Our holiday over, we started to do our specialist training as SAS troopers. The Unit was broken down into Sabre Squadrons, A, B, D and G Squadron, the last one reserved for men from the Guards Regiments. Paratroopers always refered to the Guardsmen as "planks" or wooden-tops which was not meant to be a compliment, so we assumed that we could not pass the IQ test to get into G Squadron! Within each Squadron they were divided into Troops, boat troop, free-fall troop, mountain troop and mobility troop training in each speciality.

Free-fall troops were skilled in high-level drops needing oxygen so that they could literally fly behind enemy lines; we are talking long distance that even if the enemy picked up the aeroplane on radar they would not believe men could jump out and get behind their lines.

Mountain troop, skilled to a level that a team would attempt climbing Mount Everest, mind you they did not make it and came back with bits of fingers missing due to frost-bite. I never asked with cut-backs in the defence budget did they send them up with the right kit or just army uniform. Don't laugh, it might have been true.

Then there was boat troop who trained in the use of

small boats, swimming, diving, beach assault, river crossing and how to rig up the craft and parachute with them. The Army version of the Navy's Special Boat Squadron, (SBS).

Each troop had an officer in command and a sergeant as second. The sergeants were the experts and the most experienced men within the SAS. The troops were divided into four-man teams, with each man having at least two specialist skills: Morse code operator, medic, or demolitions expert.

Down to work and we all learned to be Morse code operators, decoding and coding messages using a one-time message pad. A simple system with two identical books full of random numbers and each number had a letter, without the book it was (nearly) impossible to break the code, with one at base camp and the other with the active service operator.

We then did a demolition course, making bombs, booby traps, laying mines and finding the little buggers. I only remember the formula "P for plenty" like the IRA use but at the time we did saddle charges for blowing up pipes, shaped charges and all sorts with a calculation to use the right amount of plastic explosive to do the job. Time pencils that you crushed a vial of acid which burnt through a film of metal and then allowed the detonator to go off in a set amount of minutes, giving you time to escape. Electric detonation, trip wirers, light the fuse and run if the enemy find you, you name it they taught it. With practice we all became quite good at demolition and this was all the good stuff I had been expecting to learn and the reason I joined.

Medical lectures which gave you more permission to do life-saving work than any nurse was allowed to do but I stress only in extreme conditions behind enemy lines. Even pulling teeth out which I later did to an Arab who was in a lot of pain, he came back the next day still complaining so I must have pulled the wrong tooth, that's what you get for not wanting to pay a proper dentist. After pulling another tooth he never came back so I must have killed him or cured him!

Getting to Arabs was to be the next adventure in our SAS career, a call to the operations room where we were told that due to a mine blowing up a truck, with a troop of SAS, our training would be interrupted as we were needed as replacements to "B" Squadron a nice way to get a posting. The briefing informed us that in the early 70's the British had helped to dispose of an old tyrant and put his son in power, Qaboos bin Said, of the Arab country called the Oman, British educated and a Sandhurst-trained Officer. Since his rise to power we had been involved in a secret war (that means that you lot were not to know) and we were fighting regular troops from Aden, Omani tribesmen called the Adou, supplied and supported by Russian Special Forces, basically, the same group that had kicked the British Army out from Aden. We had on our side Omani tribesmen loyal to the new Sultan who were called Firqat, a mercenary regular army from Baluchistan trained and led by British-seconded officers and NCOs. In addition to this force but not under our control was a group of Iranian Paratroopers, nearly 3,000 men, American-trained, supplied by the Shah of Iran who was mates with the Sultan. The SAS Squadron whose job it was to train, feed, clothe, and pay the Firqat and give technical support in combat, calling in artillery, mortars and jet aircraft was rotated with another Squadron every four months. The SAS had lost 10% of its men killed and wounded in this secret conflict and "B" Squadron had the most of these casualties!

We now did a crash course in learning 300 Arabic words and off to the ranges to learn how to fire and call in mortar support. Talk about crash course, we had to go to an ammunition bunker and collect thousands of rounds, so many that it filled the 10-ton truck. We had to lie on our backs between the bombs and the canvas roof of the truck. Going down a windy, single track country lane, a young lad from Hereford was taking his girl friend for a quick shag in the countryside, dick between the ears and going too fast, he saw us at the last moment. He skidded, our driver had stopped as he had seen him coming, right into our vehicle's petrol tank, we climbed down to inspect the damage, the boy stuck a fag in his mouth. "Before you light that let me show you what is in the truck" said the sergeant in command. Had the impact been any harder and they would have heard the crash and felt the blast 10 miles away, anything to do with black cats I was thinking.

We were told to tell our wives and girl friends we were going on exercise, playing soldiers! Then we were off flying first to Cyprus with a night stopover, then to Sharsha and then our last hop to Shalala in South Oman. Besides the new boys, a couple of "B" Squadron were returning to the unit after recovering from wounds in earlier fighting with the enemy. It was obvious that the SAS was greatly under strength and that the course was too tough to get enough men to keep the unit at a healthy operational level, as they were sending back injured men the moment they had recovered.

At RAF Akrotiri in Cyprus, a party was going on in the mess hall. We were not invited but gate-crashed anyway. Lots of Brylcream boys and girls, having a merry little party. Girls, we moved in, straight to the bar but only one table with spare seats so we sat down there obviously. It just happened to be the Flight Commander's going away party and who were we now sitting with?, You got it in one. "Have you soldiers been invited?" was the question from an officer of some standing. Then this trooper replies "No we were fucking not, bloody rude of some bastard to leave us out, don't you think?" Then the bombshell. "This is the officers' table and this is the Commanding Officer who is retiring." I'm thinking we are in the shit and had better leave but the old trooper went on the attack. "Well I'm glad I have met you cos I want a few answers from you", and by the tone of his voice he was not going anywhere, so we all stayed and listened in fascination to what he was going to say next. "What rank are you men?" the officer tried to intervene. "SAS and that's all you are allowed to know so be quiet, I want answers from him not his underdog!" We all backed him up by staring direct into their eyes, and they were squirming, uncomfortable, not knowing what to do next; you could see a little fear. "What were you doing sending a crap old plane to pick up our wounded in the Oman? A fucking old plane that could not get high enough to get out of a storm, not equipped for medical evacuation and my mate bled to death because the turbulence opened his internal wounds. You fucking killed him and no excuses as there had been a VC10 available at Sharsha but you did not want to throw the officers and wives off, travelling from Singapore." This officer was having a nightmare and you could see his eyes fill up with tears, he knew he had killed a wounded soldier due to his cock-up. "How did you know about the VC10?" he asked. "Cos two SAS signallers work on the Island relaying messages back to England." No more was said, but at the time I did not put it past the old trooper doing a naughty on the officer, as he had daggers in them eyes! In fact we lost the appetite for enjoying ourselves, as the company was low-life Ruperts. I was learning, don't be frightened to mix it with officers when you are in the right, as they do not want a court martial seeing their incompetence! I was also wondering what back-up we would get in the future from the RAF.

We flew on the next day and met the team working in Sharsha, and they were glad to be able to speak with fellow SAS as it was a very barren and lonely place. We had some time to kill before our onward flight so I went for a walk and a swim with my mate Bromme O'Hare. We came across a memorial on the rocks to the crew of a British merchant vessel in the early 1900's which had been shipwrecked, the crew killed and cannibalised by the local native Arabs. We looked around for Arabs before enjoying a good swim.

Our flight then finally reached Shalala, I looked at the mountain range called the Jebal and then the wide, flat plain that was occupied by our forces. The older lads told us that they literally fought getting off the plane in the early days but now the enemy took to hiding in the mountain range but still fired the odd rocket in the direction of our base camp and airport.

We were met by a Staff Sergeant in charge of stores and base camp, an old hand near retirement. "A meal and up to the rifle range to test our guns, no messing about, you will be choppered out in the morning to meet up with the Squadron. Get some sleep because you might need it, you will be in combat tomorrow". Well, this is why we joined so nobody was complaining. After all the travelling I slept well but it did not seem long before the Staff Sergeant was giving us a call for breakfast, no fucking wonder - it was only 5am. A good breakfast and a good shit and I was ready for anything!

Two Heuy choppers, the type used by the Americans in Vietnam were waiting, up and running, as we walked to the air strip with our rifles and bergans, The sun was just rising, making the Jebel glow a bright orange. I contemplated getting another five minutes sleep in the chopper but the noise of the engine knocked that good idea into touch. The plain and the Jebel both looked very barren, sparse vegetation, sand and rock, it was the summer hot season with temperatures getting up to 40-50 degrees Celsius. We landed on top of a flat ridge, one second you could see it then the chopper blades blew up the dust. "Jump" came a cry from the pilot, a couple of feet off the deck we jumped and the chopper was away. The dust went into the engine filters so he did not want to hang about, we choked on the stuff, fine sand that made your eyes look like road maps. Our new kit now blended in with the desert, we moved out from the landing area and were taken to a hollow area were the squadron were having a briefing of about forty SAS and a couple of Officers from the regular army.

Our objective was to search a wadi for ammunition caches. When it rained in Arab countries, it tended to be a sudden downpour in the mountain areas with as much as 100 litres per square metre, with the ground baked hard it rushed down the wadis with a wall of water that could sweep away anything and anybody that was in the wadi at the time. The water cut out the rock and sand leaving deep ravines and a few caves. As the flash floods could be many years apart, the locals used the caves as homes as they were nomadic tribesmen with goats and camels. Some caves had natural springs of fresh water and when these dried up they would move on to other caves. The caves were known by the tribe in that area but this war was a civil war, with tribesmen for and against the Sultan, so now loyal tribesmen led the way to caves used by the enemy brothers. It was a search-and-destroy mission, trying to find enemy food and ammunition supplies. Us new men were assigned to different troops, but I was then told by the CO that I would take a radio and be assigned to the regular army unit that was backing up the search team with mortars. I'm thinking to myself, I have not got a lot of experience firing mortars and my Arabic was the 300 words that we learnt at Hereford and he is giving me the job as liaision officer. I did not want to complain about my first orders so I played the game. We slowly drove round the ridge a few kilometres to hill 870 which was our firing position. Two trucks filled with bombs and three mortar tubes, 20 Pakis who did not speak English. The officer that had dropped us off had gone with the empty wagons as soon as they were unloaded. He moved out with the trucks so quick I could not question him about the grid reference. Some map - it did not show the derelict buildings near the grid reference I had been given and doing back-bearings to confirm my position, either the map was wrong or I had left my brain in Hereford. The map did not show that the hill had a saddle with two peaks and as the other peak was higher I estimated that as the designated firing point. My worry was that when they called for support fire I would not be dropping the bombs accurately, short or too far from the target, with the possibility of killing my own men, so I was not confident to give the CO the all-clear to fire. One-day's training with mortars at Hereford had not prepared me for this responsibility and I was totally out of my depth. I was hoping that he would ask for fire and record some shots landing, so he had an accurate shot if we were needed to fire in close support. I spoke to the CO on the radio and expressed my concern; there was one of our choppers in the sky so I suggested he confirm with the pilot that my position was correct and accurate. Later I was to find that the maps had been made by aerial photos and were not the ordinance survey quality that we had been used too, in fact lots of errors. I was also told that an SAS mortar team had wiped out a regular Army mortar team under similar circumstances. Bad maps and men situated where they should not have been, ie wrong grid references. I could not see down the wadi as thorn-type bush obscured our vision, but the hill area was very sparse and we could be seen from a long distance but not from the wadi. I dug myself into a shell trench as a good soldier would do and should do. The regulars only put a few stones round them, offering very little protection if we came under fire, so I was a bit surprised about their attitude to the enemy. A sanger was the name used when you put a load of heavy stones around you for protection from incoming fire. You could dig down a couple of feet in the local mountain range, then you more often hit solid rock, so your gun position was finished off with the biggest rocks you could physically move. I suppose we were hunting them and intelligence said they were operating in small groups, so this was the reason for the lack of security and self preservation. An SAS Corporal turned up in my position, sent by the CO. I now felt I had done the wrong thing by putting in doubt the position of the mortar tubes, it was an embarrassment for me as I felt I had let the team down by my inexperience. The day was long and by midday the temperature was over 40. Not being acclimatised I suffered with the heat, so I rigged up my poncho to keep off the burning sun.

I was doing nothing and the sweat was running off me. I was thinking about the lads doing the search, they must be suffering, the wrong time of day still to be searching. It was so hot that the air shimmered and small tornadoes started swirling up clouds of dust and sand.

Later in the afternoon, I heard some bursts of automatic rifle fire and some exchanges on the radio, confirming a contact with the enemy. I was keeping my fingers crossed they would not ask for close mortar support, I had a bad feeling that I would be killing some of our blokes. At 5pm the officer came back with the trucks and by 6pm everyone was back at the starting point and a debriefing started.

My mate Watty got some stick about not giving enough information on a contact report. His search team had been ambushed but fortunately received no casualties; Watty had bullet holes in his bergan which is as close a shave as you ever want! You're not putting your head up at that moment to talk into the radio when you are the target. He like me should not have been given the radio operator job because he did not know the ropes and what was expected, and the map was the same as mine, where the fuck are we? Then as the debrief was coming to an end and last light was setting in, a rubble of heavy explosions, only a couple of kilometres away, made everyone put rifle to hand out of instinct. The CO was on the radio talking to static units out in the Jebel, gathering information on who was getting attacked. Fifteen minutes and the explosions did not cease then as they ended he turned to me and said that was Hill 870, the enemy had just obliterated it, his comments made my Adam's apple go up and down as I swallowed. We had been thrown in at the deep end; you had to question the CO in his decisions of command as at the beginning the first briefing he said we were hunting them. Some fucker had got the wrong information as it took a lot of men to fire that shit we had just heard and here we are sitting in a circle having a debriefing at last light. Another black cat had passed my track!

Fortunately that was the one and only operation before leaving Oman, a quick two weeks that put a lot of doubts in my mind whether I had joined the right outfit, as I had not been impressed. The CO was then removed back to his parent unit RTU'd. and a new officer, Major Snipe, took command of "B" Squadron.

Land Rover groups working in the desert

Chapter 14

Beach Landings, "Drowning Practice", Dying for a shit

At Hereford with the Squadron, the new Squadron Commander Major Snipe takes command. He starts with a 100-mile march, non-stop with full kit, back in that lovely place Wales, the weather and the sheep still looked the same as on the entrance course. Snipe was a runner, a total fitness fanatic and this march was his way of showing the lads who was now in command, what he was made of and how fit he expected the men to be. A few men did not complete the run/march which was bad enough in the eyes of the Boss but an American from the Green Berets was first back to base camp and he sure did not like that. Fitness was to be down to self discipline, maintained by all SAS at a high level and no excuses would be tolerated for dropping out on exercises or marches. Near Hereford camp was a lone hill, if you could run to the top and back without stopping you knew you were in good physical shape, so this was a regular training route for myself and other SAS men.

We were briefed that the role of the SAS was to infiltrate behind enemy lines by stealth and destroy Russian missiles, e.g. Scuds, which could carry nuclear, biological or chemical weapons. The volunteer Territorial SAS, 21 Squadron, had been practicing our role with NATO forces and our Squadron had done very little training in this field due to the small number of men within the regular SAS Regiment. At the time I was in the Regiment it was under 50% of its supposed manpower and the commitment to Oman had left little time to train at the real job as a NATO force. We were now to have some exercises so that we also could work with NATO and practice our main roll in time of war against the Soviet Block. I asked the officer giving the briefing "How far did you have to get away from a Scud missile, so that when you blew it up you were safe from its contents?" He took my question as insubordination and was not amused but I thought my question quite relevant! The trouble with soldiers that have common sense and a brain is that you ask stupid questions that upset officers, especially when they do not know the answer or want to tell you were on a one-way ticket. I was thinking what is the point getting behind enemy lines and destroying missiles, you could detonate your own bomb in England and let the wind bring death to everyone. Why bother with a rocket, stay at home with the family and wait for the fallout in the wind. (I had read the book "On the Beach", written by Neville Shute). As a writer I think he had more knowledge of his subject than most officers or politicians. With all the knowledge of nuclear bombs and contamination, I just could not understand the mentality of these officers who contemplated using nuclear bombs. Mind you, they would be monitoring the situation from safe bunkers; you and I would just be the cannon fodder. Chernobyl had not happened when I was in the Army, but it was a perfect example to illustrate to the officers, politicians and the world that a nuclear war was impossible and if you were downwind you got contaminated!

The first exercise was to be in France and we would be working in small groups with the French Parachute Regiment playing the enemy. Well you will remember I told you that we sent signals back to Hereford using Morse code and the one-time message pad and it was secure. We quickly learned that if the book was captured, that the general drift of messages to one patrol would give enough information that the enemy could calculate the route and objectives of all the groups involved. The radio operator did not have an instant method of destroying the book. Now you would think that someone would have thought up a way to destroy important info before it fell into enemy hands. Amazing as it seems with all the wars that we had been in, we did not have an effective device to destroy secret papers, eg maps, code books etc, when surprised by the enemy. So the French Paras captured one patrol early in the exercise and with the secret code book in their hands they captured nearly every SAS unit operating on the exercise, how embarrassing! My patrol, commanded by a Sergeant Morrel, a Fijian, was captured near its objective. Taken to an old barn as prisoners, they witnessed a French Paratrooper getting tortured, hung up by his thumbs for falling asleep on duty so in a real war what would the French Para do to you as the enemy, when they tortured their own men? I did not get captured and infiltrated the enemy camp which had been the patrol objective. The debriefing that followed the operation was very humiliating and the guy captured with his code book was reduced from Corporal back to a trooper. I thought the point of an exercise was to evaluate and change procedures so that in a real war the same mistakes were not made. What was the sense of punishing a man when in fact he had shown that there was a problem in destroying secret documents?

The exercise was over, we were transported to the French Para barracks for a debriefing but first thing was a good shit and a shower. The toilets had an armed guard who gave you only two pieces of toilet paper as you entered. Apparently so many Paras tried to commit suicide in the toilets that the chains to the cistern were removed and a guard stationed. From what our men had witnessed as normal discipline you could understand the suicide rate. I am still wondering why he had a gun, maybe to shoot anyone who attempt suicide! I was saying to Watty Graham in the next shithouse, obviously they do not write long suicide notes, being a bit short of paper to wipe my arse. "We will never join Europe and come down to this level of ignorant peasants," was another comment to Watty. He gave a long windy fart so I assumed he was in agreement. The French Paras could not hide their contempt for us so in a social gathering in the Sergeants' mess, I had to mention two world wars where the Brits had saved the French. I then asked my

French counterpart, how they had fucked up at Dien Bien Phu, losing all the French Parachute Regiment to the Viet Cong, in Vietnam. I could not let a fuck-up on an exercise take a bearing on past performance.

Assigned to boat troop I had my first exercise with them down at Poole in Dorset, playing with the boats. Our rubber dry suits and Zodiac launches had been in storage so long that most items fell apart as you opened them or tried to get into a dry suit. We eventually found enough dry suits and three boats that were serviceable. Down at Poole at the Royal Marines depot we inflated the boats and put in the duck boards. This was done a couple of times as only three men had ever used an inflatable. The Johnson 40 engines were now the next item to go onboard and get fitted. Again they had not been used for many years and the effort to get them started drew a crowd of Marines as onlookers. They could not hold their laughter as man after man fell exhausted trying to get these things started. I learned later that a can of Cold Start was the magic ingredient to get them going but the Marines were not saying anything to help us dumb fuckers.

I felt less embarrassed when we pulled out of Poole going down river to the open sea. We had our bergans, rifles, full kit, maps, expensive sea compass as we made our way down the coast to practice a beach landing, doing it by day before a practice at night. Four men to a boat, we now looked the part as we moved from deep water to a couple of hundred metres from the beach. I had been a keen canoeist doing white water rapids as a boy soldier and knew about reading water. As we moved closer, the swell of the water, the white tops of the breaking waves, the sound of pebbles being dragged up and down the beach, the undercurrent, alerted me to mission impossible. The Sergeant must have enough experience to know this must be called off, as the conditions were near impossible for experts and we were unpracticed novices. Then the first two men entered the water and started to swim to the beach. They had been ordered to get ashore, do a recce and then flash torches so that the rest of the troop could go ashore with the boats. If they got into swimming difficulty they must raise their hands with a clenched fist so that a boat could go in and rescue them. Good swimmers, the best, but in these conditions they were in big trouble from the start and the fists were soon raised. The sergeant moved his boat with his remaining crewman to the rescue and he was now near where the swell was breaking into a fucking big wave that surf-boarders dream about. He was attempting to pull the men in with his boat broadside to the waves, a wave flicked the boat upside down as if it was a piece of driftwood. My God, the situation was critical and there was no doubt in my mind, these guys did not have a fucking clue! The troop corporal moved his boat into rescue with now four men in trouble and one upturned boat. His boat went bow first to the rescue and had the stern to the breaking waves, the men scrambled in as the next wave swamped the boat and the engine stopped. I did not wait: I moved my boat in close did a quick turn and had my bow facing the oncoming waves. I throttled up and over each wave as they came in but allowed the boat to move close. "Throw a line", I shouted. A fellow trooper made the line secure and I gave it full throttle to pull the swamped boat out of danger. We made it to deep water and managed to bail out the corporal's boat but the engine had given up so we towed the boat, back to Poole harbour. Unfortunately that was not the end of the fiasco as we approached the buoyed channel, well marked to show the safe passage into the harbour, the Sergeant shouts to me,"cut across there it will be quicker". Now the sergeant was in a big hurry as we had lost three rifles and a machine gun in the boat and all that expensive equipment was now getting washed up on the beach! "Sergeant, that's the safe passage over there", I said pointing to the buoys." "Shut up and do what you are told". The shallow rocks are the reason for the white tops but an order is an order in the British Army and bullshit baffles brains. I set course as directed and no sooner was I in amongst the white tops which were hiding shallow water and rocks, we got into trouble. The corporal's boat which I was still towing got lifted by a wave when I was in a trough and his boat landed on top of my boat. The impact knocked a trooper called Frank into the water, so I grabbed his hand out of instinct. The dry suits were an old type with a metal clasp round the neck that clamped the suit with the hood. Unfortunately he did not have the hood on and his dry suit quickly became a wet suit. Full of water and sinking, I could not pull him to safety, as he was now a big balloon of water. I was laughing, this was like a Laurel and Hardy film, I am trying to stop this lad drowning and the rest are trying to push the one boat off the other. We all had a knife strapped to our legs. "Cut the fucking suit" I shouted "you're too heavy to pull into the boat". He only replied "they will make me pay for the suit", "It's your fucking suit or your life you daft cunt!" Yes, his brain twigged and he cut open the old suit. It just happened that a Navy survey ship was moving into harbour, saw we were in trouble and kindly rescued us, thank God for the Navy! At that point they scrapped the night practice. The Sergeant was to busy making a list of all the expensive kit now in Davey Jones locker and I was thinking about black cats! Well that really impressed me being (Kamikaze) boat troop but more was to come.

We rigged up the boats for parachuting out of a Hercules transport C130. Our briefing was that the tailgate would open when the green light came on, push the boat out and quickly jump after it. If you are slow, every second will give you an extra hundred metres to swim to the boat. The first man to the boat only had to climb aboard, pull one toggle and the boat would be released from the parachutes attached. Now this is where fun starts. Pull aboard the parachutes before you sit and start the outboard motor because if you lose them you will have to pay for them and that goes for your personal chutes also, swim with them or you will have the price taken out of your wages. These are new steerable chutes which cost a lot of money, yeh we got the message, don't lose your fucking chute! The first to the boat had to pick up the men still in the water who were last out of the plane as they had a lot of swimming to do especially towing a parachute. Once your feet hit the water hit your release to get out of the parachute, or you might drown getting trapped in the rigging lines, then put on your flippers and start swimming. This was going to be fun and I was not to be disappointed. The new lads got the rear job, last out of the plane and longest distance to swim, me again. The wind was knocking on gale force and no, they did not cancel the jump, so with the wind, the last out, I could only see the boat from a long distance. The steerable parachute needed a jet engine to get me anywhere near where the boat had landed. I was in the hands of the gods and the elements as I descended. The wind took the chute away from me as I landed in the sea, as the rigging lines had been on my mind! The sea had a two-metre swell with white horses on the crest so the first problem was getting my bearing so you knew what direction to start swimming. The chute was like an anchor, so you had to stop and roll it into a ball. From the top of the swell I could see the boat, so I started kicking my legs getting my flippers into action. The drift and current had not been discussed (we were Army not Navy) and that boat was not getting any closer with my legs going top speed. I could only laugh, had I put my flippers on back to front and I had visions of landing in France! I was thinking of all the French I knew to help me with customs, General de Gaulle, cul de sac, Eiffel Tower but fortunately a trooper had landed close to the boat and rescued the rest of us.

The three boats all completed the operation and we set a bearing to meet up with a navy landing craft. All went extremely well and the landing craft lowered its tail for us to climb aboard. Now the two-metre swell meant the landing craft tailgate was in the water, then in the air two metres, returning in the trough with a mighty crash and splash. A commonly-used American word helps me describe this big heavy armour plated tailgate as I sat looking at it going up and down from my rubber Zodiac, (awesome) and in more detail (fucking awesome)! The same guy Frank who had the trouble with the dry suit/wet suit, did not get his timing right and fell off the gate as it lifted in the air, doing a unrehearsed back flip somomersault. "He is dead" I am saying to myself as the gate returns to the water with him directly underneath. He raised his arms at the last second and the gate pushed him down under the water. To me it was another miracle I had witnessed as he surfaced unscathed and he got a grip on my boat as I moved in for him and pulled him clear of the gate. Safely in my boat, I gave it full throttle and went straight up the gate as it hit water again. Now I was begining to realise why so many SAS had drowned on exercise and had their names on the clock tower, I think they should have called these exercises "drowning practice".

If you had read the book Bravo 2 Zero, about the Iraq War, the same troop and Squadron I had served in, their mission had been to destroy Scud missiles and did you note that no officer was with the troop. Did Sergeant McNab know how far to get away after blowing up a missile? Did he ask? Was he a volunteer kamikaze or did he not have the brains to see that he had been sent up the river without a paddle and that his unit was dispensable? Was it just coincidence that the radio frequencies did not work and they had no return ticket? Talk about stealth: his unit went behind enemy lines in a jolly green giant helicopter, the noisiest possible way to announce your arrival. Which idiot officer thought up that method of secretly getting behind enemy lines? He gave information to the enemy which endangered his own men and then he has no shame in telling you a story, that as a ex-professional soldier, I thought he should be hiding his head in shame with the amount of fuck-ups he made. His men were carrying so much kit that they had to make two trips to get it from the landing zone. The explosive devices he had and their kit was captured by the Iraqis, which gave the enemy the information on how many soldiers were in his group, on the ground, working behind enemy lines. Why did he not booby-trap the equipment, seeing he was such an expert with explosives? The arsehole is still writing books telling you a load of crap of how good a soldier he was and how good the SAS are! If he had finished his book properly he should have put in more detail about his debriefing at Hereford, I would have been interested to know if the Officers and Sgt McNab had been disciplined for their actions in that they mounted an operation that was a total disaster from start to finish. The leadership was evidently totally incompetent in this mission but when you read on you may come to the same conclusions when I was in the SAS, if you have not done so already.

The squadron now organised a parachute jump on Salisbury Plain. The drop only takes a couple of minutes but driving to Brize Norton air force base then driving back to Hereford from Salisbury Plain makes a long day sitting on your arse in a 4-ton truck. As a medic with 23 Parachute Field Ambulance we often did cover for a parachute drop. On big drops you were guaranteed casualties, but this was a one-plane job on a nice day. All landed safely and we made our way to the truck that we were to be crammed into like sardines. I noticed the ambulance was empty so, as I had in the past, I decided the time would pass quicker if I got my head down on a comfortable stretcher in the back of the ambulance. Two Sergeants noticed my good idea and ordered me out so they could get the stretchers, so much for not pulling rank in the SAS. Unfortunately the ambulance had a head-on crash with another vehicle and as the two men were fast asleep they could not protect themselves from the impact. They lay with their heads near the driver's cabin which had a metal bulk head; their necks broke instantly with the force they catapulted into the metal. They were two very experienced SAS instructors and it was all over for them in a stupid car crash. I felt guilty as they had copied what I was doing but then I thought the truck could have crashed and would they have felt the same about my fate. If the bullet has your name on it you can not change fate, but to me it was yet another occasion when I felt if there was a God he had something else in mind for me and I was thinking about those black cats again! The driver had to be returned to his parent unit the next day, for his own protection, so I thought to myself, "Better not say anything that it all had been my idea." Does a sketch from Mr Bean come to your mind? Unfortunately this was a really sad event, worse than death, living death and another black cat passed me by.

The Squadron now went further a field for training, a month in the jungle of Malaya and a month with the Australian SAS, at Fremantle near the city of Perth, Australia.

Training to survive in the jungle was interesting and the instructors made it clear that they knew what they were talking about. One of the first SAS books to be published was by one of these instructors a Sgt Lofty Wiseman who did not bullshit and knew his job. Do not smoke; do not wash using soap as the enemy can smell you in the jungle. So I had to ask "Are we allowed to have a shit?" This unit did not see the funny side of my questions, they were all too serious. Anyway a month in the jungle learning to live off the land, getting eaten by creepy crawlies is just a great experience. One night I woke up, to a horrible smell, my fucking arm pit! Moving in the hot humidity of the jungle and constantly sweating and wet, my skin looked like when you have fallen asleep in the bath, all white and wrinkly. When we did come out of the jungle a whole layer of skin just peeled away and more so on my feet and hands as all the callouses and hard skin just rubbed off. I was like a new born baby, with soft white skin. By the way you shit in the jungle an army of ants appear and within 30 minutes they clear the lot away and even lick the paper clean.

A couple of nights on the town in Singapore, then on the aeroplane to Australia and a great welcome was in store for us. This guy comes on the plane and with no explanation he takes out two cans of disinfectant and sprays everyone on the plane, right in the face, it went down really well. Fortunately, after the Australian welcome on the plane which turned out to be the normal procedure for visitors from countries that had diseases or insects that had not yet infected Australia, the camp was paradise compared to ours in Hereford. Right next to a beach and because the local police had no authority over the army, the beach was used by nudists, lots of them and mainly Shielas. The only army unit in the West of Australia, did them boys have a job or a paid holiday?

Boat troop were to be trained on how to dive and place mines on ships. An intensive training course started with all the theory at classes within the camp from a British Special Boat Service (SBS) Sergeant and his Aussie instructors, then by landing craft to Rottnest Island for the practical part. Every night was free to be enjoyed playing with the Sheilas and a good piss up. Now we never realised how racially predjudiced the Aussies were! The Fijian soldiers in our SAS unit were men built like brick shithouses and not to fuck with. This Aussie SAS comes up to us as we are drinking and says "I see you have brought your niggers with you?" Our Fijian hit him so hard he flew back amongst his mates who thought twice about backing him up. Speaking to an Aussie later he tells me that they will not accept blacks because they do not want in Australia what is happening in England, meaning a black invasion with ethnics taking over our English culture. I understood his argument as I am not a do-gooder either. I treat black people with respect but do not consider we should have to change our traditions to accommodate them or have different laws that only protect them! I could not say anything about or against Fijians, as I rated them some of the best men I have ever met in my life and they had no chip on their shoulders about being coloured!

Fighting and theory over, we set sail for this Rottnest Island, famous for its protected animal reserve and a creature called a Woccas, some thing like a rat crossed with a kangaroo. These animals walked in and out of the wooden barracks as if they owned the place but beside the odd shit on the floor they were no problem.

The first dive took place within hours of getting ashore. Watty, although free-fall troop, was on the diving course and we had had a heavy drinking session the night before. I don't know if it was the drink or the travel across in the landing craft, but we both were suffering as we got rigged up for the first dive. You could have called it simultaneous spewing, as we discharged our stomachs into the face mask of the diving gear. We were only in two metres of water, as we came to the surface and emptied our masks. It was up our noses, in our hair. We were choking in spew, not a nice experience. The next day and the second dive some sixty feet below and this diving business was now quite pleasant when you were sober. A third dive and we were catching crayfish, similar to lobster and that night after a drinking session, supper was freshly-boiled crayfish.

The tanks were an old type with a rod on the side that you pulled down which gave you an extra ten minutes air when your bottle was going down. We had been tied to an instructor with a three-metre length of nylon cord and you told him by sign that you had to go up. The instructor's air bottle lasted a lot longer with his experience of breathing under water. In and out the rocks and caves looking for crayfish got us novices all excited and we quickly used up our air supply. My bottle was going empty so I pulled down on the reserve. Odd, my air supply stopped and I pulled on the reserve metal bar again. Still no reserve air supply and I had some how turned off what gasps were still in the main tank. I did not panic, swam to the instructor and gave him the hand signal that I had no air. I put my hand out so he could share his demand valve and go to the surface with me. Had he forgotten the hand signals as he did not give me his mouth piece? I did not panic but removed my mouthpiece to show him my bottle was empty, not even a bubble. He still did not give me his supply. Was this Aussie the one who had been punched by the Fijian? My waiting was over as I shouted, "I'm fucking drowning" and kicked for the surface. Now I was panicking as I had sixty feet to the surface and my lungs were now empty. I do not recommend suicide by drowning as I found it very unpleasant. None other than the SBS Sergeant came to my rescue; he had been the top diver fortunately keeping an eye on his flock of novices. He gave me his mouth piece and if he thought I was going to give it back to him and share the air, he was fucking mistaken. He was gasping for air as we broke surface and then I let him have his fucking mouthpiece. I needed to be helped out of the water, my nose was bleeding and my lungs felt like I had quadruple pneumonia, not double. After five minutes spitting out sea water I recovered and the first question from the SBS guy was why I had not shared the demand valve with him? That was going to be my question! I told him what had happened and he then questioned the Aussie Sergeant instructor. It turned out this Aussie had false teeth and had a strap around his head to keep in his mouthpiece and teeth in. I had to laugh fucking nearly killed by a set of false teeth. The bottle was examined and found to be defective as the reserve bar had a broken swivel that had not been visible before the dive. I dived again that day and for twenty years even in civilian life regularly went diving, but never again tied to someone else. I was getting regular dreams about black cats!

In Australia we had a Squadron to Squadron debrief about our active service to learn about different areas of combat. They started with a debrief about how they had operated in Vietnam with the American Forces. They had only lost four men in the conflict and gave in detail the story of their losses. They had pioneered the technique for abseiling out of helicopters into the jungle, four men jumping simultaneously so that the pilot maintained control of the craft. This technique was practiced in turn by our men and later put into general practice with Special Forces. They also showed us how to get out of the jungle when the enemy was in hot pursuit. They dropped there bergans and in the rear pouch had an American Claymore mine, they rolled out the electric detonating wire and fired it sending the seven hundred ball bearings into the oncoming enemy force. This slowed the enemy, as you can imagine. They got to the RV point to meet the helicopter and the pilot lowered his winch cable into the jungle. They then hooked onto the cable with a mountain karabiner that was attached to their belt and the pilot pulled them to safety through and out of the dense jungle. One man who had died fell from the hook-up but it was never established what was the defect that caused his death as his body was never recovered.

Another soldier had gone out of a circle of soldiers at night to have a common old shit but his modesty of going too far out was the reason for his death. He came back into the circle at a different point and was challenged but forgot the password, and was killed by friendly fire! Was that the meaning of the saying "I'm dying for a shit".

They had been given the role of collecting intelligence from behind enemy lines, finding trails from North to South Vietnam used by the Viet Cong and regular North Vietnamese troops. Later in the war, body counts became important to show the civilians back home in Australia and America that the war was being won with heavy losses inflicted on the enemy. So now the role changed into attacking the enemy by ambushing the trails instead of intelligence gathering. They used electrical detonation of mines (Claymores) and hand grenades to do ambushes from a distance. Several hand grenades (mills bombs) would be strung together, the grenade fuse removed. It was threaded onto a length of coax detonating cable, a knot was tied and this was now in the centre of the grenade instead of the standard fuse and detonator. Several bombs on one ring main with an electrical detonator, gun cotton taped to both ends of the ring cable to guarantee instant explosion and then the command wire was taken back to the detonating command centre. The rings of grenades were placed in the branches of trees and on the ground and carefully camouflaged. The same with Claymore mines, several hundred ball bearings packed with C4 explosive in a plastic case, sighted up and down the trails and the hundred metres of command wire brought back to the firing point. They placed one man up and one down from the ambush position, to count the enemy coming into the ambush, two men in the command post that carried out the detonation. All set and camouflaged, you had now to patiently wait for the enemy to be agreeable and walk into the killing area and this sometimes meant days lying in wait! A problem that occurred in this type of ambush in Vietnam was that the look outs on more than one occasion counted thousands of Vietcong walking past the kill zone and the patrol commander had to think twice about detonation and hoped that they did not see the hand grenades. Small groups of about twenty enemy were the estimated potential for this type of ambush but you had to be suicidal to take on a large force. Pictures of successful ambushes were passed out showing how effective they had been, trophy photos with lots of blood and guts.

The Americans accidentally killed another soldier and another died in a gun fight with the enemy. We all know by now that working with the American cowboys is that they are trigger-happy and can do more damage than any enemy force but they still think they are the best soldiers in the world.

Our Colonel Jeapes now gave them a briefing about our secret war in the Oman. They were astonished to learn that we had seen more active service than them and had lost one tenth of the Regiment killed or wounded. He then told them about winning the enemy over with a hearts and minds campaign to get the enemy to come over to our side. He told them about the attack on a village and how four SAS had stopped a large enemy force, one man, a Fijian, had been shot twice in the chest but still managed to fire his machine gun, killing over twenty men in front of him as he laid wounded with his back against sand bags. The men at base camp had to pack into two available helicopters to fly a rescue mission it was, so overcrowded that some ammunition had to be thrown onto the runway so that the choppers could get off the ground. The enemy retreated with the arrival of reinforcements but they were still a larger force than the defenders and reinforcements combined. The Aussies were impressed and now respected our Fijians as one called Tac was put forward for a Victoria Cross but as the war was secret it was not given to him! The Colonel told a funny story of how an officer had packed the arse of a camel with explosives and had released the constipated animal. They watched it by telescope all day as it moved up into the hills controlled by the enemy. The enemy could not believe their luck as camels are not cheap and were needed to carry supplies from Aden into Oman. Four Adou blocked in the camel on a path and moved in to secure it with a rope; the officer used the radio control to detonate the explosives and killed the enemy. A posthumous medal was suggested for the brave camel but due to possible repercussions by the RSPCA, he only got a mention in dispatches.

We now had a joint exercise in the North of Australia, an army training range the size of England. Talk about Crocodile Dundee, this place had everything, from sharks and seawater crocodiles to deadly poisonous snakes and scorpions. Dried-up river beds with the odd natural deep pool that were full of fish of all descriptions, and with a pin and a bit of fishing line the catch was more than you could eat. Big lizards walked up to the pools and drank not giving you a sideways look; they may have never seen a person and had no fear. Then there were kangaroos and lots of them which were classed as vermin by our Aussie counterparts. We had flown up in a jolly green giant helicopter but motor troop had driven up the hundreds of miles from Perth. One of the lads was telling me he was talking to the Aussie sitting next to him as he was driving, he lent across because of the noisy engine and shouted to the Aussie "I've driven all this way and have never seen a kangaroo" at which point the windscreen was splattered with blood and guts from the first kangaroo he encountered. Well at the time it sounded funny!

    Boat troop had to use two-man canoes and paddled to a small island to lay demolition charges at a mining camp. I still remember jumping out of the canoe at some rocks and climbing up the steep face of the cliff. One of the lads touched my arm and pointed back down at the canoes in the water. The full moon showed the canoes and the large number of sharks that had come to investigate "who is in my water!" Our minds lost a bit of enthusiasm about planting the demolitions and we were thinking "how the fuck are we getting back into the canoes?" The answer was with great care so that you did not tip the canoe, and I have never paddled with my hands so fucked if I was using my hands as shark bait.

    We had a few days to relax and recuperate after the joint exercise. So we did the British soldier thing that was common after war games, public relations experts, playing with the Sheilas and fighting the locals who did not like us reminding them that their grandfathers had been deported. They had English pubs and Aussie bars in Perth with the true Aussie having a chip on the shoulder and not so friendly. One came into our company and explained why the Aussies called us "pongos". Going back in tradition in England, when we had tin baths hung up on the walls, bathing was normally only done once a week, as it had been when I was a boy. Expats held onto this tradition but with the hotter climate and sweating this was not sufficient to stop one smelling. So the name (pongos), where the Brits go the pong goes! I could see his reasoning for the past name, but we now showered as they did and this brave man just had it in his mind to wind us up for a fight. So after the beating I gave him I was sure he would need assistance getting in and out of the bath. Big muscular bronzed guys who drank from little puffy glasses, poured from a litre jug of Swan Lager and not very good at fighting. We just used the litre jug and you could not take the piss out of the lager as it needed all the flavour it had. Now the Sheilas lived up to their reputation, litre for litre they kept up with you, beautiful women who got better with every litre of Swan Lager.

On our return to Hereford we started preparation for a tour of duty in Oman but on a personal note I was saddened that my son hid behind my wife as he was getting accustomed to my absence from home.

Me boat training in a lake near Hereford after sea adventure

SAS Jungle Training Camp

Diver training in Australia

Chapter 15

Four months in Combat

The squadron did the final preparation for combat in the Oman where the enemy was getting pushed back into Aden by the combined forces of Sultan Qaboos. At Hereford we had been allowed 60 bullets each to prepare for war. as cut-backs in the defence budget took priority over our lives! The standard issue rifle the SLR 7.62, was an insult to professional soldiers. The fact that it was joined by a bolt in the centre which allowed movement between the foresight and backsight made it difficult to be an accurate weapon. Many soldiers, even SAS, did not pass the annual test of accuracy because of the basic design faults in the rifle! It was rumoured that it was selected as the main infantry weapon as the Guards Regiments looked smart with it on the parade square, and as bullshit baffles brains in the Army, I did not doubt it was the real reason. The toy soldiers just do not look the part with a short compact, accurate rifle!

In Oman, outposts had been established and a fortified line consisting of a barbed wire fence and minefield had now been positioned the length of the border making it difficult for the enemy to get reinforcements, ammunition and food. The Adou were now being won over by the "hearts and minds" campaign, amnesty and gifts of money to change their loyalty. They were given work with the Sultan's forces, food, clothing and our respect for the Muslim religion, all won over the enemy. Woman being equal in the communist-led forces had not gone down well with the macho Arab enemy camp or with the Muslim religion and it had caused discontent. Now a reward system to hand over hidden supply dumps made some of the enemy very wealthy men. We would go out with them and dig up oil barrels full of weapons and ammunition which we manifested and then destroyed. In some dumps, the weapons could be brought back and used again, a lot depending on the terrain in which they had been concealed. In one Wadi a cache of British-made 7.62mm ammunition was found, so much that it had to blown up on the spot; but maybe the real reason for its destruction was that it was embarrassing. Combined with the serial numbers and date of manufacture, it could be proved our Government was selling weapons to countries which would in turn give it to an enemy force fighting and killing British soldiers. We would practice with many of the weapons captured, I fired quite a few RPG7 anti-tank rockets at old armoured personnel carriers; I found them very effective in punching a hole into most armour. They would ricochet off sloping armour so they had to hit your vehicle on a flat side to penetrate the amour plating. They self-exploded at about 800 metres, they had been designed to do this with an added shrapnel belt to engage infantry at that distance. The sight also had a built-in range-finder with a graph which estimated the distance, taking into account the average height of a NATO tank, all simple but clever stuff. In using captured weapons and ammunition we were able to practice to a better standard, thank God for the enemy to help us, as our politicians certainly did not and they still make cuts which jeopardise the lives of our men at the front line. Within a short time of arriving in the Oman most of the Squadron changed their SLR (Self Loading Rifles) weapons. Some now carried German made Hecklcock rifles; others American Armalite M16s or Russian AK47s. I carried an American M16 mainly for the reason I could hit a target with an accuracy that impressed me and the ammunition was lighter so I could carry more going into battle. The Firqat tribesmen were given Belgian FN 7.62 rifles which fired single shots or automatic fire, the basic design was the same as the SLR which could not fire automatically. When in battle I witnessed an Arab fire on automatic, his stance was his main downfall; not spreading his legs, not leaning forward, not holding the weapon tight. The power of the rifle just had him going backwards in a 180 degree arc of fire, wanker! The tribesmen were also not impressed by their issued weapon either and started to carry the Russian AK 47s.

We operated in our four man teams allocated to different tribes to do the 'hearts and minds' campaign. We gave them wages, food, clothing and brought in other supplies such as timber and corrugated sheeting so they could build shelters. We even gave them a film show once a week. It made us laugh as when they saw kissing or naked women they would start to giggle like naughty little boys, then, in an action film they would get all excited. On showing the film Zulu, with 3,000 Zulu warriors attacking a small force of British at Rorke's Drift, our Arabs started to help by shooting the Zulus, soon the white sheets that were used for the screen burst into flames amid laughing and cheering. A message was sent to base camp explaining all the shooting. 3,000 Zulus had been wiped out at Rorkes Drift with the help of many AK47 assault rifles!

The tribes literally lived in caves near natural water sources before our arrival and the establishment of Sultan Qaboos. The new reforms he introduced improved the lives of all Omanis. Originally the water was collected by the women using goatskin bags, often with a long trek to its source. We brought in pumps, pipelines and water storage tanks; they had never had it so good. Most had never seen a doctor or had medical treatment, which surprised me with a country in the 20th Century. The Sultan changed all that in just a few years, so he also won over his people like a true and uncorrupted leader.

I was the camp medic with one team and soon found that the locals quickly reacted to medical treatment, in fact you had to give them half the dose recommended because their bodies had a good immune system that had not be affected by excessive medication or prolonged use of antibiotics.

An Arab came to my tent not feeling well so I gave him an examination. His eyes were jaundiced yellow and with rotting teeth all due to the diet of goat, camel, rice and very few greens. I gave him an injection of multi-vitamins and tried in my best Arabic telling him to eat more fish and greens. He came back the next day like a hyper-active kid, demanding another injection. He got over to me that that night he had managed to fuck all his three wives and was amazed by his new virility brought on by this medicine called "vitamins". As I had a limited supply I refused more injections but then he produced a wad of notes and I thought why should I stop this man's fun? The next day he had passed the word around and I had a line of Arabs for sick parade, all wanting this expensive drug called "vitamins". When a woman was ill with the same dietary problems I wanted to give her an injection. Her husband hovered over me and allowed her to rearrange several skirts that she wore, she gave me a little square of bare skin to aim my needle. I just hoped I would not hit her nerve as they were not going to let me see any more. I did not find out if it improved her sex life.

Twice a week a plane would land and bring in supplies and I borrowed a Land Rover from the Arabs to collect them. The so called road could only be managed in four-wheel drive with low ratio gears. On the return run which was only a few hundred yards, I could hear this knocking from the engine and with a bang, a piston blew out of the engine casing, hit the ground and flew into the air. The Rover did not have four thousand miles on the clock but Arabs do not bother with such things as oil or maintenance. The same happened to all the water pumps, within a short time they all burnt out. "Oil - what's oil?" and the country has millions of barrels under ground.

The only other transport in the camp was a dumper truck, so for the next flight I was sent down in this and gave my leg a good lump (the starting handle swung back and hit me) so I was not in a good frame of mind. A Jordanian soldier walked off the plane, apparently sent out to help our Arabs and listen to their moans and groans. They would confide better to a fellow Arab was the theory from base camp. I loaded up the dumper and set out up the hill, the Jordanian was still walking and had not helped me load up the dumper. What a cheek, he jumped in front of me, hand raised trying to stop me to bum a lift. I pressed on the brake and my foot went to the floor (no brake) "Get out the fucking way!" (could not translate the phrase into Arabic) and I made gestures with my arm, to warn him. What is Arabic for "get out the fucking way you daft bastard"? My only way to stop killing the Jordanian, now going downhill, was to pull the lever that dropped the bucket and all the supplies, and then he had the nerve to start screaming and shouting at me for nearly killing him!

Our team returned to base camp for an operation to find and destroy an enemy base that had been located due to information from an Adou collecting his money and amnesty. About half the Squadron took part in the sweep on the enemy base but they had seen us coming and had managed to escape. A large natural cave had given refuge to the enemy group, we combed the area, and then I heard this crack under my foot. I though "Shit I have stepped on a mine", so I got my bayonet out and probed under my boot. A plastic syringe had given me the fright and I uncovered loads of used dressings and packaging from medicines. Obviously the enemy was doing the "hearts and minds" routine also and this camp was situated less than a mile from one of ours. I wondered if they were going from one medic to another getting a second opinion, but I am sure of one thing the enemy medic did not have a supply of "vitamins".

One member of the Adou who was given a de-brief after surrendering to our side, revealed that he had been sent to Russia for his training. He was on a political cadre, the ins and outs of communism and how to bring down a western bourgeois, capitalist regime. The teacher was pleased to inform the class that his star pupil, picture hanging on the wall, was none other than Arthur Scargill. I need to ask Arthur if he was telling the truth, or had the Arab found an issue of the miners union monthly printed in Arabic, to know his name!

Back up the hill with another team and this time I was the one-man 81mm mortar team as by now I had practiced with the weapon and was very proficient using it. I was to aim, prepare the bombs, fire the bombs and command the mortar which was normally a three-man job. Another man had a 50-calibre machine gun and another a 30-calibre, the Sergeant would be the radio operator and command fire at the enemy. As the evening closed, just before last light, we would all fire the weapons to show the enemy our fire-power. It was like the American July 4th celebrations with every man in the camp letting rip with a magazine from their rifles, tracer bullets flew in a deadly 360 degree arc out from our defensive position and I sent out at least 20 bombs from the 81mm mortar tube. Then after the fireworks display we would clean the weapons, and then get our heads down for the night or chat in the command centre. Night-time was boring so I would often turn on the radio and flick through the frequencies. I picked up messages from oil rigs, once a radio station in Australia which was a freak condition with radio waves bouncing round the world, the military did not make sets to tune into local or commercial radios as they use different frequencies. Then one night, a real SOS message which was a shock to hear, s.o.s s.o.s (save our souls). A group of SAS had been to North Oman for some rest and recuperation as the conflict had not reached that area. On return to the South the front Land Rover had gone over a mine, seriously injuring the driver and to my dismay and horror it turned out to be Bromme O'Hare, a friend and fellow comrade on my SAS training. The serious injury to his foot got him a medical discharge from the Army, a good soldier who would be missed by all. I did mention to him that his dick would get him into trouble one day as often I had gone out with him and anything in a skirt was fair game. After months in the Oman the camels and goats started to look pretty, so the few white women whose husbands worked on oil rigs were the centre of attraction up in the northern towns of Oman. I did not have to relay the message as base camp had the signal stronger than me; they dispatched helicopters and medics to the convoy.

The teams did a lot of patrolling within the tribal areas, mainly checking water-holes as water was a precious commodity that the enemy needed working behind enemy lines. We searched for their supplies and set up ambushes with information of enemy sightings given by the tribes. Our positions were mainly fired on at last light because we could call in air support and by morning they were long gone and in hiding. The trouble with working with different groups of soldiers and tribes, was that the uniform was very similar to what the enemy wore. On one occasion an SAS team and a Firqat group saw over a hundred men who appeared to be wearing regular army uniform, so they waved to them. The enemy saw white men, who stood out from Arabs, and attacked. A fierce gun-fight had dead and wounded on both sides and although out-numbered the team was able to call in artillery fire and air support. Later, a couple of armoured vehicles helped the withdrawal and the evacuation of our wounded. This support, from what we term heavy weapons, made all the difference in this war, as to group a large force was suicidal for the enemy.

Another problem I had at night besides boredom was that my sanger was infested with rats which would run over me and keep waking me. I solved the problem by putting a packet of biscuits under my sleeping frame. It makes me laugh how well prisoners are treated in England; they would have gone on hunger strike if they had to endure our conditions. We did get a rum ration which helped me sleep; a Fijian showed me how to melt down sweets from our Army food rations, add a tin of fruit, and then a simple but tasty rum punch. I soon got into the habit of watching the sun go down with my rum punch.

I was talking to an SAS Corporal one night and he told me a story that fascinated me. He was not the type to bullshit and the detail of his story was such that I did not doubt what he was saying. He had been sent to Northern Ireland, when General Harry Tuzo was the General Commanding Northern Ireland, with orders to execute a leading member of a Protestant Paramilitary organization. His back-up unfortunately was a crap hat patrol that was in the area to rush to his assistance if needed. He broke in by the rear of the house, set himself up in the bedroom and waited for the target. He was armed with an SMG sub machine gun, that fired single shot or automatic fire. This gun had been fitted with a silencer, not your standard issue. He had waited a few hours when he heard the front door open and movement downstairs. The target started to climb the stairs towards the bedroom and he prepared to fire. The intended target, for some reason, hesitated at the bedroom door and opened it slowly but sensed something was wrong! He quickly tried to close the door and the Corporal did not hesitate in firing. It was not a clear shot, (firing at a reducing angle), as he pulled the door shut and the actual rounds that hit him were the shots that penetrated the door. He screamed as the four single shots hit him in the face, but fortunately for him they did not penetrate into his brain and he ran down the stairs and out of the house before another shot could be fired. His screams brought the back-up patrol running to help the Corporal who met them at the front gate of the man's house. The distance now made the SMG useless, as it was a close-combat weapon."Shoot him!" he ordered the patrol who had standard army issue SLRs, as they had a longer range, up to 300 metres. The screams of the wounded man brought witnesses and nobody dared fire having their green cards. The wounded man made his escape and told his story to the police who then investigated the incident and arrested the SAS Corporal. He was charged with attempted murder and held in police cells. The SMG was not a powerful weapon but with the silencer and then the bullets going through the door, the velocity was greatly reduced. Hitting a Paddy in the head, say no more. The powers-that-be found it all very embarrassing as the SAS were not supposed to be in Ireland and General Tuzo had not been informed of the operation to carry out an act of assassination, and with it "State Terrorism". The Corporal went in front of a judge who asked him if he had been cautioned by the police, he had been told by an officer to say "NO" and the case was dismissed. Questions about the special weapon and the Soldier's unit caused the General to order the SAS operations out of Northern Ireland while he was in command. I did not think this man had any reason to invent the story he had just told me.A few weeks after hearing the Corporal's story, the SAS were sent to Northern Ireland with publicity in all the papers and television.

    I was talking with a couple of lads having lunch, army rations, I finished my meal and was moving back to my sanger to clean my teeth. A young Arab was talking to the Sergeant and Cpl Cooper as I walked passed them. A few yards further and near my sanger, I heard a weapon being cocked. I turned and saw the Arab pointing his AK47 weapon. I could not understand enough Arabic to follow the shouting from this man, but you do not need to know the language. The voice was raised enough to know this lad was not a happy Arab. I walked into my sanger, put my rifle under the blankets, and cocked the M16 so the Arab would not get excited on hearing the sound. I went back out and took aim; this guy had the drop on all the team, a trooper was making steps to his rifle each time the intense conversation got the Arab's eye away from him. I could kill him but things went through my mind; if I shoot he could pull the trigger just out of a death reaction with nerves twitching. I moved my aim to the rifle but that would be a harder shot, I moved my aim to his head and took a squeeze on the trigger, I was calculating the situation, then I thought this friendly Arab had a hundred mates a few yards from our camp within the main camp! He was shouting, but time had passed, and I could hear the sergeant still talking obviously trying to calm the situation. When the talking stopped would be the time for me to fire, so that made me hold from the final squeeze. I purposely coughed so he would know I was there and he would die the moment he pressed the trigger. He then started to back out of our position and I moved back with the team, "What was his problem?" I asked. He wanted some new socks, and he acted like that for a pair of socks! He then fired a shot over our base to remind the Sergeant about the socks. No wonder we were making a fortified camp within the friendly Arab camp. This particular Arab Firqat unit had been on the enemy side and some still were undecided about which side to be on!

Colonel Jeapes then arrived in the Oman for a briefing with all members of "B" Squadron. He turned up by helicopter to all the teams out in the Jebel, visiting all locations. He arrived at our position and asked us all to sit around for a briefing. "You have heard about our new theatre in Northern Ireland, well when you finish here you will have a month's holiday and then be sent to Ireland for six months". No one was impressed with the statement as most of us had served with our parent Regiments/Corps in Ireland and after four months in the Oman, then six in Ireland it was asking a lot from any unit. In a major world war you could expect to be away from home, fighting for your country and family, but Oman and Northern Ireland did not give me the feeling, or many other soldiers, that we were risking our lives for a good cause or one worth dying for. In any conflict you need to know that the nation is behind you as it was in the Falklands War, to motivate and give moral support to soldiers. The country was not united over the Ireland conflict and this war in the Oman was so dirty it was carried out under strict secrecy.

Jeapes starts knocking the Parachute Regiment and their behaviour on Bloody Sunday which did not go down well with me or another trooper being both ex Para. The Parachute Regiment had always been sent to the toughest areas of Northern Ireland, had killed and captured more terrorists, weapons and ammunition than any other Unit, so this officer who had never served in Northern Ireland did not have the right to his conclusions. Once a Para always a Para and we did not like any crap hats, SAS included, insulting our parent Regiment.

"You will be given a list of IRA and you will kill them. If they put up their hands to stop a bus that is sufficient reason, I want them dead". Heavy stuff. He made it very clear that we would not be issued a green card and he had ordered the "shoot to kill policy" which even today is denied by our Government. Soldiers like myself, who had seen first hand the atrocities of the IRA, initially liked what he was saying, justice at last to the IRA bastards. Then the corporal who had been the first to attempt an execution in Ireland asked the question "Would we be backed up if anything went wrong?"

I understood his reasoning, as nothing the Colonel was saying would be put in writing. How did we stand if we accidentally killed the wrong man? Accidents do happen! Who would be making the list, the same incompetent secret service, and the bigoted, biased police? You could just imagine someone making a death list, with that power, why not put someone on it that has been fucking your wife, where does political killing stop, and why not put on a few trade union leaders? "Nothing to worry about our orders have come from the top and I mean the top." He did not mention a name, but the way he put it over we took it to be the Prime Minister! At this point his briefing was interrupted by a coded message that started to arrive and I decoded it. An officer had captured the number 3 on the list and was informing the Colonel that the prisoner was a Sean McKenna and that he had been handed over to the RUC and I think he was looking for a pat on the back from the Colonel. Totally the opposite-he blew a fuse, ranted and raved, "I told them I wanted them dead not taken prisoner. Take a message and code it back to Hereford. You have not carried out your orders and this will be noted on your military record." This brought back memories of how I had been treated by Major Burke, so I knew how this man would be feeling when he got this message. A man doing his job at the front line, a soldier, not a murder and the Colonel was going to finish his career!

The next man whose name was on the list was caught by an officer commanding a four man team was executed, as ordered. His men were sent to each corner of a field so there would be no witness and then the suspected IRA man was shot a few times, twenty if I remember correctly, as the unarmed prisoner tried to escape by attacking the officer. (using minimum violence which could be interpreted which way a judge was guided by his political or Freemason leaders). Yes, he then faced a murder charge from the police but he had protection as this was a "STATE" execution, the officer was protected in the court and found not guilty. The man executed was Peter Cleary on the 15th April 1976! He would be the first of many and so as not to complicate these orders of State Terrorism, Jeapes would be promoted and become General Officer Commanding Northern Ireland, top dog, licensed to kill. Then our Government sends to prison for life, Corporal Lee Clegg of the 2nd Battalion Parachute Regiment for killing a woman in a stolen car, for crashing through a road checkpoint, to show the world we did not have a shoot to kill policy in Ireland. It's funny how the British system protects Army Officers and the Police who order killings or carry out illegal execution but lower ranks in the army do not get afforded this protection. Not in the right circle! A political prisoner, Clegg would serve a few years in jail. Pressure by serving and none serving ex Para's helped to release him. I personally sent a letter to him offering to give evidence about the shoot to kill policy of the British Government.

Now the reason I had not killed Gerry Adams that day

was that I had not found any weapon and did not think that the shit was worth spending 20 years in jail for, a life sentence. The system protected him, the police had been incompetent and had not done their job. Adams was guilty in as much as he was part of the kill team and then the bastard has the cheek to write about it in his memoirs. I agreed that the system did not have a punishment to fit the crimes they were committing, but doing the same as them in cold blood was bringing our Regiment to the level of the IRA. Caught in the act with a gun, I could kill and live with it on my conscience, but asking me to murder in cold blood, I was not up to that. I could not now serve in the SAS with these orders. It was officers and arse-licking soldiers who carried out General Pinochet's ruthless regime in Argentina, and here we were taking lessons from the murdering bastard. Is that why our Prime Minister was so friendly with him when arrested in England? Could British Officers and Special Forces do similar crimes, like throwing prisoners from the rear of an aeroplane, still alive? Men and women falling to their deaths to land on water with such a force that it split their bodies open? British Prime Ministers can shake hands with the likes of Gerry Adams and Pinochet, knowing the crimes they have committed. Being poorly educated must be the reason I do not understand, as to me a spade is a spade.

In the Oman, I did a silly thing and confided, a Cpl Dave Wohersky that I was a dissident and would be purchasing my discharge from the Army on return to Hereford. I was instantly an outcast for not being one of the sheep and I did not realise that I had put my life in danger. One day I decided to look down the water hole that I was told was an underground lake made by a volcano. Two groups, (eight SAS men) were in the camp and the area was protected with a large friendly Arab force so I told Worhersky that I was going down to explore this crater. The track was difficult and I slowly made my way down. Women had filled goatskins and done the journey daily but now the pump was installed and running, so nobody else was on the track. I estimated I was halfway down when the crack of a rifle echoed down the hole and the bullet just missed my head. I took cover and aimed my rifle back to the rim. The sun was in my eyes and a heat haze around the rim made it impossible to pick out the gunman. I waited for my SAS team to come running to investigate the shooting but after five minutes no one appeared. I moved my position and skirmished all the way back to the rim of the crater and then entered the team bunker, nobody looked up, some were cleaning rifles, Dave Wohersky had his rifle stripped down, someone had tried to kill me and nobody heard or saw anything.

The next day I was transferred to base camp by helicopter and was told to report to Major Snipe. He had been informed that I was bad for morale and should be RTU'd which was the biggest insult to an SAS trooper, I protested, yes I want to purchase my discharge but why send me back when I am prepared to serve to the end of my tour? He said he would think it over and inform me of his decision. I was fuming that I had been shopped to the OC by this Corporal Wohersky and went for a drink to get pissed. I could not imagine they would try and kill me in the base camp. In the camp bar a couple of lads were having a drink and one was Kevin Walsh, the "airborne wart" and the other was one of the cooks, so we got talking and drinking. The cook was upset as he had reported the day before that one of the Paki cleaners was nicking food from the rations store and today they had cut his hand off. He then said he was not even 100% sure that it had been him, so now he was getting pissed out of remorse for what his loose tongue had done to the poor Paki. In the end, with the drink, I told Kevin that I was the nurse in charge of him at Netley when he was a mental patient and he was the reason I had joined the SAS. What drink does to loosen the tongue! I never wanted to say anything but we were all on a downer and I told him of my problems with the CO and how I had been reported by

Wahersky. He was not a lover of Wahersky and he put me in the picture about him and the reason he also did not like him. It only turned out that Wahersky had joined from the TA and was an arse-licker, to such an extent Kevin revealed that he had had several accidental discharges, nearly killing people in the process. Normally and especially in the Paras, you would be reduced to the ranks if an NCO. A private would do thirty days prison but this guy was into the officers' arses so much that he was never punished and had not one but several accidental discharges-some professional soldier!

Kevin Walsh said leave it with me and I will sort things out with Major Snipe. Next day Major Snipe told me I was now under his command and ordered me to drive a ten-ton truck to his out post in the mountains. I had never driven a lorry in my life so I had kangaroo petrol in the tank to start with till I got the hang of driving it. I was just getting into driving it well when I was told to take a dirt track and the kangaroo action started again till I mastered the technique of this difficult route that was full of deep potholes and boulders. I found out when I arrived that the track was often mined and the rest of the team were sitting on sandbags in the rear for that reason. "Is this what they did to people who were dissidents in the SAS?" I was thinking. Yes, I was getting a complex and dreaming about black cats.

This camp was to be fortified with an SAS inner camp, so the work started immediately. The barren area had very little topsoil so then we encountered hard rock which we worked on with picks and sledgehammers. It took all day in the blazing sun and we only managed to get down to our knees. A request was sent down for some Bee Hive charges, a shaped explosive charge designed for sending the force of the explosion down, to break open a concrete bunker, mine clearing, but also was effective against solid rock. A helicopter arrived with supplies and our requested explosives. Kevin set up and detonated the first charge which did the job and cracked up layers of once solid rock. We got down to our waists before running into solid rock again. Our Arabs had been building their own shelters and to them it was too much hard work to dig so they just made positions on the surface. Kevin set up another charge and warned everyone to take cover, the Arabs in their new bunkers. This time some rock flew into the air and one piece landed on an Arab position, so badly constructed, that it went through the roof landing on an Arabs head! The Arabs, screaming with excitement, sent us running to their flimsy shelter to find out what had happened. None other than the macho leader, and he was in hysterics about the blood running down his face. He needed a few stitches so I set about to fix the wound. I was giving him an injection to stop infection when this tough Arab fainted and his mates got so excited they demand we call in a medical helicopter and take him to hospital, so to keep them happy the chopper was requested. Kevin and I went as escort, so I was to get another couple of days down at base camp. In base I met my mate the civilian, we did a bit of fishing. I was glad to get out of the company of my comrades, we had a few day's fishing and diving for crayfish which helped me to relax. The crayfish were on a shelf and so plentiful it was like being in a supermarket, selecting the biggest and the best. The sharks did not bother us and there plenty of them in these waters but the big Moray eels would swim up to us and take the crayfish from our hands. You took one look at the teeth and did not argue, I was in his terrain and he was the boss, nice little eel you can have my crayfish! I felt safer with the eels and sharks but I only had to last out a few more weeks to get out of this unit and the army.

  A sergeant from the Royal Engineers was at base camp, having arrived from England to help with some construction for the Arabs. An officer was also with him and they went to the armoury to get some explosives for their work. In the armoury the officer had asked the sergeant how they set trip flares, so he unpacked one to show him! Incredible as it sounds, the sergeant removed the safety pin and he accidentally dropped it-right in the box packed with other flares. They panicked and ran out, slamming the armoury metal door behind them. It took several days for all the exploding ammunition to stop. It was very embarrassing for the both of them. The system protects Officers, so no action was taken against the pair, but they were sent out to the Jebel. So now Kevin and I had the Sergeant with us as a new addition to the team as we flew back to our encampment.

Our position was now complete, we had a area within the main camp secure from the enemy and any Arab on our side that wanted a pair of socks. The engineer built a water-storage tank, showers and a few other things to improve conditions, and with nothing else to do I helped him!

I would train every day by running around the main camp perimeter and other lads did press-ups and sit-ups to keep in form. For hours I would run to kill time, and think what I would do in the future, out of the Army. A message came into camp, that the Major was organising a marathon run to raise money, to help buy paraplegic bungalows in Hereford, for men that had been shot and paralysed, as well as for the two Sargeants that had saved me by ordering me out of the ambulance. I was more than happy to try and raise money by doing this sponsored run, so my training around the camp had not been for nothing. Men who had been in positions where they could not do physical training were going to suffer, as we had now done over three months of our tour. In base camp Snipe had been training daily so it was no wonder that he came in first and then had the cheek to badmouth men for not being fit enough to complete the run. The good thing was a lot of money was raised and some civilian Companies that had large multi-million pound contracts to construct roads and a port, added to the fund. Taylor Woodrow and Air Works had to be thanked. Mind you, if we had not been defeating the enemy, they would not have a contract, as these big contracts were the

Government would commit and sacrifice our unit. Yet here we were, begging for money to build houses for paraplegics!

That night a big party was organised by the civilian companies and the drink and food was the best and plentiful. CO Snipe did a walk around to talk with most of the men and guests. I was with my friend from Air Works when he stopped to talk with us and seeing I had nothing to lose by saying what I thought, I asked him why he had not taken the serials numbers from the captured British manufactured ammunition and sent a bill to them for the much needed houses! What a reaction! "Say another word and I will have you out on the next plane to England." I must have hit a nerve!

The next day we were flown back up the Jebel to look after our flock of Arabs again. For some reason, Kevin Walsh was ordered to send our team down a slope that offered no protection, if we made contact with the enemy. An enemy force was suspected to be down in the wadi and we were the bait to draw the fire. With someone trying to kill me, I was not a happy Geordie. The couple of lads with me were also against this suicide mission. What his intention was I don't know, but Kevin never left the safety of his bunker and now I was becoming more of a dissident by saying what I thought. I had nothing happy to say about being made live bait for the enemy to shoot at. I was now a lone wolf and would look after myself till I was out of this man's Army. As it was afternoon, the enemy must have been having their siesta and I lived to be the bait another day.

My accommodation in Oman

Me on the Jebel

Me running a marathon in the Omanian Desert

Chapter 16

Attack on the Sherishitti Caves

The Officer was called Neil Lawson, and he was about to die. It would be his decision. Unfortunately his men did not have the same choice, they had to carry out his orders. He was a British training officer attached to Sultan Qaboo's regular Army. On the day of his death he was working as a platoon commander. He had been in the briefing with the rest of the British officers and the SAS taking part in the attack on the Sherishitti caves. Had the information gone in one ear and straight out the other, was there a hollow gap in between, did he have delusions of being another Lawrence of Arabia or was he just a Rupert?

"B" squadron SAS were arriving in base camp ready to fly home the next day and the advance elements of "D" Squadron had been in the process of taking over. As the helicopters brought in the four-man teams, you could see the chopper arrive, then an incredible dust bowl. As the dust cleared after the chopper had departed, only the team was left. Faces covered with Arab headdress their only protection, but that fine dust found access in every part of the human anatomy. Your eyes looked like road maps, nose hair was more prominent and a good fart was the only way to get it out of your arse. The only way to protect your weapon and I mean your rifle, was to roll on a condom and if AIDS was desert dust you would have no chance to escape. We had been met by the quartermaster. "Dump your gear in my office and debrief in the bar." No argument about that order; the "Boss", Major Snipe, was handing out the beer as we entered. Other teams had arrived earlier, with the same welcome, and looking at the cans on the table, they were getting a shower inside out. "Relax today and hand over your kit in the morning," was the pleasant order from the "Boss". If that was an order to get pissed, every man was doing his job and some men had already won a medal. The base camp personnel stayed sober and the advance group from "D" Squadron had to learn to be teetotal, since arriving from Hereford. I had downed a good few pints and now suffered the after-affects, I somehow bounced off a few walls and managed to get to the mess hut and downed a bit of grub, then found the first vacant bed. I knew my limit but some of the guys had no limit.

God, 5.30 a.m. and some cunt is shouting "Everyone to the briefing room or mess hall, same place." Major Snipe and the General in charge of the Sultan's regular army were there with maps and drawings. "For fuck's sake what is going on?" I said to one of the lads. Hot coffee was being handed out, thank God, as I must have snored my head off during the night and my throat felt as rough as a badger's arse. If I looked and felt like shit you should have seen some of the other poor bastards, rough; a gathering of Alcoholic's Anonymous, eyes like piss holes in the snow.

The General started; unfortunately a British officer attached to the Iranian Parachute Regiment was overheard in the officer's mess, criticising how the Adou had managed to inflict heavy losses on the Parachute unit. The Shah of Iran was an ally to the new Sultan Qaboos and had sent 3,000 of his best paratroopers to fight against the communist Adou. They had sent in a battalion to attack the Sherrishitti Caves which was the main supply base for the Adou. They had hit the area using heavy artillery, also using a navy destroyer just off the coast to give the enemy a good pasting. A Navy gun was able to fire at a much faster rate than a battery of Army guns due to computers and automatic loading and firing mechanism. With helicopter gunships constantly giving top cover they had advanced to Hill 830 near to the caves, and then made sangers to rest for the night before the final assault. When the artillery fire stopped, the Adou had come out of their caves unscathed and counter-attacked. It had been near last light and the gun ships had returned to base: known as Midway airfield. The Yanks trained the Iranian Army so I assume some connection with the name of the base, which had every conceivable item for war and comfort, so it had to be American!

The Adou had used mortars to keep down the heads of the Iranian paratroopers; the Adou fighters had followed in with the barrage close behind, so brave to be so close to their exploding mortar bombs. They were at the top of the sangers before the paratroopers had time to see what was happening and then it was too late. They had wiped out the first platoon of Iranians still crouching down in their sangers. There was no love lost between Iranians (Persians) and Arabs, and thus no mercy was shown, hands up to surrender, it made no difference to their fate. The rest of the Paratroopers, seeing they were getting overrun, had deserted their positions and escaped back to their base camp at Midway airfield. An officer who was family to the Shah of Iran heard the British liaison officer make some comments that had offended the Iranians. Making an excuse for the officer, the General had said the officer's words had been taken out of context. So now we have been ordered by London to organize an attack on the caves and to show the British can do it better. The Shah of Iran had personally been in direct contact with the Foreign Office to complain about the British officer's lack of respect for his soldiers. "Some dumb officer is in the shit to say the least", I said to the lad next to me.

The General then said "I knew you would not want to miss out on this mission to attack the caves, so I will let Major Snipe give you a detailed briefing". This comment got a general indescribable murmuring from the lads, "arsehole, wanker, stupid mother fucker" all combined and daggers from the Major's eyes, for being so rude to the fucking General!

I said to Watty sitting next to me," I think we are going to pay a price for the comments of a drunken Rupert". I looked at Watty, he was still pissed, you know the look. As Snipe started to speak Watty got up and walked outside, everyone could hear him pukeing up, which made all the lads smile and added a bit of humour to the atmosphere.

After fighting the IRA in Northern Ireland, who would shoot you in the back and run or quickly surrender if cornered, the Adou were a different ballgame. They were brave and had balls, they would fight a larger group right up to the wire. They mainly carried AK47 assault rifles, RPG7 rocket launchers, RPD machine guns, Katooshia 122mm rockets that fire a large high-explosive warhead, mortars and here I mention new British GPMG machine guns, but Russian equipment in the main. We had similar firepower but had the advantage with artillery at our disposal, three Hawk training jets that had been fitted with GPMG machine guns and could also drop a five-hundred pound bomb. We also had a squadron of armoured vehicles called Saladins led by a fellow Geordie, called Charlie Skelton from Newbrough, a small village up the River Tyne. He had helped the SAS on a few occasions and managed to back us up with his armoured cars. He became a good friend of mine after we did a deal to sell some 303 ammunition to local tribesmen who carried the old Lee Enfield 303 rifle.

The Major's briefing had stated that two tribes would be fighting with us, one from the Shirrishiti area, (brother fighting brother) and another flown in from a different area. The SAS team that trained them would liaise with the tribal leaders. A sergeant from the SAS team that had been training the Firqat tribe had flown in, reassured us of their loyalty. The other tribe was reported to be a mixture of old men and boys with many of the tribe still fighting with the enemy. Their soldiering ability was pointed out. One had tried to clean the dust from his rifle but the grit had jammed the working mechanism, a bullet was in the breach; so he kicked down on the cocking handle, the gun had fired and blew the top off his head. The team leader thought the Adou had the best men from this tribe.

With the whole of "B" Squadron and the advance unit of "D" Squadron, we would be used as a basic infantry unit. A costly group of specialists being used as cannon fodder backed up with two light tanks, artillery and the Sultan's jets, two tribes, four companies of regular army totalling just over seven hundred men would be in the attack. The tribesmen would lead and guide the way to Hill 830 followed by the SAS, then the regulars would follow the SAS and the armoured cars would be on a flank to cover the advance.

Once the hill was secured, the four regular companies would move down these ridges, pointing out the separate ridges leading down to the caves, with the Arabs as scouts to show the way and the two four-man SAS teams that had trained them. Boat troop and freefall troop would then move down to the front of the caves after the ridges were taken. Mountain troop would absail down from above the caves and throw in satchel charges (large packs of plastic explosives). This part of the op would be done while boat troop and freefall troop would be firing into the caves. Immediately after the explosions boat troop would lead the attack into the caves, just my luck to be in boat troop and them cats came back to my memory!

"The regulars have been moved up to the starting point during the night, you will be flown up to Midway in the Shorts sky vans as soon as you have had breakfast and got your equipment and ammunition." At that remark the shutters rose from the kitchen but not many fancied bacon and eggs, more important was to sort out your weapons and ammunition. Ammo had been laid out by the quartermaster, you just helped yourself. I had my American Armalite rifle (M16) so I filled up my pouches with ammo, a couple of hand grenades and a phosphorus grenade. Two hundred rounds of 7.62mm for the machine guns, everyone carried this communal ammo to keep the GPMGs supplied. A day's food ration, fresh water, one bottle and an extra five litres in a water-bag. We all carried about 50 lbs in weight, but one of our Fijians in the unit, built like a brick shithouse, was carrying the GPMG machine gun and more ammo than I could physically lift. With the experience fighting the last four months we were well trained in what to carry into battle and any special equipment would be allocated by the troop sergeant.

We moved out to the runway to wait turns in the sky van, a 10-minute flight. With four planes doing the taxi run, it did not take long to get on a plane. My turn, but last up the tailgate and what a start to the day. The pilot did not bother closing the tailgate and he had full throttle in seconds. I still had not made it to a seat when he lifted off. It was so steep and with all the equipment I was carrying: if Watty who had fortunately sobered up, had not grabbed me I would have fallen out the back of the fucking plane. I was also given a bodybag to carry and I thought if I travelled with that pilot again I would get into the bag for the journey. Attacking a defended position in daylight the quartermaster thought many bodybags would be needed. From the bad moment in the plane, the rest of the day was to be a disaster.

The sky van did not need the mile long runway, he braked and stopped in such a short distance that, had it not been for the seat belts, we would have been sitting with the pilot. I hurried off the plane to avoid a return trip. The runway was impressive with mountains of kit stacked in neat rows nearly half the length of the mile long runway. One Adou, with one rocket could have made the 4th of July look insignificant. A bulldozer was at work filling in a large hole; a couple of occupied body bags were being thrown in without ceremony, to fill an empty space. Watty and I looked at each other, raised eye brows but said nothing.

The last of the men landed and we moved out to the starting point, a couple of kilometres from the airfield. Snipe was giving orders. First to move out were the Arab tribes in one long frontal line, not twenty yards behind we moved out in similar formation, then the regulars in a long column behind, and finally Charlie's two cars which I could see on a prominent ridge to my rear left. At first there were no problems, we moved a few kilometres but then the Arabs started to look back and then gestured for us to move forward with them. These moves were noticed by Snipe who shouted out "This is their war and they take the main risk, keep your positions". The young Arab in front of me did not look a day over 15 years old and the guy next to him could have been his great-granddad and they were looking worried. Then they stopped on masse and interpreters were telling Snipe they would not move forward until he called in artillery fire and the jets strafed the hills to our front. There was a heated exchange of words, Snipe red in the face. They were not British Army so they could stand up to Snipe and tell him to "fuck off" in Arabic. Some had manned positions to the front when they had been in the ranks of the Adou and knew where the enemy was waiting. Snipe did not want the advance to stop because of the time factors; he must have assumed the Adou would not have the balls to attack his force! "SAS to the front", he commanded! Now I was twenty metres in front of the same Arabs that had been suggesting I should walk with them. Pat Mc Donald was to my left and I said "Who's war is it now?" I gestured to the young Arab that he should join me, the next thing, he runs up to me and holds my hand. Arabs often walked hand in hand as a show of friendship, not to be confused with being a poof. Now I am stuck with this young kid holding my hand, walking into battle. Thank God it was a secret War and no BBC camera crew were capturing my embarrassing moment on television.

    We got about 50 yards before the Adou opened fire on this long line of slowly walking figure 11 targets; our Arabs had been right and Snipe now knew it big time! Shouts for "MEDIC" as some of the lads were downed with AK47 rounds and shrapnel from exploding RPG7 rockets. I had no cover but to the forward right was a hill that would protect me, so I ran for that cover, 40 yards ducking and weaving till I got to the base. Damned if I saw my Arab friend again but Pat had come to the same mound and now passed me. "What are you doing, come on to the top and lay down some fire to help the lads stuck in the open." He was right so I followed him, we looked for the enemy but they were so well concealed we could not locate their position. All we could do was fire a few mags in the general direction. Artillery called in by Snipe, now started to impact, and yes, planes started to strafe and bomb the hills to the front. I felt a sting in my right thigh and grabbed it, thinking I had been shot. Lo and behold, the old Arab was standing behind me a few yards away, his sights might have been over the hill but his muzzle was not, bullets were impacting into the rock near my leg. I screamed at the old cunt then he recognized his stupidity. Who trained that arsehole?

While I had my problems on this first contact with the enemy, unknown to me till later, when talking to Charlie Skelton, I was not the only one. He had moved forward with the armoured cars to give support firing his 30-calibre machine guns. He soon came under fire, rounds pinging off the armour-plating, and anti-tank RPG7s just falling short. One round of incoming fire cut his radio antenna to a short stump, putting him out of contact with the officers who were trying to direct his fire and his main gun a (75mm). As he got out of the armoured car to repair the damage, he heard an explosion a couple of metres from the car. Soldiers from the Baluchi Regiment were passing the car, first using it for cover and then they were ordered to skirmish forward to help the SAS at the front. The bang was an anti-personnel mine finding the target. Anti-personnel mines are designed to maim and not kill and they were easy to hide. Charlie never forgot this soldier standing there on one leg, he was in deep shock. Moving his weight to the right leg and lifting his left, detonated the pressure release mechanism of the mine. White bone of his shin, muscle and tendons hung down, blood spurting from torn veins and arteries. The foot had disintegrated. Charlie did not hesitate and jumped down to give first aid to the wounded soldier and moved him to the relative safety of his armoured car. Other men stepped on mines and lost limbs, obviously now in a mine-field they had to find a way through, still under fire from the enemy.

The shooting died away and now it was decided to advance again, this time skirmishing forward as it should have been done in the first place. One group was ready and in position to give cover while another group advanced. As we climbed Hill 830, the shrub and bush which had given the enemy good cover now slowed us down. As we entered it, we could not see far to the front, caution was the only answer and more delay in reaching the summit. No further contact with the Adou was encountered at this stage of the advance. As we reached the summit the undergrowth thinned out with a better field of vision. One final push and the hill was in our command but now it was about five in the afternoon and impossible to fight on to the caves. We had no night-sight equipment as cutbacks with the British Army deprived us of specialist equipment.

It took another hour before all the force were on the hill, command post was established and the officers had an "O" group. Helicopters brought in 81mm mortars and plenty of ammunition, and they also removed the casualties. When our troop officer returned he informed us that only seven men had been wounded on the advance, so we had been lucky. One bullet from an AK had hit an SAS GPMG gunner in the shoulder and hit bone, then ricocheted into the leg of the number 2 on the gun that fed the bullets; both men were from "D" Squadron. Now we had to make sangers but it took nearly another hour to fit in all the different groups, move to the left, move to the right, move further forward, move to the right, talk about sergeant major fuck the troops about, and time was getting on. Now we could get busy building our sangers. I teamed up with Pat, digging down till we hit solid bedrock, and with the plentiful supply of loose boulders in the area we soon had a defensive position. A couple of lads were ordered to put out landmines forward of our sangers. These were called Claymores, which we worked with a 100-metre electrical cable and a handheld detonating device. If fired, they sent 700 small ball bearings forward. I had been trained with the Paras that a forward listening group should be sent out while this type of work was carried out. This was mainly protection for the men concentrating on laying the mines and trying to hide the cable ,but this basic training was not carried out. Our boat troop officer had a couple of men lay mines and they returned, job completed. "Geordie, start a brew up while I finish the sanger," suggested Pat and as an experienced SAS lad I had confidence in any advice he gave me, he was a born leader. The water was just boiling in the dixey as Pat entered the sanger. At this moment a rocket passed over my head and I felt the heat off the propellant; then an enormous explosion as it impacted behind us. As I instinctly ducked forward under the wall for protection, I knocked over the dixey and spilt the water, "For fuck's sake Geordie, you spilt the tea" moaned Pat. Green tracer, red tracer, impacting rounds rained into the hill, the main attack was against freefall troop just to our right. Again those cries for help "MEDIC" as men were wounded!

Now that lack of using basic training , protecting the guys laying mines and not standing to before last light, would be the reason for our casualties. Every group - troops, squadrons, platoons, companies, had officers in command so no-one could pass the buck onto non-commissioned men for the incompetence in not complying with basic infantry procedures. The Ruperts were in command and totally responsible. A good commander needs to be like a good chess player and take advantage of the other commander's blunders and this enemy Arab leader was no sloth. He possibly could have attacked earlier, but men out in the open, laying mines that would be a problem for him if he waited any longer. Surely this had changed his plans! Two new men, Watty and John Forsyth in free fall troop; both men who had passed the SAS with me, had been sent out by their troop officer to lay the mines. They were personal friends, men who had gone through the extreme SAS training which gave you an extra bonding and sense of comradeship. They did not even have their personal weapons as protection. Was the officer assuming the enemy were stupid? Under-estimation and lack of respect for the enemy by British Army officers in this war and in Northern Ireland, were the main reasons for most of our casualties and an incredible lack in the use of basic training.

    John had taken the first two rounds in the stomach, bursting his intestines, a wound which caused intense pain, and rapid evacuation to a hospital was his only chance of survival. Watty told me that he could only lie flat on his back doing his best to adapt to the contours of the ground beneath his body. A bush where his head rested was cut in half by the density of the bullets used by both sides in the fire fight. If he moved it would be a bullet from either group that would take his life, so he just stayed motionless. The Adou moved forward to take the SAS sangers but the difference in calibre of the individual SAS soldiers would win the battle. We did not get our heads down but traded bullet for bullet, unlike what had happened to the Iranian paratroopers. An Adou machine gun group moved close to Watty and John but the troop saw the move and concentrated their fire on this group quickly stopping them dead, the threat sent to Allah. With this gun team out of action, the Adou leader realised he had taken on the wrong group of soldiers and called his men back. As the fire was reducing, an SAS trooper broke cover and bravely rescued John. Watty also took the incentive and scrambled back behind a sanger.

    The firing stopped and now you could hear the cries of the wounded! The enemy wounded and not evacuated by their own, were murdered by an SAS trooper who threw a few hand grenades in their direction. Yes, we certainly had some psychopathic sick bastards in the SAS but I will not mention his name. Medical treatment was given to John, a strong dose of morphine, shell dressing to the wounds and an urgent call to base for a medical chopper to evacuate him.

Again a burst of fire and another scream but this turned out to be our Major Snipe shooting the troop commander Lt Garside in the foot. The Lt had gone out to count the enemy dead but his lack of basics by not telling everyone, nearly cost him his life. He cursed at the Major but the "airborne wart", who attended his wounds; shut him up by stating he should be dead, and due to his own stupidity. While bringing in the wounded officer, the enemy machine gun was also brought into our position. It was a brand new British made gun; and our guns were at least ten years old and no fucker knew they were selling them to Arabs: that would give them to men killing British soldiers. Some British politicians and civil servants were so low that they would sell their mothers to make an arms sale. This really inspires men fighting on the Country's behalf and I start to wonder "What the fuck am I fighting for £70 per week?"

Total darkness had now set in, incoming mortar rounds and Katooshia rockets hit the hill and we started a return of harassing rounds with our 81mm mortars. No lights could be shown so we ate cold ration and to Pat's still grumblings; no cup of tea! After what had happened all he could only moan about the tea! I was not on the same wave length.

A helicopter now arrived but without moon light he was finding it difficult to locate the landing pad that had been prepared for his arrival. A low, fine mist now made matters even worse; so after fifteen minutes passing back and forward he turned on his lights, making himself a target but now low on fuel he had no choice but to risk his life to evacuate John, Garside and a couple of our Arabs who had also been shot. He was later given a DFC, Distinguished Flying Cross as he was an RAF pilot, attached to the Sultan's Forces. I had my fingers crossed for John as I knew he would need major surgery, I honestly did not give a damn about the Rupert, Lt Garside.

We took turns to try and sleep but with regular explosions it was impossible, the only consolation was that the enemy was not getting any sleep either. This time, before first light, some clever officer remembered the basics and stood-to the whole force but the enemy did not try again, more because we now had air-power and artillery at our disposal.

Another day. It had to be better than yesterday, you can live in hope, be an optimist! The original plan would continue stated the troop commander, but leave in the sangers what you could; food, water, other than the litre on your belt and leave your digging tool. Now this item was used for digging a rapid shallow trench to protect from incoming fire and I was not pleased to be told to leave it behind, something to do with my sense of self-preservation! Orders are orders and I was too junior in the SAS to speak out against my so-called betters.

The plan, well there must have been a change that I had not been told about; the whole force was walking down the same ridge, directly towards the caves and the enemy. Had our Arab guides been unable to find the correct start lines for the advance, were the officers confused, or had this been the Will of Allah? Someone in command was making the biggest fuck up in his life. Basics, control, management, brains all had been left in the sangers along with our digging tools, as nothing was going as planned. Not one officer questioned the fact that the whole Unit was going down one ridge, as a trooper you could not know of a change in plan so you could only follow like sheep to the slaughter. My troop was fortunately at the back and still at the top of the ridge. I could see a wadi; a deep ravine to my left and looked across to another ridge which was not occupied by any regular company. I thought to myself, "Into the valley of death walked the 700". Had this fuck up not happened before in British military history?

The Russian chess-player could not believe this bad, bad, bad move, as our officers knocked over the back row and were only using the pawns. We walked down a foreward sloping ridge which had a lot of bush cover; but bushes do not stop bullets. The column of 700 in one line now spread down from top to bottom of the ridge. They enemy let the first company reach the bottom before making the play. Then the "King" must have also known British tactics, which were drilled into Ruperts at Sandhurst. The British sense of fair play, we allowed people from other countries to enter Sandhurst and learn our Army's basic training and they had remembered more than our Ruperts. Some countries that went the communist way, had passed on all the information necessary for the Russians to train any terrorist group or Army to counter our moves in the chess game.

Neil reacted like a robot as two men behind a hill opened fire with AK47s, he put down his gun group who opened intense fire so that he could move to the left flank with his riflemen. Then he led the forward charge with his riflemen, to kill the two cheeky Adou gunmen. That bit of open ground just before the hill - he led all his men and entered into the killing area that had been chosen by the "King".

Not two men with AK47s but 30 men stood up and fired, full magazine of 7.62 short from 30 AKs, a wall of bullets that downed. Neal and his men - instantly killed or wounded. A deafening barrage that made everyone in the column realise we were in shit street. Then from different well-camouflaged positions, the wall of fire extended away from the inert bodies of Neil and his men and now rained fire on the whole forward slope; even reaching us fortunate souls at the back. The bullets whacked through the bushes making an instant autumn season, and not the season of goodwill towards mankind! Where was my fucking digging tool? Yes, in my fucking sanger!

The "Boss" Snipe was to my forward left and I could

hear the radio conversations even above all the explosions. Mortars and artillery fire were being directed towards the Adou. Then Adou took more initiative, another move by the "King," he ordered his men to attack front on, hand-to-hand combat with the foreword company. The shells were no good if you mixed it with the front positions of the enemy. The Regulars started to break, men started to run, dropping their rifles and running back up through and into the other companies, causing even more chaos. No one could give support fire and stop the assault because our men were in the line of fire. The Adou had started a rout but then met the first SAS team that had been with the Arabs. Ginge broke with radio rules, "We're being overrun, help we are being overrun". That frantic message was heard by all the SAS on the ridge. The lads with the Arabs ran forward, taking GPMG machine guns off the regulars and heroically they ran down the slope to support the team in big trouble. A big Fijian SAS corporal reported that he had engaged a group of fifty Adou and stopped their attack; they were forced to take cover. The other lads engaged the frontal assault and ground them to a halt. The Forward Observation officer, regular Army Rupert, now brought in a jet to strafe the enemy, but he must not have had much practice at the job, as the jet shot him seven times, one bullet shattering his spine. More chaos as another officer stepped in to direct the jets. Then I heard Snipe and this General having a verbal argument over who was responsible for this total and utter fuck-up. What a time to start passing the buck, in the middle of a battle and arguing between them selves. Snipe would have been better taking command and sorting out the mess, putting an end tp the confusion and panic from our troops. He was on the ground and the General was up in a helicopter above the fighting.

    I took out a tin from my emergency ration pack, opened it and ate the food. Then I said to myself "fuck it", I dug a small hole and put my arse and balls into it, "at least I won't get my balls shot off!" The leaves were still falling off trees like a heavy wind in the autumn season however it was not wind but bullets causing this effect! I looked at the other ridge and made up my mind to say my piece to our troop officer. "You see that ridge Sir, if the enemy move up it and get this lot in a cross fire, the situation is going to get a lot worse. Put some spotting rounds down so you can quickly call in heavy fire". He agreed with me and did what I said. Then to this day with his best effort at reading his map he could not hit that mile-long ridge (I think he was not where he thought he was, a bit lost) like every other incompetent officer on the ridge. A sergeant told him to stop trying to hit the ridge in the end when we heard a mortar bomb explode behind us. This Rupert was later a General in the Gulf War, so I saw in a newspaper, so his incompetence got him promoted with the class system that protects stupid officers.

A donkey led by a soldier came up the hill in a big hurry. As he passed me I could see he was terrified, he had two dead comrades tied onto the donkey. I must admit I was also afraid but my fear was because of what I was seeing and hearing from our officers. These idiots were going to get us all killed and I was thinking about them black cats! Then shit; I noticed the donkey had been wounded and was bleeding from a bullet lodged in its neck and the animal was also terrified. The donkey may have had more brains than all our officers put together and it had not needed a carrot to get him up the hill with a dead weight on its back. Then two regulars came running without their weapons, there was no stopping them, the fear of God written on their faces.

Snipe then got my attention; "Yes they are all dead" he was reporting to the General. He was looking with his binos down at Neil and his men, all lying prostrate and not moving, if I was alive or wounded down there in the open, I would be not moving either. Even doctors with a stethoscope can find it difficult to pronounce death and here is a Rupert 800 metres away, giving these men a death certificate, via a pair of binos. Then they told the officer directing the jets to drop a 500lb bomb on our own men! I could not believe what was being said and done; if they were dead why drop a bomb on them!!!!!!!! They did it, and strafed the bodies and repeated the exercise, as if one bomb was not sufficient to kill dead bodies. What was the reason? I wanted to protest, but as British soldiers we did not have any rights to protest, as the officer knew better. Then the orders came to withdraw back to base camp. We led the withdrawal for the battle group, last out and first back. We returned to our sangers at Hill 830 to lick our wounds and reflect on just what had happened to the so-called best Regiment in the British Army. My description was what I saw, heard, understood or misunderstood and many people in different areas of the battle could describe it totally different as it was hard to see the full picture with the limited visibility in this bush area. Let's put it this way: no officer is going to agree with my assessment.

  The execution of our own men was for the obvious reason that the British Government and our secret war did not allow for us to be taken prisoner and used as propaganda. I also now realised that the killing of enemy wounded and mutilation of their bodies was encouraged by our officers so that the enemy would do the same to us and then they had no hostage problem. The wounded and dead carried out by comrades were evacuated by helicopter and ammunition and rations were flown in.

  The silence of our own men was demoralising, everyone had been affected by the carnage inflicted upon us, and sorrow for our killed and wounded. Then the Adou could be heard rejoicing their victory, shouting and firing their rifles in the air, bastards were rubbing it in. Snipe ordered in mortar fire to send the enemy back into their caves. We ate, had tea and like typical British soldiers started to make light of a bad situation. One of the lads was called Tom the leg; because in a previous fight with the Adou he had been shot in the leg, and had now been shot in the arm. One of the lads had said to him while waiting his turn to be evacuated, "What are we going to call you now, Tom the Leg or Tom the Arm?" We stood-to before last light and suffered another night of incoming and out going fire; the eyes needed matchsticks to keep open even with all the explosions.

    Stand-to came before first light and we then prepared our army rations for breakfast. We got orders to attend a briefing, regulars moved into our sangers and we assembled at Snipes HQ sanger near the mortars. "Right lads, we are going to attack the Adou caves, SAS only. We will form a square, I will be in the centre with my O group and we will take a donkey with a 50mm calibre machine gun; move to a point where we can see the caves and fire the gun, Cpl Cooper will take charge of the gun. I whispered to Pat "How many donkeys will be in the centre?" I think the last time the British used square formation was fighting the French at Waterloo, yesterday we had had the charge of the Light Brigade, into the valley of death walked the 700, and now we were using tactics as were used fighting Bonaparte at the battle of Waterloo. Boat troop got the front part of the square and I was fourth from the right, a lad from "D" Squadron was to my left as we moved out. Moving out I spoke to Pat, "Can we make a pact that if I get shot, or you, we will get each other out dead or alive?". I was quite serious and we shook hands on the pact, I had no confidence in anybody else. We moved slowly, Snipe controlling and maintaining the square formation, his radio was so loud we did not have to tell the enemy we were coming. We moved on a different ridge from the previous day, we stopped on occasions to see if we could engage the caves but moved again and again. A burst of AK47 came through the bushes and hit dirt inches in front of my feet. Had I dived forward, the gunman would have got me. I knelt down and peered down the line of fire from the first burst. He fired again; I could see the line of fire and returned fire down the same line. He stopped firing; the lad from "D" also saw the line and fired a grenade from his America M16 fitted with a 40mm. M203 grenade launcher. Another burst of AK and I returned fire again, I pointed to face the men on my right the direction of the enemy. In the dense terrain of low bush you could not see more than twenty yards. There was no more incoming fire, so I stopped firing but I had a good angle of from where it had come from.

Snipe was on the radio talking to base camp and reporting the contact. He was on for some time, talking to different officers. He then ordered us to move forward again, twenty more yards and now he had a line on the caves. You could hear but not see the gun being removed from the donkey and assembled. I took out my digging tool and dug a shallow trench, self preservation, fuck anymore what officers told me. Just what we wanted; a heated debate in the middle of the square. Apparently on the way down the back plate had fallen off the donkey and without a plate the gun was impossible to fire. We moved back to base without further incident but the moment we arrived back an officer from the Regulars was having a go at Snipe. "Who shot my men?" he was demanding to know. Now remember the briefing - "SAS only" would move out and shoot into the caves! Yes, there had been friendly forces out there and we had not been told. Two men were dead and it was me that had killed them but I never felt blame as the Rupert should have given us the information in his briefing. You always give the location of friendly forces, basics again and there were now two men dead because of this officer. "Who fired out there?" Snipe demanded to know. I was just about to confess when I had eyeball contact with the lad from "D" squadron; he shook his head telling me not to say anything. It was the Arab guides who were dead and the Arabs were getting a little excited, blaming us. Ling came to the conclusion that it must have been a group of Adou that had fired at both groups. I had hit one in the head, the bullet had entered his eye but the back of his head was missing and the brains had been sucked out leaving a shining empty hole. The other had taken a burst in the chest and both had died instantly. I had taken over a couple of body-bags and helped zip them up, in more ways than one.

My professional army career was over, as I could not possibly accept being under orders of these incompetent idiots.I had made my mind up to pay for my discharge. Helicopters returned us to base camp and brought in fresh troops. The caves were never taken by force, but because of constant mortar fire and harassment from the overlooking hills, the enemy withdrew from the position. When inspected later they were found to have concrete blast walls and machine guns that completely protected the entrance. God or the Devil had protected me again from the charge that would have been suicidal. I visited John in base hospital which was none other than 23rd Parachute Field Ambulance, I still knew all the doctors and male nurses. He asked me to contact his parents to tell them that he was OK, so I assured him that I would do that for him. We returned to Hereford, with orders that we would have a month's holiday and then go to Northern Ireland on active service for six months. I bought my discharge and when Colonel Jeapes asked my reason, I told him I would rather shoot British officers, than the IRA which put me on the Regimental black list, of non-returnable and not to be talked to.

Fighter doing low level attack in support of troops in the Sherishitti Caves

Working with local army near Sherishitti Caves

2

(This page to be entirely free from erasure)

Assessment of Military Conduct and Character

Military Conduct ___EXEMPLARY___

(*Note*—The Range of Military Conduct Gradings possible is:—

(1) Exemplary (2) Very Good (3) Good (4) Fair (5) Unsatisfactory).

Testimonial. (*To be completed with a view to civil employment and with relation to the Certificate of Qualifications and the Job Description*)

Corporal Mumford has been an outstanding NCO both in the Parachute Regiment and Special Air Service: the SAS only takes the highest grade of soldier, Mumford is a fine example of this selection.

While serving in Northern Ireland as a medical orderly he was awarded a commendation for efficiency. I recommend this soldier most highly for any job for which he is technically qualified. I am sure he will carry it out to a very high standard.

The above assessments have been read to me.
Signature of Soldier ___N.J. Mumford___

Signature of C.O. ___[signature]___
Date ___2 August___ Commanding ___[illegible] 22 SAS Regt___
Address ___Hereford___

My Discharge Book

Chapter 17

My Discharge from the army

Although I was the first SAS trooper to buy his discharge, many soon followed my example, and to this day it is hard to keep men in the Regiment. The seeds of discontent were well sown in the Regiment before I left but I did the wrong thing by confiding to a fellow comrade of my disappointment with the command structure and being used as a political pawn. I wanted to be one of the best and proud of my unit but I was totally disillusioned; It was time to go. In my day the money was not important as it was an honour to have been capable of joining the toughest Regiment within the British Army. I have nothing but praise for most soldiers I met in the Parachute Regiment and the SAS, a group of young British men who were then and still are the backbone of British youth.

While I was waiting for my papers to leave the Army, the Regiment gave me a bad time. Friends were warned not to talk with me, which hurt. In the pubs, down in Hereford, I was given the cold shoulder but my mind was made up, I would resist this childish behaviour and be the first SAS trooper to purchase his discharge. I was being watched and followed (ok, they will call me paranoid). One night in a bar a young man approached me who remembered me from the Parachute Regiment, he had been in B company. He told me he was trying to join the SAS because he looked up to me as a professional soldier. I was honoured by his remarks but I did not want him to join the SAS because of me. I started to tell him it was not worth the effort and that in my opinion the officers were a bunch of crap hats when a Fijian stopped me from talking to him. I hope he had listened and returned to the Paras! Another recruit who approached me was a man called Phil Carras, who was one of the first men I met when I had joined the Royal

Army Medical Corps as a boy soldier. He was the physical training instructor at Keogh Barracks in Ash Vale and again I did my best to talk him out of joining the Regiment. Unfortunately he did not listen and later was killed serving with the Regiment during the Falklands War.

What I said to Colonel Jeapes about "rather killing officers" was an over-statement but the officer system was my main reason for leaving. I have no doubt that this book and what I have stated will be called a pack of lies and my character will be brought into disrepute to counter the attack on the system and foundation of the Army. Soldiers do not normally write books and the system does not like it. Officers write books, as they can do a better job of making a total disaster and fuck-up into a glorified act of bravery. There are long lists of books that document the true incompetence of British officers going back in history to the present day.

I read for example, in World War I that in a major offensive against German lines, the British troops were ordered to walk straight and tall so the Germans could see they were not afraid. Then an officer leading one division did so, kicking a football to show an example of bravery to his men. Had these soldiers ducked, dived, taken cover in shell holes, used the terrain to its best advantage, skirmished forward, used supporting artillery fire right up to the enemy trenches, used camouflage and smoke, then and only then might they have won the day. The Germans could not believe the total stupidity that allowed them to kill nearly every man and football in front of them, and thus the war to end all wars dragged on. Not for the lack of bravery of the British fighting man, but the total stupidity of its leaders and the class system that did not respect the lives of its working class men. We now, this year, honour the last surviving men from this war but when 20,000 men can die in one day, the truth about officer incompetence and the class sytem that sent these men to be slaughtered has never been fully told.

Then, in World War II, after kicking the Italians out of North Africa a brilliantly led German counter-offensive had most of the British officers surrendering to the Germans. A British division of fresh soldiers, straight from England with new weapons and equipment were ordered to surrender without firing a shot or even seeing an enemy soldier. They obeyed their orders in total disbelief. Even the famous German, General Rommel, stated "give me British soldiers and German officers and I will conquer the world", as he witnessed first-hand the true grit of the British soldier and the incompetence of it's officers.

The British Army is the last bastion of the English class system and a job for the boys whose daddy was a General. They are the dregs that can not make it in business or even want to. They see fame and fortune by being an officer first and then going into civil service and both services will hide their incompetence and even promote individuals to preserve the class system. We witness it on a daily basis with highly paid civil servants who do not have a clue what their right hand is doing. They are good at entertaining but cannot run a business in or out of government and the politician in charge of the ministry will be the fall guy and not the incompetent civil servant, ex-Officer. You ask about polo horses and they will be experts but the 1,000 people who should have been deported for crimes they did in Britain, not a fucking clue!

What is the reason for Prince William and Prince Harry joining the Army? Is it not a perfect example of what I am saying? With all the private education, would they not be better helping with big business, bringing trade and commerce to our shores? Then, with all that one-on-one private tutoring, we see they did not do that well. Better send them into the Army where we can minimise any event that may occur. Do you think it is for their killer instinct that they are joining the Army? Even I am laughing, writing that. Soldier's lives will be put at risk protecting them as they cannot be allowed to get harmed or captured. They will be neither use nor ornament for the fighting soldier at the sharp end and take away more money from equipment needed at the front. Literally, putting lives at risk. Resign now, stop the class system and then the British people will be proud of you and the Army will then become professional.

The SAS Regiment suffered heavy losses during this Falklands campaign. More internal conflict, was due to a suicide mission dreamed up to execute Argentinean pilots, with no return ticket for the Squadron that was to carry out the mission, "B" Squadron again was given the job. This time officers would go with the men and they questioned the orders, "If we execute the Argentinean pilots, would they in turn not take revenge by executing all the SAS captured?" Although the mission was cancelled, some officers that objected to the mission were RTU'd a the great insult for a SAS soldier. Neither the Americans nor any other Army would dream up a mission that was suicidal for its men. You have to take risks which any soldier is prepared for in the time of war but this attitude by our senior officers has to be questioned. Unfortunately, serving soldiers do not have the right to complain about orders. There is nobody to protect them against mis-management or abuse by officers that can, and have ordered them, to commit war crimes. British soldiers are professionals, with the ability to fight any Army, given the right equipment and training, without the need to have kamikaze, suicide missions. The wrong men were kicked out of the SAS and morale must have taken a nosedive.

Adolf Hitler, Doctor Caraditch, Franco, Stalin, Pinochet and Gerry Adams are all famous for the same reason. Their ability to manipulate the masses to commit genocide and then have the incredible arrogance to be able to stand up and convince educated people that they had not committed a crime against humanity. Gerry Adams has hood-winked many famous, people, Tony Blair, the Pope and many an American President and the American people with his gift to talk to the masses. He would now like to be seen as the man who is seeking peace in Northern Ireland and will personally benefit with praise and financial reward. He unfortunately recruited the pack of killers and criminals that are called the IRA. As they are what would have been the criminal element in the ranks of the Catholic minority, Adams is finding it hard to control them. A comparison can be seen with Adolf Hitler, an accomplished ethnic cleanser who used his famous "Brown Shirts" criminals to get into power, and then once in command of the German Army, had the Brown Shirts wiped out as he could not control the criminal scum. The IRA have not gone away, these killers still collect state social security payments. While waiting they plan bank raids, sell drugs and make money from protection rackets, as they know nothing else. They are the type of men that are the scum of the earth and the conflict is a way of appearing to be heroes fighting for a cause, but in reality they see the financial benefit in the conflict and dying for the cause is not in their thinking. Bobby Sands and a few others were the real IRA and were dying for a united Ireland. Gerry Adams and his forty thieves are such dedicated freedom fighters that they have stopped because they are being paid off. The British Army does not have enough soldiers to fight the Iraqis, Afghan Rebels and the IRA at the same time, so they have been warned that their massive funds available in American banks could be confiscated. The Americans still do not class them as terrorists and we are fighting, helping America, yet they do not support us in return.

So, the unemployed killers can only sit in bars drinking, the landlord would never dare ask an IRA man to pay, as he would lose his life or have his pub burned down as has happened to many decent Catholics that have had to abandon their business to this mafia. In a petty argument with a pack of IRA, even Catholics that support Sinn Fein (the political wing of the IRA) can lose their life as happened to Robert McCartney. He only intervened to help a friend but these killers who see themselves above the law had no second thoughts about killing two Catholics outside the bar, cutting their throats, slashing their bodies from the chest to navel and leaving them to bleed to death on waste ground, amazingly McCartney's friend survived. The IRA returned and carried on drinking, warning other Catholics to say and do nothing to help their neighbours, friends and fellow Christians, on threat of death.

The sisters and family of McCartney had the cheek to complain about the murder. Their story was highlighted in the press and they even had a meeting with President George Bush and other high ranking Congressmen in America. In relation for shaming the IRA to the American people as vicious, hardened mafia killers and not "freedom fighters", the family has had to leave the area where they live for generations.

The IRA see their leaders, Adams and Martin McGuiness, living the life of Riley and how saintly they appear as political men and naturally, as their merry men, they seek the same hero status. Mind you, some do get sent on missions to help fellow terrorists around the world. Adams and his Education Minister, Martin McGuiness, have been sending terrorist experts to Columbia to fight the democratically-elected Government there. What would you think might be payment for this assistance? Surely not drugs, but I suppose as Northern Ireland Minister of Education he has got one hell of an outlet, or was he put in that position for his academic qualifications? Then the two of them spend their holidays in the Pais Vasco of northern Spain with a nice group of terrorist called ETA and its political wing. Are they giving advice on how to form a democratic government or how to run the Mafia? Both groups have very similar ideas on fund-raising activities. The Pais Vasco has never been an independent state; we Geordies have more right to statehood than the Pais Vasco people. Again, the leaders of this area talk about ethnic cleansing, which means anyone who does not vote or think their way are going to be removed one way or another.

Terrorists have no humanity left in them when, with cold blooded determination, they can plant a bomb knowing the intended target is going to be innocent civilians, women and children. I do not understand what goes on in a person's mind when they contemplate such an action which is a crime against humanity. If a democratically-elected person also commits such a crime he brings himself down to the same level as the terrorist. He then becomes a state terrorist, which is just as barbaric. Bush, Blair and Sharon come under this group when they can order the bombing of a house, only with suspect intelligence that it is being used by terrorists. More often women and children are the only occupants and casualties in this State execution. The spies and informers are the same that tried to convince the world that Saddam Hussein had weapons of mass destruction. If the same rules of combat used in Iraq were used in Northern Ireland ninety percent of Irish Catholics would be wiped off the face of the earth. It makes the inquiry by Blair into Bloody Sunday a total farce, as in one house alone in Iraq we see more people killed than on that unfortunate day. I have to ask if we have different standards against Muslim and Catholics, as what we are doing to the Arabs would never have been permitted against white Irish terrorists.

One aspect of Irish history I hope will be repeated and that is the murder of its leader at the hands of the Irish! Adams and the IRA have achieved nothing in 30 years of fighting that could not have been achieved by moderate men peacefully around a table, and they still do not have a united Ireland.

I finish with statements made by people within the IRA about Gerry Adams and how he killed and butchered his way to fame. Tony Blair has all this knowledge and more about this terrorist, yet he still smiles and shakes his hand. It is an insult to every man and woman who has been a member of the Armed Forces and more for the men wounded and the families of those that died in the conflict. That hand shake shows that all their sacrifice was in vain and not necessary. Its hard for men to swallow with missing limbs, physically or mentally scarred by this man. If Blair wants to give Northern Ireland to the decent people of Southern Ireland I do not have a problem, but to Gerry Adams and his terrorists never!

On Monday 29th May 2006 there was a traffic accident in Kabul, Afghanistan, where one civilian was accidentally killed. A riot developed due to anti-American feelings against these soldiers. Stone-throwing against the soldiers caused an over-reaction, the Americans shot dead 14 civilians. Will there be an inquiry? Will the soldiers be prosecuted for murder? Will Tony Blair condemn the Americans, and will he withdraw British troops in protest? How would these soldiers, who Bush says are the best-trained in the world, have reacted on "Bloody Sunday" where the British paratroopers were being attacked by a stone throwing rioting crowd estimated at over thirty thousand and then shot at by members of the IRA, not to forget the petrol bombs? Martin McGuiness was the scholar who created the situation, no wonder he is head of education! The politicians must think twice about putting young soldiers into situations where they are the middle men. Prosecuting young, often frightened, soldiers is not the answer as they are put in a position that is impossible to not over-react on occasion. The "do gooder" critics do nothing but insult these young soldiers. They find that easy, never having been at the sharp end and under enemy fire. A Para Military Police force with better training to take command after a military conflict is what should happen, and the Army should only be held in reserve. Soldiers are not policemen and vice versa, a mature man or woman can often defuse a situation better than young boys. Is it not time we went back to electing Members of Parliament with moral fibre who stand up for principles and put the great back into being British and back up the soldiers whom they order into conflict?

" The Honourable member for Belfast West"

"The Honourable member for Belfast West" (Gerry Adams MP) was the title of an hour –long ITV programming "World in Action". Broadcast on the 19th December 1983, the programme referred to The IRA car bombs in London, outside Harrods and in Oxford Street. Five innocent people were killed, and several maimed for life. The programme said it would "investigate the politics behind the killings and ask who ultimately runs the IRA".

Well at this point I have been stopped using quotes from the programme and have been threatened with legal action. The reason given by ITV Granada on there "E" mail -----------. I can not even repeat what they said on there "E" mail without threat of copyright action.

Anyway I have had to withdraw five hundred books and it has cost me a lot of money but I will not be stopped telling you the truth. What was in great detail with extensive quotes taking twenty pages from a programme that lasted sixty minutes I have had to condense into a general account of what the programme was about.

It looked into the history of Adams and his family, his rise to power in the ranks of the Irish Republican Army and then his crowning glory to be head of the killing machine. How he personally organised and modelled that machine into what it is today. World in Action Granada and the Sunday Times quoted Peter McMullan who told how he, Adams took control and ordered killings of men, women and children in some of the most barbaric acts committed in the terrorist war against the British people. How he never showed remorse to his victims in his hunt for power. I will say no more other than you should protest to ITV Granada and demand they show a repeat of the program. Do not let the system treat you like mushrooms, feeding you on shit and keeping you in the dark.

Look at the latest budget of the labour party and Mr Brown,

how we are pumping millions into Northern Ireland. You are paying the bill to appease these fanatics, at the cost of our pension and health system. No wonder Adams the terrorist and Paisly the Religious fanatic sit smiling at a table that they vowed never to share, our government are trying to buy "PEACE". Tony Blair has to look good before he leaves power and gets his rewards for being an American lap dog and I am sure Bush will find him a kennel to end his days in luxury. There will never be peace in Ireland till it is united with the good people of both islands coming to a solution where English and Irish can live in harmony and respect for each other. We must remove religious bigotry and forget the past history as the people of today can not be held responsible for the sins of our fathers.

The Irish must be in control of there own destiny and we must let the Irish solve there own problems. Only if the Irish or the United Nations ask for our help should we give our support but not meddle politically, we have made enough errors in the past.

Remember Francis Bell and do not let his death or the other victims be in vain, you can not let terrorists win, be proud to be English and show courage in uniting Ireland.

If it is not in breach of copyright I will list as many soldier victims as possible with there age. I am sure they do not mind me insulting and telling the truth about Jerry Adams.

Sgt Michael G, Willets. 27.
Pte Kelly 24
Pte Christopher Stephens 24
Pte Frank Bell 18
Cpl Stephen Harrison 24
LCpl Terence Brown 24
LCpl D,A Forman

WO2 R. Vines 36
Sgt John F Wallace 31
LCpl Philip James 22
Private Roy Bedford 22
Pte William Snowdon 18
Pte James Borucki 19
LCpl David Jones 23
Pte Jack Fisher 19
Cpl R Adcock
Major Peter Fursman 35
LCpl Donald Blair 23
Cpl Nicholas Andrews 24
Pte Gary Barnes 18
Pte Raymond Dunn 20
Pte Anthony Wood 19
Pte Micheal Woods 18
Cpl John Giles 22
Sgt Ian Rogers 31
WO Walter Beard 31
Pte Robert England 23
Cpl Leonard Jones 26
Pte Jeffery Jones 18
Pte Robert Vaughan-Jones 18
LCpl Chris Ireland 25
Pte Peter Grundy 21
Lt Simon Bates 23
Pte Gerald Hardy 18
Sgt Brian M. Brown 29
LCpl P Hampson

LCpl M. May
Sgt Alister Slater 28
Sgt Michael Mathews 37
Pte R Spikins
LCpl Stephen Wilson 23
Pte Donald Macaulay 20
Pte Mathew Marshall 21
Pte Tony Harrison 21
LCpl P Sullivan
Pte M Lee
Pte P Gross
Pte C King
Pte M Ramsey.   All Paratroopers

Driver Laurance Jubb 22
LCpl Micheal Bruce 27
S/Sgt Joseph Flemming 30
Driver Peter Heppenstall 20
Driver Stephen Cooper 19
Driver Ronald Kitchen 20
Driver Micheal Gay 21
Sgt Thomas Penrose 28

Lt A Shields. RN
TA Samuel Gibson 28
Cpl B Criddle. BEM
Spr M Orton
Cpl D Hayes
Cpl T O'Neill

Cpl D Brown
C/Sgt W Boardley 30
Cpl James Burney 26
Pte O Pavey 19
Pte John Bateman 18
Pte Sean Walker 18
LCpl Anthony Dacre 25
Pte Hatfield 19
Pte Martin Thomas 19
Pte Darren Millray 20
WO11 M White

Pte Terence Adam 20
Pte Paul Delaney 18
Pte Richard Biddle 20

Cpl Gerald Bristow 26
Fusilier Kerry McCarthy 19
Cpl David Smith 31
Cpl Alan Coughlan 28
Fusilier Andrew Crocker 18
Lt Steven Kirby 22
Cpl Barry Cox 28
Trooper Anthony Dykes 25
Trooper Anthony Thornett 20
SQMC Roy Bright 36
Lt Denis Daly 23
Trooper Simon Tipper 19
LCpl Jeffery Young 20

Cpl Arthur Smith 26
LCpl Steven Bagshaw 21
Pte Steven Smith 24
LCpl Clinton Collins 20
Pte Neil Williams 18
LCpl Philip McDonough 26
Pte Anthony Williamson 21
Pte David Murrey 18
LCpl David Wilson-Stitt 27

Cpl Joseph Leahy 31
S/Sgt Barrington Foster 28
Pte Micheal Swanick 20
Pte Brian Allen 20
Pte John Randall 19
LCpl Kevin Pullin 28

Pte Micheal Murtagh 23
Pte Edwin Weston 21
Pte Stephen Keating 18
Pte Gary Barlow 19
Pte John Green 21
Pte Ian O'Conner 23
Pte Joseph Leach 21

Pte Ian Caie 19

Pte Roger Wilkinson 31

LCpl Ian Curtis 23
2/Lt Nicholas Hull 22
Pte John Ballard 18
Cpl Kenneth Mogg 29
LCpl Martin Rooney 22
LCpl John Boddy 24
Cpl John Barry 22
Pte Ian Burt 18
Pte Robert Mason 19
Pte Anthony Goodfellow 26
Pte Paul Wright 21
Pte Anthony Anderson 22
Pte Martin Pattern 18
Major Andrew French 35
Pte Mitchell Bertram 23
Pte Carl Davis 24
Pte Nicholas Peacock 20

Cpl David Powell 22
2/lt Andrew Somerville 20

LCpl David Wilson 27

Cpl Leonard Durber 26

Pte Martin Robinson 21
Pte Martin Jessop 19
Cpl Leon Bush 22
Cpl Stephen McGonigle

RAF John Baxter 21
RAF John Reed 22
RAF Ian Shinner 20
Cpl Ian Learmonth
Cpl Maheshume Islania
Sqd Ldr Micheal Haverson
Flt Lt S Roberts
Flt Sgt Jan Pewtress

Major John Barr

Pte John King 22
Cpl John Leahy 31
Pte Alan Watkins 20
Drummer Frank Fallows 18
Sgt Micheal Unsworth 31
Pte Collin Clifford 21

Cpl Ian Armstrong 32
2Lt Robert Williams-Wynn 24
Cpl Micheal Cotton 36
Cpl Micheal Herbert 31
Sgt William Robertson 22
Pl Gary Fenton 29

Sgt Robert McCarter 33
Sapper Ronald Hurst 25
S/Sgt Malcolm Banks 29

Sapper Edward Stuart 20
WO2 Ian Donald 35
Major Richard Jarman 37
Sapper John Walton 27
Sgt David Evans 28
Sapper Howard Edwards 24
Colonel Mark Coe 44
Lcpl Micheal Robbins 23
Sgn Paul Genge 18
Cpl John Aikman 25
Sgn Micheal Waugh 22
Sgn Leslie Walsh 17
Sgn Paul Reid 17
Sgn Paul Reece 19
Sgn Brian Cross 26
Cpl Micheal Ward 29
Cpl Derek Wood 24
Cpl David Howes 23
LCpl Graham Lambie 22
Sgt nmicheal Winkler 31
Sgn Mark Clavey 24
Cpl William Paterson 22
S/Sgt Kevin Froggett 34

Ranger William Best 19
Ranger Cyril Smith 21
Pte R Jones 21
Pte R Rowe 21
Pte T Stoker

Pte T Rudman 20
Pte S Hall 27
Pte g Curtis 20
Pte N Blythe
Pte J Willby
Pte B Bishop 19
Pte P Bullock 19
Pte J Burfitt 19
Pte r Greener 21
Pte A Lewis 18
Pte M Norworthy 18
Pte S Wilkinson 18
Pte J Winter 19
Pte G Smith
Pte A Richardson 20
Pte J Rudman 21
Sgt A Whitelock 24
Cpl T Taylor 26
Pte J Gaskell 22
Pte R Roberts 25
Pte Ronald Stafford
Pte P Turner 18
Pte P Eastaugh
LCpl A Kennington 20
LCpl C Miller 21
Pte R Turnbull 18
Pte M Harrison 19
Pte L Harrison 20
Cpl D Salthouse 23

Cpl I Morrilli 29

Reverend Father Gerry Weston MBE

Marine L Allen 22
Marine Anthony David 27
Marine John Shaw
Marine Andrew Gibbons
Marine Graham Cox 19
Marine John Macklin 28
Cpl Robert Miller 22
Marine Gary Wheddon 19
Marine Adam Gilbert 21

LCpl William Jolliiffe 18
Cpl Thomas Lea 32
Sgt David Ross 31
Sgt Sheridon Young 26

LCpl John Warnock 18
Trooper James Nowosad 21
Cpl Steven Smith 31

W/Pte Ann Hamilton 19
W/Pte Caroline Slater 18

Gunner Robert Curtis 20
L/ Bomb John Laurie 22
Bombardier Paul Challenor 22

Gnr Clifford Loring 18
Sgt Martin Carroll 23
Gnr Angus Stevens 18
L/Bomb David Tilbury 29
Gnr Ian Docherty 27
Gnr Richard Ham 20
L/Bomb Eric Blackburn 24
L/Bomb Brian Thomasson 21
Gnr Victor Husband 23
Gnr Brian Robertson 23
Sgt Charles Coleman 29
Gnr William Raistrick 23
Bombardier Terrence Jones 23
Gnr Leroy Gordon 21
L/Bomb David Wynne 21
Major David Storry 36
Gnr Robert Cutting 18
Gnr Paul Jackson 21
Gnr Idwal Evans 20
Gnr Kerry Venn 22
Sgt Thomas Crump 27
Gnr Joseph Brookes 20
Bombardier Heinz Pisarek 30
Sgt John Haughey 32
Gnr Leonard Godden 22
Bombardier Terence Griffin 24
Gnr David Farrington 23
Lt/Col John Stevenson 53
Gnr Kim MacCunn 18

Sgt Bernard Fearns 34
Gnr Richard Dunne 42
Gnr Cyril Macdonald 43
Cfn Colin McInnes 20
Gnr Mark Ashford 19
Gnr William Miller 19
Gnr Anthony Abbot 20
Gnr Maurice Murphy 26
Gnr Edward Muller 18
Gnr George Muncaster 19
Gnr Paul Sheppard 20
Gnr Richard Furminger 19
Gnr Alan Ayrton 21
Gnr William Beck 23
Gnr Simon Evans 19
Gnr Kieth Richards 19
L/Bomb Kevin Waller 20
Gnr Lyndon Morgan 20
Gnr Miles Amos 18
L/Bomb Stephen Cummins 24
Major Micheal Dillion-Lee 35
L/Bomb Paul Garrett 23
L/Bomb Stephen Restorick 23

Pte Charles Stentiford 18
Pte David Champ 23
Sgt Ian Harris 26
Cpl Steven Windsor 26
Cpl Gerald Jeffery 28

LCpl Stephen Taverner 24

Pte Paul Carter 21
Pte Robert Benner 25
Pte Richard Sinclair 18
Pte Stanley Evans 19
Pte Peter Woolmore 21
Pte Alan Stock 22
Pte Neil Clerke 20
Cpl Alec Bannister 21
Sgt Charles Chapman 34
Pte Anthony Aspinwall 22
Pte Kieth Bryan 18
Cpl Ian Bramley 25
Pte Geoffrey Breakwell 20
Pte Christopher Brady 21
LCpl A Bennett

Pte Micheal Prime 18

Cpl terence Williams 35
Trooper John Gibbons 21
Trooper Kenealy

Cpl Paul Harman 27
S/Sgt Charles Simpson 35
S/Sgt John Morrell 32
2Lt Micheal Simpson 21
Pte Christopher Shenton 21

LCpl Stephen Anderson 22
WO2 P Cross
Dvr C Pantry
Fusilier A Simmons 19
Cpl P Barker 25
Cpl T Agar 35
LCpl R Huggins 29
LCpl P Gallimore 27
Major J Snow 35
Fusilier K Canham 24
Fusilier A Tingey 25
Cpl D Napier
Fusilier G Foxall
Fusilier T Foxall
Fusilier A Grundy 22
LCpl M Beswick 21
LCpl J Davis 22
Fusilier C Marchant 18
Cpl D Llewellyn
Cpl E Gleeson 29
Sgt S Francis 28
Fusilier M Sampson 20
Fusilier James Duncan 19
Fusilier P McDonald 19
Cpl D Traynor 28
LCpl W Makin 22

Sgt Robert Irvine 43
LCpl Ian Warnock 27

Pte Stephen Walker 27
Pte Stephen Waller 23
LCpl Mervyn Johnson 38
Pte Chris Wren 34
Pte reggie McCollum 19
LCpl Stephen Rankin
WO2 Hugh McGinn 40
Sgt Trevor Elliot 38
Cpl Trevor May 28
LCpl Thomas Gibson 27
Ranger Robert Dunseath 25

Cpl Alan Buckley 22
Pte Eustace Hanley 20
Pte Marcel Doglay 28
Pte James Jones 18
Pte Brian Thomas 20
Pte Rennie Layfield 24
Pte Roy Christopher 20
Pte Christopher Shanley 21
LCpl Stephen Rumble 19
LCpl Andrew Webster 20
Pte Stephen Beacham 20
LCpl Stephen Burrows 30
Pte Vincent Scott 21
Pte David Sweeney 19
Pte Paul Worrall 23
Sgt S Reid 28
LCpl D Moon 24

Cfn Brian Hope 20
LCpl Colin Harker 23
Sgt M Seldon
Cfn Colin McInnes 20
Sgt Micheal Burbridge 31
WO1 James Bradwell 43
LCpl John Hillman 29
LCpl Alan Giles 18
Pte Brian Soden 21
Pte David Meek 24
Pte John Williams 22
WO1 Mike Heakin 30
Pte William Davis 19
Pte Micheal Hatton 19
Pte John Robinson 21
Pte George Crozier 23
LCpl Peter Herrington 26
Pte Peter Sharp 22
Pte Raymond Hall 22
Pte Frederick Dicks 21
Major Peter Willis 37
Cpl Ian Metcalf 36
Pte George Lee 22
Cpl Terrence Graham 24
Pte James Lee 25
2Lt Howard Fawley 19
Cpl Micheal Ryan 23
Cpl Errol Pryce 23
Cpl Robert Bankier 24

Rfn David Walker 30
Rfn Joseph Hill 24
Major Robin Alers-Hankey 35
Rfn John Taylor 19
Rfn James Meredith 19
LCpl David Card 21
Cpl Ian Morrill 29
Rfn David Griffiths 20
Rfn Raymond Joesbury 18
Rfn Micheal Gibson 20
Cpl William Smith 29
Lt /Col Ian Corden-Lloyd 39
Rfn Nicholas Smith 20
Rfn Christopher Watson 20
Rfn Micheal Bagshaw 29
Rfn Andrew Gavin 19
Rfn John King 24
LCpl Grenville Winstone 27
LCpl Gavin Dean 21
Rfn Daniel Holland 19
Rfn Nicholas Malakos 19
Rfn Antony Rapley 22
WO2 Graham Barker 36
Cpl John McKnight 29
Bandsman John Heritage 29
Bandsman Robert Livingstone 31
Bandsman George Mesure 19
Bandsman Keith Powell 24
Bandsman Laurence Smith 19

Rfn David Mulley 20
LCpl Thomas Hewitt 21
Pte Philip Drake 18
Pte Sohan Virdee 20
Cpl Derek Hayes 28
Major Christopher Dockerty
S/Sgt Arthur Place 29
Pte David Wray 18
Drv Laurence Jubb 22
LCpl Micheal Bruce 27
S/Sgt Joseph Flemming 30
Dvr peter Heppenstall 20
Drv Stephen Cooper 19
Drv Ronald Kitchen 20
Drv Micheal Gay 21
Sgt Thomas Penrose 28
Sgt Micheal Muldoon 25
Drv Norman McKenzie 25
Sgt William Edgar 34
Drv Paul Bulman 19
LCpl Norman Duncan 27
Capt Robert Nairac 29 George Cross
Guardsman Graham Duggan 22
Guardsman Kevin Johnson 20
Guardsman glen Ling 18
Cpt Herbert Westmacott 28
Guardsman Danial Blinco 22
Sgt Anthony Metcalf 28
Guardsman Robert Pearson 19

Guardsman Micheal Shaw 23
Guardsman Micheal Doyle 20
Guardsman Anton Brown 20
Capt Anthony Pollen 27
LCpl Simon Ware 22
Guardsman Brian Hall 22
Guardsman George Hamilton 21
Guardsman Norman Booth 22
Guardsman Stephen McGuire 19
Guardsman John Van-Beck 26
Guardsman George Lockhart 24
L/Sgt Thomas Mckay 29
Guardsman Alan Daughtery 23
Guardsman William Forsyth 18
Guardsman John Hunter17
LCpl Alan Swift 25
LCpl Damian Shackleton 24
LCpl Graham Stewart 24
Guardsman Samuel Murphy 21
Sgt Philip Price 27
Guardsman David Robertson 25
Guardsman Paul Fryer 18
Trooper Geoffrey Knipe
Sgt Frederick Drake 25
Gunner Timothy Utteridge 19

I am sure there are hundreds I have missed from the list but the government have not got a full roll of honour for our soldiers who died because of the Irish troubles.

"Gerry Adams takes over as IRA chief"

"Gerry Adams takes over as IRA chief" was the headline over a Sunday Times article by Barrie Penrose on 4th August 1985. Here is the article in full:

> Gerry Adams, the MP for West Belfast and the president of Sinn Fein, the IRA's political arm, has replaced Martin McGuinness as the chief of staff of the Provisional IRA. As a result, Adams is now in complete control of the IRA, commanding both the political and military wings of the terrorist movement.
>
> The IRA's seven-man executive and 13-strong army council are believed to have ratified the decision last month in a move that now gives Adams unprecedented power in the IRA. His promotion to chief of staff stems mainly from his master-minding of Sinn Fein successes in Ulster's local and national elections and in the propaganda war against the British government. It is also tacit acknowledgement by leading Provisionals of the fact that Adams has been their dominant military tactician for more than eight years.
>
> Adams was elected MP for West Belfast in 1983, though he has refused to take his seat in the House of Commons. That a Westminster MP is also the terrorist mastermind of the IRA is bound to cause the government problems, and to pose even more difficulties for journalists covering Ulster.
>
> The furore over the BBC's interview with McGuinness, which was first revealed in last week's Sunday Times, has no connection with the appointment of Adams as chief of staff. In recent months, Adams has demonstrated to the Provisionals' rank-and-file that his successful policy of winning Sinn Fein votes in elections can be run to political advantage with the IRA's campaign of violence in Ulster and mainland Britain.
>
> Before last May's local elections in Northern Ireland, Adam's bullet-and-ballot-box strategy came under fierce attack

from hawkish Provisionals among the active service units. They demanded a policy of unrelenting violence, unaccompanied by the requirements of election politics. But Adams, then adjutant to McGuinness, expelled five top IRA hardliners, including the veteran gunmen Ivor Malachy-Bell, Anto Murray and Eddie Carmichael. Adams and McGuinness told their rivals they would be court-martialled and shot if they formed a break-away group or joined the Irish National Liberation Army, another republican terrorist group in Ulster. The removal of these five allowed Adams to capitalise on his political successes and gain complete control of the IRA.

Last week, senior officers in the Royal Ulster Constabulary and the security forces expressed no surprise that Adams had replaced McGuinness. A prominent Whitehall figure commented: 'I've picked up a bit from what I know from our own sources.' The Sunday Times has confirmed Adams's position as chief of staff through its own republican and intelligence sources. What IRA role McGuinness will now play has yet to emerge. He had been chief of staff since February 1983 and for some weeks had been expected to hand over the job to Adams, who is well qualified to lead IRA terrorists.

Adams, aged 36, was born in the republican stronghold of West Belfast. In 1965 he joined the old IRA 'D' company but four years later, at the start of the present Ulster troubles, he sided with the emerging Provisional wing of the IRA. He became, in quick succession, an intelligence officer, battalion quartermaster and finally commanding officer of the second battalion of the Belfast brigade, a post he held from May 1971 until March 1972. During that time the battalion, which covered the Ballymurphy and Clonard areas of Belfast, killed three policemen, 19 soldiers and 27 civilians.

On March 14, 1972, Adams was arrested in the midst of a wave of bombings in Belfast and Londonderry and taken to the Palace barracks in Hollywood. He gave a false address and the alias Joseph McGuigan. Under interrogation he admitted he was Gerry Adams and an IRA member.

Adams was interned in Long Kesh (now the Maze) until May 1972, when he was released to take part in secret 'truce talks' in London with the then Northern Ireland secretary, William Whitelaw. McGuinness also attended the Whitelaw meeting, as did three former IRA chiefs of staff, Sean MacStiofain, Daithi O'Conaill and Seamus Twomey.

Adams had attended the negotiations on condition that he was released from interment. Back in Belfast he became adjutant of the IRA's Belfast brigade, then made up of three battalions. Adams was responsible for discipline and the day-to-day running of the brigade. The breakdown of the Whitelaw talks prompted the IRA to step up its campaign of violence.

He helped to plan 'Bloody Friday' on July 21, when 21 bombs were planted to go off in Belfast's city centre between 2.15 and 3.30 pm. By the end of the afternoon four civilians and five soldiers had been killed and another 130 people injured.

A former IRA leader, Peter 'Pete the Para' McMullan, who now lives in the United States, said in a TV interview, Adams was very concerned about the routes to and from the bombing, which Adams checked personally. McMullan added: 'He was one of the ones who actually thought up the economic bombings' (ie the bombing of economic targets).

With such 'successes' to his credit, Adams continued to rise in the IRA hierarchy. When MacStiofain, the then chief of staff, was arrested in November 1972, Adams formed a committee of three with O'Conaill and Joe Cahill to run the IRA in his absence. Five months later Adams took command of the Belfast brigade and under him the brigade killed six soldiers and 11 civilians and exploded 91 bombs against economic targets.

On July 6, 1973, he was interned again. He tried to escape and was sentenced to 18 months' imprisonment. In the jail compound reserved for Provisional prisoners he became commanding officer of fellow IRA men such as Bobby Sands, Brendan 'Darkie' Hughes and Brendan 'Bic' McFarlane, initiating education and discussion programmes for all the Maze IRA men.

While in prison in 1976, Adams drafted a blueprint for the IRA, which was seized by police in the Irish Republic when they arrested the then chief of staff, Seamus Twomey, a year later. From prison Adams set out his political and tactical ideas in the 'Brownie' columns of Republican News. There he pushed his wish for a new cell structure for the IRA and a raised profile for Sinn Fein under IRA control 'at all levels'.

When Adams was released in 1977 he was elected to the Sinn Fein Ard Comhairle (central committee) and later that year became chief of staff of the IRA. Shortly afterwards he became vice-president of Sinn Fein.

According to McMullan, Adams and McGuinness met in a Dublin flat in late 1977 to discuss plans to assassinate Brigadier Frank Kitson, then a senior military figure in Northern Ireland; a bombing campaign in Britain and Adam's strategy of 'economic target' bombings. On February 17, 1978, the Le Mon House restaurant in Comber, County Down, was firebombed as part of the so-called economic war: 12 people died and 23 were badly burned. Next day Adams was arrested and charged with IRA membership but charges were later dropped. Adams resumed his seat on the IRA army council.

It is not certain when Adams stepped down from being chief of staff the first time. However, in 1981 the IRA hunger strike produced more sympathy in Catholic areas and enabled Adams to start fighting elections and to take the ground from the old Provisional leadership based in Dublin, who saw taking part in elections as collaboration with the British. Adams consolidated his personal standing a year later by topping the polls in the Ulster Assembly elections. William Whitelaw, then home secretary, banned him from entering the British mainland after he was invited to visit London by Ken Livingstone, the GLC leader. But in 1983 Adams became the Westminster MP for the West Belfast, winning because the moderate Republican vote was split between two other candidates. The ban on entering Britain was lifted, but Adams has never taken his seat. Adams now heads a slimmed down active-service IRA modelled on his strategy. It is thought by the police and army in Ulster that there are no more than 50 seasoned operators who handle information on a strict 'need to know' basis. Behind them is a larger 'civil and military administration', in IRA parlance, whose members are known as the 'auxies' or 'the sweeney'. This force is used for punishment, back-up work and intelligence-gathering.

To demonstrate his support for his bullets-and-ballot-box strategy, Adams agreed in May, after his local election successes, to an upsurge in IRA violence. He is also believed to have agreed to the blitz of English seaside resorts, which was foiled by the British police. Last week's bombings of economic targets in Belfast and Ballynahinch was further evidence of Adams's hand at work.

There are reports emanating from Sinn Fein that Adams has decided to take part in the next general election in the Irish Republic. He is said to have chosen Louth as the seat he will contest. There is bound to be an outcry from the public and politicians for the arrest of Adams. Sir John Biggs-Davison, Conservative MP for Epping Forest, and chairman of the party's backbench Northern Ireland committee, said Adams's new role confirmed there was no distinction to be drawn between Sinn Fein and the Provisional IRA.

Watertight evidence, however, is hard to secure. Moreover, the security forces rarely arrest an IRA chief of staff. A special branch officer in the Republic told The Sunday Times: 'Once you identify him you can have him watched. Lift him, and the IRA will appoint somebody else. Then you've got to start the surveillance process all over again.'

However, Adams's appointment is part of a continuing process moving the centre of IRA operations from Dublin to Belfast, and in Britain, Labour's Northern Ireland spokesman,

Peter Archer, called on the government to adopt a clear strategy towards men like Adams. 'Either they treat him like an elected representative, or if they have evidence of his criminal involvement, they (should) treat him accordingly.'

There are also likely to be renewed calls for the proscription of Sinn Fein, but this would be complicated by the fact that there are now elected Sinn Fein councillors in Northern Ireland. Biggs-Davison said the government should now reconsider whether all candidates for elections in Northern Ireland should be required to sign a declaration that they did not support violence.

The secretary of state for Northern Ireland, Douglas Hurd, said he was not in a position to confirm or deny reports about changes in the IRA's chief of staff.

Seamus Keenan, a Sinn Fein spokesman in Londonderry, said yesterday: 'Martin has consistently denied that he is chief of staff. We would regard any suggestion that Gerry Adams was as ludicrous.'

© News International Newspapers. Reproduced by permission.

I hope you find this book a talking point. Nobody is too old to learn, so with my web page we can exchange comments, insults and praise. Stops life being boring and if we can save one soldier or stop one conflict, I personally will be a happy man.

My "E" mail address is: geordiemumford@yahoo.co.uk

I dedicate this book to Sophia and a smile that could stop all Wars.

Questions for Tony Blair
1. Is the Pope a Catholic?   Yes / No
2. Is Gerry Adams a terrorist? Yes / No

Young boy soldier, then proud of his country